What are the implications of the American economic involvement in Europe? What effect has the world's oldest consumer society had on the world's newest?

In these pages, a tough-minded business analyst makes a penetrating survey of the successes and failures of Americans and of American companies in the Uncommon Market. He arrives at fascinating questions and answers. One of them: can Europe and the United States be drawing together to form a new, supra-national society?

Recently, the author spent many months inquiring into all aspects of the European business community, asking literally thousands of questions of European and American businessmen to ascertain what impact U.S. products, U.S. representatives, U.S. marketing methods, advertising, and cultural exports (like Rock 'n' Roll) are having on the Old World.

What he discovered first, of course, was the surface Americanization of the Continent — supermarkets, superhighways, credit systems, disc jockeys, Yankee management techniques. But is this breeding Ameropeans? Or is Europe undergoing a far more subtle, significant, almost revolutionary changeover to a consumer society akin to, but not identical to our own?

Is the new international company breeding men without a country? THE AMERICANIZATION (EUROPE will make stimulating   absorb-

THE AMERICANIZATION OF EUROPE

The Americanization of Europe

THE IMPACT OF AMERICANS
AND AMERICAN BUSINESS
ON THE UNCOMMON MARKET

EDWARD A. McCREARY

DOUBLEDAY & COMPANY, INC.

GARDEN CITY, NEW YORK

1964

Library of Congress Catalog Card Number 64-19223
Copyright © 1964 by Edward A. McCreary
All Rights Reserved
Printed in the United States of America
First Edition

To Edward A. McCreary, Sr., an old American

To Jean Monnet, a new European

FOREWORD

This work was conceived as a fairly simple, perhaps semi-technical, report on American companies in Western Europe. In the background were a few implications. Almost immediately, however, the implications of American economic involvement began to move to the fore. There are a number of reasons why.

For one, the collection of specific company figures and general statistics in Europe can quickly become an exercise in pointlessness. These figures are rare, incomplete, seldom comparable—and undergoing change. In Europe, industry facts, figures, and trends which marketing specialists can pick up in the U.S. by reading the trade papers are guarded like Spanish daughters. Consultants sell for a handsome fee the kinds of industry gleanings businessmen in the U.S. casually and almost unconsciously pick up over drinks.

Then too, with over 3000 U.S. companies established or at least implanted in Europe, it is too easy to "prove" virtually anything one might wish about U.S. companies. Within this great mass of companies and happenings there are significant trends, but for any one point there are multiple contradictions. There are no specific "How To" rules for success.

Moreover, what is most fascinating about Europe today is what American companies are helping to do to it. The changes taking place are not necessarily those which most Europeans see evolving. Most American businessmen in Europe, because of familiarity and because of the nature of their preoccupations, do not think, or at least do not talk much, of these changes—which is, strangely, one of their strengths overseas.

What is happening is that portions of the economic structure of the countries of Europe are changing and growing, and from this flows much more change. The status and value systems, the arts and social attitudes, the very "cultural essence" of a people are in large part a reflection of their economics past and present. The world of ideas and cultural traditions does much to shape the manner and style by which men think and live. But the substructure on which a culture rests is the way in which men earn their daily bread and organize their workaday lives. New developments at this level create and spread new ideas and relationships throughout the whole structure. Sometimes these changes are so profound that the participants only vaguely realize what is underway. At other times, as at present, at least some of the effects are immediately obvious.

Business developments are by no means the only forces acting on Europe but they are cardinal factors on which much else swings. They permit a non-emotional and non-nationalist view in a vital part of the world. To understand what is happening in Europe one must understand something of its economics.

What follows is a working-level view of some of this economic change in Europe. It is a work of reportage and comment based on over 300 interviews with American and European (but mostly American) business and government (but mostly business) representatives.

This book is designed for easy, rather rapid reading.

Specialists or students may find it useful to go through particular sections in detail. As much as possible I have tried to
avoid jargon or overprecise hedging. The intention in this
series of rapid sketches is to provide a flow of factual points
and pictures which can combine to give the reader a "feel"
for the *ambiance* of business in Europe, a sense of the direction in which things are moving, and why, as well as an
awareness of some of the intangibles at work in the change-
process.

To these ends the text is liberally sprinkled with direct
quotes from men involved in the mechanics of developing
new Europe. Regrettably, many of these quotes cannot be
specifically attributed. In the United States, the top management of a company, accustomed to speaking for themselves
and their companies, often talk forthrightly—and for the
record. Middle-rank managers, however, are leery of making any comment that has not been cleared by the front
office. It happens that most U.S. managers in Europe are of
the middle rank in their home-company hierarchies. Moved
to Europe, they are triply shy of being quoted.

European managers are, from long habit, even more quote-
wary than the Americans.

In order to develop meaningful, candid comment and
solid information, a researcher often must promise his inter-
viewee anonymity. Many of the sentiments quoted here,
however, were expressed in one way or another by enough
individuals so that they took on general validity. For instance,
the somewhat surprising comments on the quality of U.S.
managers in Europe were echoed throughout Europe by
Europeans—and by Americans.

There were surprises throughout. For instance, thoughtful
Americans discussing life in Europe sooner or later mention
their shock at discovering how provincial in outlook many

Europeans are. This is a reversal of old roles. Moved to Europe, where their businesses and outlook tend to be as wide as the Western world, these Americans find well-educated men and women in many capitals who are influential members of an elite, who speak several languages, but who hardly think in terms beyond those of their own social group, much less the continent on which they live or the world beyond. Such Europeans confuse social sophistication with knowledge of the world.

A European businessman's favorite expression for Americans is "naïve." All too often it may be applicable. But one sometimes sees European businessmen suspecting a convoluted thread of motives for an American action that is dismayingly simple in motive and effect.

Many American companies in Europe become involved in complex, important, and intimate multicountry acquisitions, joint ventures, and licensing or pricing negotiations with European companies. After a series of delicate negotiations in Italy, a bright and quite worldly American staff assistant was impressed by top managers he met there. He found them urbane and highly intelligent. About their general outlook or attitude, however, he said, "Either they're way beyond us in maturity and understanding of how things really are, or they're cynically shortsighted and selfishly irresponsible. For all our sakes, I hope it is the latter because this can change."

Actually, any businessman in any country is a child of his environment. Laissez-faire European businessmen in Italy or Belgium or mercantilist business chiefs in France are acting and thinking within accepted or expected and established patterns (as are public relations-conscious chiefs of U.S. companies).

The point is that in present-day Europe these patterns are changing.

I wish to express my thanks to the hundreds of men who gave so courteously of their time to make this book possible. I am especially indebted to those (relatively fewer in number) who had the self-confidence to divulge something of their personal thoughts and problems in the new Europe. Also, I wish to thank those who, having no ax to grind, shared food and friendship with the passing stranger. I am forever grateful.

Finally, I owe a long-term debt of thanks to the Harvard Graduate School of Business Administration which can, sometimes, help a man begin to learn to see and think.

Edward A. McCreary

CONTENTS

THE AMERICANIZATION OF EUROPE

CHAPTER I

INTRODUCTION

Throughout Europe the words *american* and *americanism* vary curiously in meaning. They run the scale from implications of openness and freedom, or ingenuity and high quality, to grossness, bad taste, even a certain vague but inherent evil. It is quite enlightening, to an American, to find the word *american* used in some circles in Europe very much as *communism* is used in some circles in the U.S. This generic, lower-case usage makes the word a catchall for anything of which the speaker morally and emotionally disapproves.

In Britain, for example, at least one point on which right-wing "Suez" tories and the more emotional left fringe of the Labor party see eye to eye is in their dislike and distrust of what they call "the americanization of Britain." Quite often, as it turns out, what they mean is change, virtually any change, which is not a reversion to pre-1913 Britain or a move towards the more perfect socialist state. To call so many of the changes going on in Europe "americanizations" is highly inaccurate or incomplete but, under the circumstances, understandable.

Modern Europe is in the midst of a peaceful yet intensive revolution. On the face of it this revolution is economic; it has to do with the rise of consumer economies. However, as the people of Europe are discovering, there is much more to a consumer economy than the happy, oversimplified idea of more people with more money buying more things with more credit. In Europe a consumer economy means new technologies; new and giant systems for making and distributing products; new kinds of companies and value systems. A consumer economy means new wealth, new centers of power, new habits, and new attitudes growing out of the old. The new consumer economies of Europe bring in their train new educational systems, new opportunities, a cracking apart of established class systems and a quickening of the society. They represent nothing less than extensive social upheaval. This means they make a great many people, at all levels of a society, decidedly uncomfortable.

America happened to evolve the first consumer economy. As a result, America and things American—the most obvious symbols and prototypes of many of the changes now underway in Europe—draw much of the emotional fire and blame for changes underway there. Essentially, what is happening in Europe, however, is not an americanization of Europe but the parallel development in Europe of consumer societies somewhat similar, especially on the surface, to the one in the U.S. If America were to vanish tomorrow, Europe (if not overrun) would still evolve in its present direction. But the facts remain: America is a readily available model for any developing consumer economy; America and Europe interact strongly at many economic and social levels; and, in the new Europe, American companies are very much on the scene. There is more to the so-called americanization of Europe than semantic hysterics on the part of Europeans who dislike aspects of the new Europe.

Since the changes underway in Europe are basically economic, one way of finding out about americanizations there would be through a study of American companies in Europe.

AMERICAN COMPANIES IN EUROPE

Depending on whom one talks to, U.S. firms in Europe have (1) no real impact on life in Europe, or (2) are daily transforming it. The fugitive truth flutters between these extremes. American companies do keep establishing themselves in key industries such as chemicals, electronics, and foods. (Autos, oil, cosmetics, and pharmaceuticals they are already well into.) But Americans do not have as strong an impact on European lives as this implies. Rumors to the contrary, extensive use of Kleenex, Esso gas, Elizabeth Arden make-up, or Campbell's cream of chicken soup does not turn Europeans into facsimile Americans—any more than a recent craze for scotch whisky seems to have turned Frenchmen into Britons. Most important of all, in no one country of Europe do all the American companies there, when lumped together, account for more than a few percentage points of total industry investment or employment. The real levers to change in European life are in the hands of Europeans. For instance, one of the main keys to economic change in Europe are the channels and systems of distribution—that is, the retail stores and organizations for getting goods into the hands of consumers. But, since most American companies in Europe are manufacturers only, for them, trying to change distribution patterns is like trying to push on a piece of string: much action at one end and little at the other.

Of course, sheer availability of goods at one end of the distribution chain does fertilize change. And American companies in Europe, while not primary agents, can be catalysts that accelerate and influence change.

THE AMERICAN INVASION

American companies such as Singer Co., American Radiator and Standard Sanitary Corp., and International Harvester Co. have been in Europe since the late 1800s. Many more, including General Motors Corp. and Ford Motor Co., set up shop in Europe during the booming twenties. But the greatest U.S. influx was post-World War II. Between 1950 and 1963, U.S. investments in Europe jumped from $2 billion to over $8 billion. The bulk of this investment, usually with the active encouragement of local governments, came after the creation of the Common Market in 1957. Between 1958 and 1963, over 300 American companies settled in Belgium, over 250 chose Holland, possibly 600 set up operations in France. More than 1000 American companies established subsidiaries in non-Common-Market Britain. Many of these companies set up separate subsidiaries in two, three, or more countries, and 3000-plus U.S. companies now maintain European manufacturing activities of one type or another. Some U.S. subsidiaries and joint ventures boast no American managers; a few, such as Chrysler and Du Pont, at their peak, may have carried over 200 Americans on their payrolls in Europe. In all, U.S. companies now maintain an estimated 40,000 American men, women, and children in Europe.

These postwar American companies and managers poured into Europe in such numbers that they annoyed, and eventually frightened, national industrial and government groups. The new arrivals were blamed for rising rents for luxury apartments, "unnecessarily high" wages and salaries, and "the disruption of orderly marketing" (i.e., lively competition). (Some of the severest critics were "old-timer" U.S. companies in Europe.) As more and more big and medium-sized U.S. companies increased their stake in Europe, complaints about the americanization of Europe, then of "American domination of national industry," grew. In 1962 an Englishman came out with a popular book to this tune, several French ministers made unfavorable public comment on the same score, and a number of German editors and industrialists chimed in with loud alarums over this new American invasion. The next year the French Government requested a meeting of Common Market ministers to discuss curbs on American investment in member countries. A new reaction to the Americans had set in.

However, to all intents and purposes the Yanks are already an integral part of the new Europe. The profitable, protected national markets of old are dwindling, and sellers' markets, like the street singer and organ-grinder, are disappearing. This marketing move was becoming obvious in 1962 as Italian refrigerator manufacturers swooped in to take huge pieces of the French refrigerator market, as agricultural equipment producers throughout Europe moved into each other's markets, and as the auto industries of Europe braced for a headlong crash of production lines.

There is continuous resistance. In France the refrigerator industry, caught napping by foreign competitors, was able to get a special six months' tariff imposed on Italian refrigerators while it "adjusted" to this new competition.[1] In Germany, meanwhile, a number of important industries were simultaneously lobbying their usually pliable government for a special tariff increase so they too could adjust to the outside competition. Meanwhile, German auto manufacturers growled that, in Italy, Fiat had a fat 80 percent of the market and the Italian government would not drop tariffs

---

[1] Since refrigerators are still a seasonal (summer) sales item in Europe, this seemingly innocuous six-month summer tariff would be as effective as a one-year tariff.

sufficiently to let Volkswagen and others compete. In Brussels, at the same time, the antitrust section of the Common Market Commission was having no real success getting information about European industry, much less competitive rulings into effect within it.

But the above are rearguard actions. The new Europe is fast building, and in the new Europe American companies are doing very well. It is revealing to see the obvious frustration and annoyance of highly competent Europeans when they see U.S. managers, for whom they have little individual respect, taking away markets from their much more "clever" European rivals. Not all Americans do that well, but enough so that it is worrisome. One commonly cited reason for this success is that many American firms are so large by European standards that they can afford to buy a market. But there are also other factors, such as the American emphasis on setting and meeting schedules; habits of co-ordinating with others; familiarity with a consumer economy; a willingness to try something because it might work, and if it doesn't, let's try something else. How long these differences and advantages will exist is a question. The Europeans are openly and avowedly out, as one Belgian put it, "to beat the Americans at their own game." This will be hard on some Americans and good for the new Europe.

AMERICAN STIGMATA

Advertising in Europe is growing, and is going American. Most of the major U.S. advertising firms have opened offices to speed the process. These firms have virtually transformed English advertising, and are hoping to do the same thing on the Continent.

American marketing concepts have met little resistance in Europe. "In fact, we have taken them over and improved them," says a German marketing executive. Faced with competition from the smooth-working teams that run Procter & Gamble Co., Henkel, the German soap company, has more than held its own. Giant, Holland-headquartered Unilever may not be the liveliest competitor in British markets, but on the Continent its food and soap lines blanket all channels, crowd the competition. Most major European consumer-product companies are rapidly improving their studies and controls of, as well as their approaches to, the market.

Management consultants, especially American Management consultants, flourish in Europe. By and large these American consultants sell techniques and technology—e.g., they offer special advice on steel-mill design and operation, on marketing analysis, on checking new products or new (other country) markets, and on budgetary, cost-accounting, and sales-control systems. Like most U.S. advertising agencies in Europe, U.S. consulting organizations backed into Europe at the behest of U.S. clients, but work hard at getting European accounts. American executive-recruiting firms have come to Europe. So has Manpower Inc., an agency that specializes in part-time office help.

Meanwhile, throughout Europe one discovers the Ameropeans, Europeans who have studied and/or worked for some time in the U.S. These men make ideal idea-bridges, serve as important information-translating centers in European and in American companies (where you find them in key slots and on their way up through the hierarchy). These men have drive, speak American-management lingo (which in U.S. firms is evidently vital), and, as Europeans, get along with Europeans. They serve as cross-cultural lubricants. That is, most of them do. One hard-driving, up-and-coming, U.S.-trained Anglo-Swiss who works with an American consumer-products company in Europe is referred to as "The Ugly American" by his European workmates.

Then there are the new Europeans, usually young men, often of good family, who are neither resentful nor fearful of the changes going on around them and who expect to run the Europe of twenty years from now. Those in their thirties may have a slight chip on their shoulders, but they are out to prove something—and very likely will. The younger men are more relaxed (the ice is cracking ahead of them) but every bit as hard-working. All are beginning to think and work in Europe-wide terms. They enjoy twitting the Americans but are essentially very serious. They have so much to do. It is they who must bridge the gaps between the old Europe and the new.

Does all the above represent an americanization of Europe? If americanization means the takeover of Europe by essentially American ideas, attitudes, and prejudices, the answer is no. If americanization means the development and spread of American or American-like products, techniques, and organizations throughout Europe, the answer is a qualified yes.

But the adaption of new, American-like techniques and organizations would undoubtedly lead to the development of new attitudes and viewpoints in Europe. Is this, then, a form of second-order americanization?

To find out, let us take a closer look at the evolving new Europe and at American companies operating within it.

PART I

THE NEW-OLD EUROPE AND ITS CHANGING MILIEU

CHAPTER 2

EUROPE, NEW AND OLD

New building is endemic in the new Europe. Major cities are a mixture, sometimes pleasing, of modern glass-walled buildings, nineteenth-century homes and offices, winding medieval streets and ancient houses. Frankfurt, Germany, which had its share of night visits during the war, has much of the new face. Zeil Weig, its main shopping street, is all flat-sided multistory stores and offices set down like table radios end-to-end in a giant discount store. Rotterdam, Holland, which had its heart burnt out in one night and a day, is a series of straight lines, open squares, and gleaming windows set to catch the cloudy North Sea light. Other cities seem less extreme, but at the edge of every city are the inevitable ten- and fifteen-story apartment blocks. Ancient cathedrals, Gothic look-alikes, lovely reminders of an antique partial European unity, are everywhere. But today's profane symbol, the glass-walled office building, rises higher. No city is complete without one; more are building. The new is everywhere, not just in buildings but in people, their goods, and their pleasures.

The working classes of Europe have for generations been just that, no more. They worked to eat, walked to work, and were not considered an important market for goods. The working class still works, but many drive to work, and somehow they are now almost middle class and a very important market—in fact, the basis of the economy. It happened after World War II.

Take Theodore and Anna Halsman, a German couple near Wiesbaden. He is thirty-eight and she is thirty-four years old. Theodore earns $2650 a year as a machinist; Anna also works, as a $1500-per-year secretary in a construction company. They have two boys.

In 1945, shortly after the war, Anna remembers being glad to get potato peelings for dinner and walking five miles with her older sister to an already stripped woods in search of twigs with which to cook the meal. Now a new supermarket has opened near her new apartment and she does her buying there; frozen foods are coming into use. Anna once made her own dresses (when she could get material); now she buys her clothes. "It is important to be neat at the office," she explains. Her husband, who before the war might have owned one suit, now owns three. Her boys start to school each year in brand-new gear. Anna reads the fashion and women's magazines, does not clip menus but does file etiquette notes and decorating tips, and worries about doing things "properly." Over the past six years, Theodore and Anna have bought a new stove, TV set, auto, and refrigerator; a washing machine is next on the list. All their appliance purchases to-date are first-time buys. A nice, unexceptional family. Multiply Theodore and Anna by eight to twelve millions in a single country, and one begins to see what consumer wants plus a little money in many pockets can do.

Anna matured early in a time of chaos, United Nations Relief Organization food lines, and black markets. A pack of cigarettes bought food or love (of a kind), but this is a vague, unwelcome memory. The change began in 1950, the year of Korea; Anna was twenty. By now things were tidily organized though nothing was plentiful, and this was the year the rest of the West decided to rearm Germany. The investment impetus of American funds, plus hard work, turned the trick; Germany spiraled toward prosperity. The improvements came only gradually for working people, but they came. Around 1956 something new, a mass-consumer boom began.

With varying degrees of lead or lag, the other peoples of Europe began to find themselves living through a similar process. The first sign of change was the girls. They began to look stylish, well-dressed, even sleek. (American cosmetic and foundation-garment companies spotted the trend and moved to Europe to help extend it. They got there early, did well, and still do.) The European Economic Community's Treaty of Rome, signed in 1957, gave added push and confidence to the national boomlets, and the new Europe began to rise, complete with motels, new restaurants, vacation resorts, well-attended clubs, and fine profits. The new Europe, grown out of destruction and poverty, is wealthy. Clubs in Germany and Brussels that charge $1.25 to $2.00 for drinks scare few customers away. A workman or an office clerk supporting a family on $30 a week doesn't go, but plenty of other Europeans evidently can and do. Many clubs in Germany that started out as G.I. entertainment spots now would just as soon the G.I.s stay away; the soldiers' complaints about prices embarrass tired German businessmen who have come to watch the show.

It is in summer, though, that the new Europe bursts into bloom. By plane, train, cycle, or bus, but preferably by car, roughly one third of France moves to the Mediterranean during August. Italians also catch the move-to-the-sea-or-lakes-in-August fever. During the summer season almost half the German nation (20 million out of 50 million people) leave Germany for just about everywhere. The Britons and other North Sea Europeans also filter down to taste a bit of sun. Europe becomes a summer sea of open-collared colored shirts and cameras. And each year the Americans get harder to spot. But if one single item were to epitomize the new Europe it would be the auto.

America's long love affair with the automobile is pale and cold compared to the intensity and ardor of Europe's happy lust. More than transportation, a car is the symbol of power, of arrival, and of escape in countries where all these things are harder to come by than in America. Only Americans travel Europe in dusty cars; Europeans stop to polish theirs. Englishmen now polish cars instead of tending gardens. European bumpers are not really bumpers but a specially fragile and cherished portion of the car. Drivers who touch bumpers with the car behind when parking in Switzerland will sometimes find that a bystander has called the police. This is a sin which deserves, at the least, a reprimand from authority. Among America's upper-middlebrows and high-brows the auto isn't considered fit for conversation. In Europe, serious-minded young things will break up lesser conversations to learn what make of car somebody drives. Gossip columnists, as a matter of course, report on the cars their personages are sporting.

"It's a shame to see what the car is doing to these beautiful old cities; they keep paving over lovely little parks around here for their autos," says an American in Zurich. In Frankfurt cars are parked on sidewalks, where pedestrians respectfully skirt them. Americans, who have seen this movie before, wonder if European citizens and government planners have any real idea of what the car will mean, for by and large the European road net is narrow, town-and-village-choked, and, increasingly, traffic-clogged. There is also a truck boom in Europe. Low-geared, two-trailer, hard-to-pass trucks form long commercial convoys that pound the roads day and night. Each year five-million and more new private cars put rubber to pavement, and road-construction work is minuscule compared to already evident needs. But new loves tend to get what new loves want, and this will change. Overpasses, underpasses, four-leaf clovers, and superhighways are on the way.

The auto is changing the form and location of Europe's entertainment, its courtship patterns, and is giving new mobility to labor. However, the new Europe means something more than well-paid workmen and shiny autos. It also means language schools flourishing in all the capitals, a new sense of personal potential, and, especially among middle- and upper-level government and business people, a sense of pride in what has been accomplished to-date. There is also recognition that much more can be done, realization that this calls for Europe-wide industries and markets, plus an excitement—and hesitation, too—about this new factor. In varying degrees the Europeans realize that social change will follow a broadening of the economy; but, as in the case of autos and road nets, they don't realize yet just what pressures and changes are due. Prodding them to move ahead with the new greater-Europe trend is not the threat of Russia ("We have America against that," explains one) so much as a primordial interest in profits and, most widely, the memory and still felt shock of World War II.

The ache and a general sense of guilt and loss after World War II hang over Europe like winter clouds. The war is a watershed in time, and its memory (out of nowhere, like pieces in a dream) pops into conversations, then fades out again. It comes, almost as out of context as these fragments:

"But that was during the occupation."

"When I see one over 40 I wonder; and what did you do during the war, Mr. German?"

"They shot three men against my wall."

"We were cowards; the British fought."

"Among ourselves we don't discuss the occupation; too many people did too many things."

"Of course, the British had the Channel. . . ."

"Your bombers did not leave us very much."

"After the war was harder than the war."

Youngsters in their teens and early twenties have only hearsay memories of the war and its bleak aftermath. Says a 21-year-old Dane: "The Germans come over here, drink beer and are jolly. The old people don't like them, but we younger fellows get along." With reservations, a companion agrees. Paris universities and language schools are favorites with German students, and a German psychologist says of today's young Germans, "They are different in several ways, but mostly they are not nationalistic. They think about Europe." And yet, enough scar-happy students are flocking to the dueling clubs in German universities to keep tribalism very much alive. The new Europe is not skin-deep as yet, while the old Europe still grows out of the bone. Behind World War II lies the memory of World War I, back of that is the War of 1870, and so it goes through time. Europeans have long memories.

OLD EUROPE

Most Americans are descendants of Europeans who, in moving to the New World, consciously severed their European memories and acquired new ones. America is young, and for us the beginnings of time go back little more than 300 years. Now that we are tying ourselves back to Europe it is becoming necessary to revive some of the old memories because one can't clearly see the kaleidoscopic new Europe without them. One has to "see" and "feel" something of the presence of the old tribes and kingdoms, the old cities that nurtured present Europe, and the class systems that still support and restrict it.

Years and dates are an arbitrary and numbing way to measure human time and changes in attitudes. There is a more natural system at hand. The average span of years between a father and his sons varies between twenty-five and thirty years. This is a useful measure. Looking at the Norman invasion of Anglo-Saxon Britain in 1066, the time gap is nearly 900 years. But it is also something that happened thirty fathers ago. The event comes even closer psychologically if we take yet another measure of time. Anybody who has known his grandfather and/or other people's grandfathers will have observed that the differences in thought and attitudes between these generations is not nearly so great as the similarities. For all the arguments between generations, there is much in grandfather's attitudes and ideas which we admire and accept.

A robust grandfather talks with his son and grandson: these three form a natural human unit of time. Let's call it a grandfather-unit of time. Only fifteen grandfather-units ago the Normans won the Battle of Hastings. A short twenty grandfather-units back takes us to the fall of Rome. At that time our North European grandfathers had the tribal organization, ethics, and mores of the people now trying to learn to rule themselves in the Congo. And twenty grandfather-units isn't very long ago. This realization helps put some of Europe's origins in a new, more realistic perspective and proximity—for the old tribes and people are submerged but still there.

In the valleys of Wales, west of England on the island of Britain, dwell the ruddy, heavy-browed Celtic Welsh and the ancient Dark Welsh, round-headed, slimly built, black-haired people with deep features. These Dark Welsh bowmen, moving up from Spain before European history began, mixed with the earlier immigrants who built the ancient megaliths, the gigantic stone barrows of old sagas and legend. In Southern England, as in Holland, one sees lank-haired blonds whose faces were as familiar to the local fens 1000 years ago as now. In artificial light, a long-faced North Italian woman, with sculptured nostrils and lips, becomes a fifteenth-century painting. Hours after a visit with a Tuscan university professor you realize why he looked so familiar; his portrait was painted over 2000 years ago on the wall of a nearby Etruscan tomb. The light-haired Lombards (the Long-beards) gave their name to a province of North Italy, and one can tell those of Lombard descent by their name endings and their looks.

Time, plus the upheavals of World War II, the urban emigration of labor in the new Europe, and the auto have combined to break down the old tribal settlements, and are turning parts of Europe into something closer to the racial melting pot America claims to be. But the process is slow and has far to go; there are many pockets undisturbed. In 1962, for instance, sociologists stumbled across a Scottish village in the Alps. Some twelve or thirteen grandfather-units ago, a company of Scottish archers, freebooting their way through Europe, hired themselves out to the losing side in a battle between Florence and Milan. With the Milanese winning the day and their employers in flight, the archers formed a compact body and retreated toward the Alps. (Nobody would have been anxious to pursue a determined body of men armed with armor-piercing arrows.) Moving deep into an Alpine valley, the Scotsmen fortified a village and settled down. Some undoubtedly went to war again, a few may have gone home, but the majority stayed put. Their descendants carry Scottish names, speak Italian laced with Gaelic, but have lost the Scottish burr.

Near modern Paris a high-cheekboned Frenchman gesticulates with hands and eyebrows and explains the world to visitors much as his fathers did to stolid Romans. The French sometimes try to explain themselves by saying, "We are a Latin people." In truth, the bulk of them are less Latin than the Rumanians—Slavs who happen to speak a Latin language. It is the brilliant and quarrelsome Gauls who stride through France today as yesterday. And, all over Europe pieces of yesterday lie round about. In parts of Italy country people still lay flowers at ancient pagan shrines (with little pretense that they are Christian shrines). Villagers in Breton France bring gifts to the local witch to seek her help in matters mean or large. In Holland an intelligent and sophisticated lady whose dog strayed recently went to a medium for aid in the search.

Old beliefs, and old national memories, too. In Scotland the Scottish National party, emotional heir to Bonnie Prince Charlie's "rebellion," seeks a local parliament, and is a factor in elections. The ancient Welsh, whose king, Llewellyn, was killed in 1207, fitfully try to revive old freedoms, right old wrongs; there is a weak but active Welsh underground independence movement. In fact, Europe, as colored on the map, seems a grouping of strong national states; actually, however, it overlays a collection of different, more ancient nations. On the Mediterranean, from Narbonne, France, to Tarragona, Spain, the people share similar feast days, costumes, dances, and a patois that is neither French nor Spanish. They still speak wistfully of the almost-nation at Catalonia. Further north, in Provence, a historical source of heresies, poets and Protestantism, there is another local tongue and, again, memories of another almost-country that never came to flower.

Modern Europe is a four-dimensional montage (the fourth dimension is time) of peoples and memories. No major war, social or political, or religious struggle is forgotten, but is merely built on by new ones. In Holland today (population ten million) an American businessman who wants to reach a mass audience must advertise in four sets of papers; there is a Catholic, Protestant, Socialist, and Liberal (i.e., conservative) press. The Liberal-Socialist division is new, hardly 100 years (two grandfather-units) old. The Catholic-Protestant differentiation goes back a bit further, to the Reformation, and to the wars against Spain 300 years (about six grandfather-units) ago.

In Belgium (population nine million) an advertiser must use two languages: Flemish and French. Local citizens hold protest marches and conduct street riots from time to time, reminding each other of these and other differences between them. In Switzerland, a confederacy very much on the lines of that proposed by the Civil War American South, there are four languages: Swiss-German, French, Italian, and Romanche (the ancestral tongue of a Celtic remnant swept into a corner of the mountains). In Italy, which became a country only two grandfather-units ago, in 1870, a businessman must think not of the Italian market but of the North Italian market (lively and prosperous) and the South Italian market (an improving but in many ways depressed area). Today, in the era of the Common Market, a service company intending to serve both France and Germany usually ends up with its offices in psychologically neutral Switzerland or possibly Brussels. A German manufacturer visiting Copenhagen speaks American-accented English with just a touch of slang; it makes life easier.

"There are no dead issues in Europe, just indefinitely postponed ones," says one businessman. There is still a French pretender to the throne and people who would like to see him reach it; and in an OAS court trial in 1963 a French defense attorney quite seriously challenged a prosecution lawyer to a duel. One must not let the shiny new cars and buildings and the business logic of the new Europe delude him into thinking he can ignore the old.

CITY LOGIC

The old Europe that lies under the new, the old Europe that is most obviously influential, comes out of its cities. Of the three secular groupings of the Middle Ages—the nobles, peasants, and burghers—the burghers prevailed. They created industries and wealth and tightly organized societies where power was shared by trades and guilds and individuals or families of wealth. These cities, usually run by oligarchs, had histories and traditions of their own which are still cherished. Europe's cities are older than its countries. Marseilles, London, Zurich, Florence, Hamburg, all antedate the national consciousness that dominates them. Once they were free cities. Now there is possibly one left in Europe: Geneva. As the extreme of a type, it can help explain something about European thinking.

Geneva, Switzerland, is an international financial center of almost 200,000 people, with a jet airport, modern office buildings, a view of the Alps, and frontage on a lovely lake. It shelters more American company headquarters than any other city in Europe. Over 10,000 American men, women, and children live there. But, more than a city, Geneva is an entity.

The town lies at the spot where the Rhone River pours out of Lake Leman to start the long fall south to Marseilles and the sea. Men have lived there since the Stone Age; the pile supports of their lake huts still stand in the water. When the Helvetians, a truculent tribe of Celts, burned their corncribs to migrate west towards France and claim new lands (about thirty-three grandfather-units ago), Julius Caesar and his troops met them near Geneva and, after unsuccessful parley, followed by numerous marches and battles, sent them bleeding home to a hungry winter. As ambitious Caesar pushed into Gaulish France, Geneva, situated on a main trade route, prospered and grew.

Left on its own after the fall of Rome, Geneva gradually built itself into a free city-state; wealth from trade, a loyal citizenry, and strong walls making it a match for local medieval overlords. With the Reformation the rectors of the university and town fathers became Protestant and welcomed John Calvin as spiritual and temporal leader. Through the years they went to church, attended to business, and withstood intermittent assaults by the neighboring Savoyards. Napoleon tucked the city into his capacious empire for a time. It became independent again after the Great Man left the European scene. Then, coming full historic circle, in 1830 Geneva cast its lot with the loose Swiss confederation of cantons, the Helvetic Confederation. Shades of Caesar's Helvetians.

For all its gambling casinos, naughty cabarets, and restless international sets, Geneva, today as yesterday, is a close-knit, close-run, proper little town-within-a-town where the heads of the banking clans run the city for the good of the clans—and therefore of the city. Social life is a matriarchy controlled by clan grandmothers. Business and family life has a strong New England flavor. A young Genevois temporarily in London remembers his gray-bearded Old Testament figure of a grandfather. The old man used to wake his sons at 6:00 in the morning for family Bible reading and, after a breakfast of porridge, walk off to his bank. The abstemious Boston bluenoses who bankrolled New England's profitable rum, slave, and molasses trade would have approved.

But Geneva is under siege. It is an island: of French-Swiss in a sea of German-Swiss; of genuine Genevois in a rising tide of outsiders and foreigners; of Calvinists in a sea of Catholics; of nineteenth-century attitudes under assault from all directions. An American resident notes: "Only about 50,000 of the people here are native Genevois of more than two generations, and of these about 5000 are the people that count. The 5000 pull together, cling to the old ways, don't quite know whether to embrace the change, but don't really feel they can do much to stop it—and they like the money too much to try." But there are the first hints of a question: Can they continue to run their city and their banks as they used to?

For two-dozen deep-habit-forming generations Geneva was far enough away from the turbulent centers of Europe, so that it could follow its own patterns of life. Now, sudden as an air strike, a new world has dropped in and is growing around it. The companies moving into Geneva are not just tenants, they are also important clients—and you can't socially ignore a client who lives across the street. The patterns of world finance are changing. Size is becoming a major factor in banking. The Swiss-Germans seem to be taking over the great banks in Switzerland, and no one is sure just yet what can happen, or should happen, to the small family banks. There is worry. The old order is changing.

The present Europe, as noted, grew out of its ancient cities. From the mid-1800s on, industries began replacing crafts; but the men who owned and ran the new industries sprang from the cities and took their attitudes, values, and practices from the city. Controlled markets, restricted competition, agreed-upon prices, the blocking of new competitors, the social hierarchy of European business and social control through oligarchical senior bodies—all came from established city patterns. These systems, cherished as morally and logically correct, clash with a new, more subtle, and sometimes contradictory logic, with competition and change as constants.

A QUESTION OF CLASS

Over the generations the rulers and peoples of Europe have constantly striven to hold back or slow change. One of the most effective tools for resisting change is a tightly organized class system, and class differences are the cement of European societies.

Class lines in America are vague, and movement between them is easy enough so that many Americans can pretend we have no class system. In Europe there is no such pretense. Class lines are carefully delineated, and the broad gap between top and bottom is often marked by genuine disdain and sometimes fear.

When the Franks moved in to give their name to Gaul, they assumed overlordship of an existing population. The Normans in England came as conquerors, and so did numbers of the ruling groups in Italy and Spain. However, this "rule by strangers" may only have accelerated the class differences that came out of the Middle Ages and continued into modern times. They were extreme: at the Battle of Agincourt the massed French knights, eager to get at a British invasion force, rode down and trampled their own advancing skirmish line of foot troops. This was only twelve impatient grandfathers ago, and the remnants of this fine contempt for the lower orders is still evident in Europe. Peasant revolts have given way to workers' strikes and socialist parties, but the term "class war" still has meaning in Europe (so much so that in the 1920s fear of it helped create European fascism).

It is almost as difficult for a (white) American to conceive the extent or nature of the gaps between classes in Europe as it is for Europeans to bridge it, because these differences are formed of carefully nurtured emotions. And it is one of the old memories Americans worked hardest to erase; few came to America from the comfortable top of the old social order.

Class systems are not a mere extension of the snob instinct; they are a carefully developed technique for promoting stability by freezing the existing social order. They make it easy for a man to stay at the level in which he was born, difficult for him to move. European class systems, like all others, are based on money and power; but once a system is established, since money and power will not come easily to those not already near the top, less "materialistic" measures are possible. A man's family, profession, education, degree of culture, and "time in grade" are weighed as status marks. The individual who first breaks into a new level of the society is seldom fully accepted socially; his children may be; his grandchildren are. The essence is a slowing down of any change.

Once established, class systems can become virtually self-sustaining. Conscious of Gresham's Law, as it were, groups at various levels of the hierarchical ladder devote considerable energy to keeping those below them at a distance and in their place. There must be no cheapening of the social coin. Class distinctions are maintained by careful family indoctrination, by withholding or granting economic opportunity, by manipulation of educational systems.

It is the English who have developed the stigmata of a class system to the highest degree by emphasizing manner of speech. England is a land of dialects, and people of working and lower-middle-class station or background are spotted and placed in the social scale by the kind and degree of local accent they display. Above this level the England-wide public school (private boarding school) accent takes over. It is the Great Delineator. Children learn their attitudes and accents at public schools, and families on the way up (or down) will make painful financial sacrifices to get a child into a proper school. One even determines delicate class gradations by shadings in public school accents. Oxford and Cambridge universities, at the social and educational apex of England, supply a special patina (including a peculiar stutter affected by some Oxonians). Acquisition of a proper accent is socially so important that scholarship students arriving at Oxford from a non-public-school background (i.e., grammar schools) have been known to hire elocutionists to help them pick up the proper grace notes. In another social world—but growing in size and quality—are the red-brick provincial colleges, where the many boys who could not make it into Oxford and Cambridge get their degrees.

"Put twelve Englishmen in a room together and within three days they will range themselves in social pecking order from one through twelve," says an American of more than ten years' residence in England. He believes that this will change—in fifty years. "It is already changing in business," he says, "not just in technical areas but in any large company. A young fellow who wants to get ahead can do so faster than in the U.S. It is only the stockbrokers and banks that are holdouts; in large companies it's the job that counts." Then he adds, "But these class things matter so terribly in a man's private life. On the one side there is this heart-searing business of being locked out; on the other, a sort of bland arrogance."

The most insidious (or perhaps successful) aspect of a closed class system is its effectiveness in convincing a man that those above him in the social order are his betters. In this respect, it is a form of highly selective emasculation. A red-brick-college graduate says, "If some perfectly stupid clod is firmly convinced that he's intrinsically better than you; if everyone else around believes the same thing; then you begin to think there may be something to it, in spite of all the evidence to the contrary. No matter how hard you try, you are never going to make it."

The answer for many is not to try very hard, to accept the system but be sticklers for their "rights" within it. An American executive working with Britons notes, "You have to worry about their susceptibilities, and the lower down the scale you go the more sensitive they get." Certainly at the level of the laboring force there is much good humor, but also an obvious resentment which leads laborers to speak of themselves as a forgotten people who are taken for granted. Their quarrels are not so much between labor and management as between *them*, the upper class, and *us*, the workers. As a result, besides unions, steeped in doctrinaire 1890s socialism, parts of British industry are plagued with low productivity and wildcat strikes. An American plant manager in Britain, exasperated by a long series of grievances and quickie walkouts at his factory, bursts out, "Sometimes I think all they are looking for is attention." He is almost right. Not fifteen miles away a couple of other American plant managers, who have realized this, have little labor trouble at all. (Among other gestures, they play golf with the regional union representative.)

The different class systems throughout Europe have varied earmarks, social safety valves, and routes to the top. In France a principal route to the top is one of the grandes ecoles, government-sponsored technical institutes that date from the time of Napoleon. In Belgium and Holland family background and connections are still the main criteria for a smile from fate. In Germany and Italy the class systems, at first glance, are more open than in many other countries, but have their own hidden blocks and deadfalls. In all Europe, though, the old order is under pressure. The old class system will not be swept aside and forgotten. It is being partially bypassed and overlaid by new systems and new logics.

Just under the skin of the new Europe are the still live memories and attitudes of all the ancient peoples, nations, and classes that make it up. If you doubt this, talk to a well-educated "modern" European, ask him why things are the way they are and why they should or should not be another way in changing Europe. Chances are he will be glad to give his views. Once he gets underway, listen carefully. Sooner or later you will begin to hear grandfather talking.[1]

---

[1] When General Charles de Gaulle, priest-chieftain of the Frankish-Gaulish nation, spoke of the "Anglo-Saxons," he was not toying with romantic euphemisms. De Gaulle is of an ancient line. Think of a strong-willed grandfather; twelve such grandfathers back a group of third-generation Norse pirates who had seized the north coast of France crossed the English Channel to take control of that island from the loosely organized tribes that lived there. A handful of generations later these same pirates, now thoroughly integrated with their rough Saxon cousins, came back to France armed with a powerful new weapon—the Welsh-invented longbow. For generations these bandits laid waste the body of France. It took the efforts of 40,000 men and a girl to drive them out.

Ejected from the Continent, these Anglo-Saxons reverted to the sea, from whence they came, and took up trade. Ever since, usually for petty mercantile reasons, they have been frustrating the high-minded efforts of Europe's major nations to conquer each other by the sword. Their American cultural cousins are no better, and now they are in Europe.

CHAPTER 3

THE MILIEU OF CHANGE

"What's it like doing business in Europe? Six years ago I could have told you. . . . Maybe in another six years I'll know again."
A U.S. EXECUTIVE IN GENEVA

A number of American businessmen report that business life in Europe is different, but no more difficult or confusing, than in the U.S. Many more, however, find their European experience closer to a walk through uncharted swamp with a faulty compass.

What confuses and distresses these unhappy explorers are the hauntingly familiar yet different, even illusory, paths and landmarks they encounter. Underlying the new Europe are various forms of nineteenth-century capitalism complete with *caveat emptor* and "the public be damned" overtones of America's turn of the century. All the fine old business-jungle ethics (highly refined and carefully stylized, of course) are also preserved. Ubiquitous governments exercise a paternalism which ranges from carefully detailed solicitude for workers (and sometimes consumers) to active control of, or competition with, private investment. This is as if, in America, the onetime hopes and plans of financier J. P. Morgan to organize key U.S. industries into a "gentleman's club" controlled by its banks, and the most doctrinaire dreams of Roosevelt's New Deal, had come true together.

Says one American, "Working in Europe is like stepping into the world of one of those distortion mirrors in a funhouse at the carnival; everything is familiar but the proportions are different."

Italy, for instance, is a surrealist's study in Early Laissez Faire. Through early 1963 the Italian Government did not enforce international patent agreements. Italian drug companies made a lucrative business of pirating expensively developed U.S. and European drugs as quickly as they came on the market (and in one or two cases, through industrial espionage, a little sooner). Government-owned or -controlled companies compete with private industry in chemicals, oil, steel, electronics, and dozens of other industries. Labor is watched over, social-service charges (fringe benefits) are among the highest in Europe—up to 50 percent of the basic wage. And yet there is little or no food and drug legislation or inspection for the protection of consumers; every year a major scandal erupts over adulterated products. Bribery of public officials and the press is commonplace. Dozens of new fortunes and industries have been created in Italy since World War II. Conspicuous consumption is a favorite pastime, and tax dodging a national obsession. All in all, it is enough to warm a Commodore Vanderbilt's heart—except that government holding companies have the frightening habit of buying up private companies' stocks.

Belgium is an extreme of another type. Whatever competitive struggles there may have been have long since largely been resolved. Today, what is good for the Société Générale de Belgique is likely to be what Belgian society gets. To understand what this giant holding company represents in Belgium, try to visualize an American economy wherein the Chase Manhattan Bank, the Bank of America, and the five largest investment houses in Wall Street have merged with General Electric, Westinghouse, U. S. Steel, Du Pont, Union

Carbide, and several other major manufacturing, mining, and shipping companies.

The Société Générale is not so much a company as a chunk of the economy (possibly 10 percent of it), and major firms that do not belong to the Société Générale are usually affiliated with one or two other Belgian trusts. Belgium is a young nation. It was created in 1839. Through judicious intermarriage and investments its "nobility" and rising industrial burgher families joined forces to create a series of family-linked industries. The royal family, for instance, has important holdings in the Société Générale. "But it's not even as simple as that. Actually, just about everybody owns at least a little bit of everybody else," says a banker in this familial country.

Americans in Belgium find their hosts easy to get along with, "interesting" to do business with. "Hire a top accountant, read the contracts for what they don't say as much as for what they do say, and be sure to keep some kind of a trump up your sleeve. If there is a way of backing you into a corner, somebody will find it." That, in effect, is what half a dozen long-term residents in Belgium say. Curiously, they almost always say it with a grin. "The Belgians are so cheerfully, blatantly piratical you almost don't mind it," an American entrepreneur remarks.

Serious Switzerland, land of mountains, international banks, and precision machinery, has another pattern and tempo. There are a few large and many small firms in Switzerland. If a company wishes to move into new technology, that is its own affair; but generally, in an established field a company is expected to maintain the industry price structure. Legal (and enforced) markups for wholesalers and retailers are set by manufacturers' associations (cartels). Efficient companies gain by making more profit than less able firms, but seldom sell at a lower price.

Here's one example of how tidily a national cartel can work. Through 1962 the cost of having a man's suit dry-cleaned in Switzerland was seventeen Swiss francs (about $4.25). Four American businessmen in Geneva decided that for $16,000 they could open up a modern dry-cleaning shop, charge $1.25 or $1.50 to clean a suit, and get their money back within a year. They applied to the city for a license. The city gave its blessing and referred them to the canton, which looked over the application, formally acquiesced, and in turn referred the would-be capitalists to the central government at Bern. The authorities at Bern solemnly studied the project and O.K.d it, but said the company would have to be an accepted member of the national association of dry cleaners. Representatives of the association then looked over the group's plans and financial arrangements and, after due consultation, agreed to accept the new group. There was only one condition: the new members, like all members, would have to charge seventeen Swiss francs to clean a man's suit. Says one of the businessmen who experienced this four-step process and punch line, "And up till then I'd always thought the Swiss had no sense of humor."

France, Germany, Holland, Britain: each boasts a different pattern of development and of economic practice. Sometimes there is lively competition within national markets, but generally it is subdued. "You've got to remember these are old, close-knit societies in Europe," cautions a U.S. banker. "They have had a long time to organize and to resist any change that threatens the status quo. That's why their early industrialists never went to the excesses ours did, but that's also why their system has never undergone any real reforms." American companies in Europe soon find this out for themselves.

One American electronics company, emboldened by its strong technical lead and patent position, moved to the Continent, built a modern plant, but made no sales inroads to speak of. The reason: established major suppliers in Europe had quietly let dealers know that while, of course, anyone was free to buy as many of the newcomer's new products as he wished, there might be some "unavoidable" delays and cancellations in delivery of the remaining items these dealers needed from the major suppliers. (In America this sort of behavior is strictly illegal. In Europe it is strictly good business.) After bleeding dollars for a number of months, the new company managed a tie-in with one of the "Big Four" of the industry. Under patronage of its new sponsor, it was permitted into the market.

Again, a large U.S. company with long-established companies managed by Europeans has in recent years been spending large amounts of money and energy to co-ordinate its subsidiaries. This effort involved sending U.S. marketing experts and staff people to "advise" local managers. Pleased with himself and the good work he was doing, one American reported to an American colleague: "These fellows in France are plenty bright, but they've never even been through the basics of sales territory analysis. Why, there was a major potential customer fifteen miles away from the main plant they had never called on." However, what the polite senior French executives who received his various sales analyses had not found it politic to explain to this American member of middle management was that the "major potential customer" fifteen miles down the road was the "marketing property" of another supplier.

The ground rules, then, are different in Europe. Poaching of customers is discouraged, not only in cases where companies have split markets between them, but sometimes on general principle. In England, advertising agencies in good standing with the association of advertisers never directly solicit accounts held by other agencies. They must wait an invitation from prospective clients. In Holland, banks are not supposed to solicit accounts.

And yet, business in Europe is no matter of carefully shared profits and pleasures. In Belgium an American chemical company with useful patents and technical know-how entered into a joint venture with a subsidiary of the Société Générale de Belgique. When the new plant went into production, the Belgians, who held a controlling 51 percent of the stock and had charge of sales for the joint concern, sold the product virtually at cost to one of their own subsidiaries. This all-Belgian subsidiary then processed the low-cost material and sold it again at a happy profit. The Americans were left sadder, maybe wiser, and with a very low return on their investment. In France, after setting up a fifty-fifty joint venture with an important local appliance manufacturer, an American company expected to rush into production and to capture an important part of the market. Once this American potential competitor was carefully tied up via a joint-venture agreement, however, the European partner saw no point in moving quickly and upsetting the market. It kept the operation on a low-volume, high-markup basis.

Europeans cite the above as fairly typical instances of American naïveté in dealing with "sophisticated" European businessmen. In that the Americans ignored the different motives of, and the alternate courses of action open to, their European partners, the judgment is deserved. But there is a reverse side of this coin too. Many Europeans are prone to a curious form of unrealism or naïveté of their own. Take the case of the French company which, in effect, tied up its potential American competitor by entering into a joint venture with it. Ten years ago, tucked safely into a national market, it could have felt smug about its finesse. Today there is the Common Market. At the moment, German and Italian producers are invading this firm's home markets and un-derpricing it—when, with the U.S. partner's help, the reverse could have been true. As Europeans like to explain to Americans, the ground rules are different in Europe. But the uncomfortable realization that the game may be changing is slowly taking hold. Meanwhile, Europe is a marble-cake mixture of new and old.

SOME RULES OF THE GAME

To get a new product launched in Switzerland one non-Swiss manufacturer decided to offer retailers a higher-than-normal margin. The first retailer to whom he suggested this, however, reached up to the counter behind him, pulled down his industry association listing of standard markups, and said, "Look, 22 percent—*that's* what I'm supposed to be getting. Now, don't try to offer me any more." Here we have the ancient, city guild system gone nationwide. Its objective is not to turn out more or cheaper products but to keep anybody who is already in business comfortably maintained without worry or much labor. Buying a business is like buying a piece of land; the customers, like the trees, come with the property.

Commercial legislation in Europe seems designed not so much to protect consumers as to protect producers and sellers—and the status quo. In Germany in the 1930s, for instance, at the behest of food retailers, department stores were forced to move their then newly established food departments from the ground to the top floor. In Germany today special sales are permitted only when a firm is giving up business or a particular line of goods. There is a legal winter sale period and a legal summer sale period (12 days each). Firms are also allowed a 25th-anniversary sale. Promotional contests using box tops or labels as entry blanks are illegal (because they are a buying compulsion). They are illegal, too, if potential participants have to get their entry blanks at a store or office of the firm running the contest (because, once in the store, many people would feel obliged to buy something). Free promotional samples are legal but they must be small (not more than one fair usage of the product), and it is illegal to give samples to 100 percent of the households in an area (because this temporarily clogs the market for competitive brands). Only passive competition is fully acceptable.

"Anytime you find a strange system of distribution or obvious gaps in product lines in a region or country, look for a law or local regulation," says a Belgian marketing consultant. "Everyone is surprised at how much beer we French-speaking Belgians drink. Well, the beer companies achieved a tax on wine. Also, at one time I wondered why no one had introduced a clock radio in Belgium or in Europe generally. They are quite popular in the United States and would seem a natural attraction. But clock radios have clocks, and this means jewelers' stores, a limited form of outlet with very, very high markups. Therefore," he shrugs, "no clock radios."

In Holland, land of tulips and merchant cities, supermarkets are difficult to establish because by ancient law stores can sell only what is in their guild charter. This slows any experimenting with supermarkets; licenses are hard to get. Gradually, however, more and more convenience items are moving to the "free list" (i.e., they can be sold through numerous outlets). In the meantime, supermarket operators have taken to buying up various small specialty stores for their licenses and pooling these licenses in one big store. Again, in Milan, in Northern Italy, the more than 200,000 retail establishments in that city have been applying political pressure on town authorities to hold back necessary licenses for would-be supermarket operators. Nevertheless, there—and in all Europe—self-service stores are spreading.

A EUROPEAN POINT OF VIEW

To Americans it sometimes seems that in a corner of many European minds there must be the firmly imbedded conviction that their society is virtually perfected, immutable, needing only minor rounding and burnishing here and there. Four hundred years of evidence to the contrary, few Europeans think in terms of process or evolution. Even rebels think in terms of change only in order to establish some other immutable system. These attitudes spring, possibly, from a combination of Europe's stable class systems, its small countries, and its city societies.

People in small groups do not compete with each other: they establish a pecking order. This, by turns, both explains and describes much about the business practices Americans encounter in Europe. From large firms down through medium and small firms, each has had its own preserve, rights, and status. European concepts of what business is for, what responsibilities it has, what rights and duties an individual has, are of many shades, but all are different than American concepts. In this sense the modern American businessman in Europe is truly an alien. The Americans, however, are aliens of omen, the outriders of a new order.

There are large international companies in Europe—for instance, Shell Oil, Unilever (soaps and food), and Nestle's (foods). There are good-sized national, and increasingly international, companies such as Imperial Chemical Industries of Britain, Renault and Fiat of France and Italy respectively, or Siemens (electrical products) of Germany. These hired-manager-run companies are a part of the new Europe. In structure they grow closer and closer to many American companies. Not so the thousands of smaller fry who make up the bulk and still set the tone of European industry.

The American chief of a machinery company selling to hundreds of European firms says, "Our customer is usually the son. Whether he is twenty-five or forty years old, he operates as president with the permission of his father." In this sense Europe is a full generation behind the United States, where the nonowner-managed, publicly held company is dominant.

Traditional European companies differ from American companies in a number of ways. For one thing, European firms are "smaller," about one-tenth smaller, than their U.S. counterparts. In Europe a company with $3–$4 million in yearly sales is considered medium-sized; anything over $10–$15 million in sales per year marks a large company; and concerns with sales of $40 million and more rank among the giants. European companies, especially the smaller ones, have invariably been more profitable than their U.S. equivalents. Acquisition specialists say actual earnings for a property in France, for instance, may well be twelve times those shown on the books. Company owner-presidents tend to enjoy company-financed autos, servants, homes, and other benefits not normally available to U.S. executives.[1]

---

[1] Mistresses, who present a special bookkeeping problem handled on a purely individual basis, are not so prevalent as legend indicates. However, an American eight years in Belgium reports, and a number of Belgians and fellow Americans tentatively confirm, that in that country the mistress may lately have become a top status symbol, superseding the chauffeur-driven car. In these cases she has often been on, but discreetly to one side of, the scene. Since there is no point in having a status symbol unless others know of it, she is now more prominently displayed than before, and preferably in the chauffeur-driven car.

There is also another less specific, more important difference.

Consciously or no, many Americans tend to think of their
companies as social entities, creations with a survival drive
and rudimentary conscience, operating in a universe occupied
by other, similar entities. Few Americans think of themselves
as working for the owner or owners of a company; they
think of themselves as working in, being part of, the company. With their fellows, they *are* the company. Persons
working in a company as part of the "team" or "organization"
create and reflect a mass personage, the "we" of the company. Possibly the corporation supplies some Americans with
the kind of identification Europeans derive from their class
system. In any event, this extra corporate ego exists in varying degrees in many companies and individuals. There is a
whole business and social literature, both satirical and serious,
that touches on this phenomenon. One man may start, direct,
or own the company, but most often, especially after it
reaches a certain critical size, his fellow workers (those in the
upper and middle management level) take part of it away
from him to create a joint entity. Generally the owner goes
along; he, too, comes to see the business not so much as a
means to an end or reflection of himself, but as an organism
with needs of its own.

The European owner, by contrast, looks at his company
as property, as the human and mechanical equivalent of an
orchard which he and his family tend. The orchard is alive,
in the sense that trees are alive, but passive. The people
who work in the company are not, like their American
counterparts, a part of the company; they are *his* faithful
gardeners, loyal and respected servants who help *him* harvest
his fruits. Significantly, one can expand an orchard, or buy
more orchards, but orchards do not of themselves expand,
and gardeners work only where and as directed. This par-

ticular concept of the European firm does not preclude growth, but neither does it automatically assume growth and change as does the American view.

It is easy to find European companies with absolutely no intention or temptation to grow. American equipment salesmen and Americans in search of reliable subcontractors commonly report on company owners who say, yes, they could double their businesses, but this would only triple their worries, bring the tax people nosing around, and complicate an otherwise comfortable life. "And how can you argue with that?" asks a U.S. engineer. The answer is that you can't. All one can do is point out that . . . well, the world is changing.

The rise of technology and new products, wherein plastics and aluminum compete with iron and steel, as in autos; mass national markets, which demand volume production (and create a base for exports), as in appliances; the Common Market, which encourages new kinds of companies and intercountry intrusions of a galaxy of products—all these are combining to crack once cozy little national markets, and comfortable patterns of business. They are putting thousands of family companies under mortal pressure to adapt or be bypassed.

Historically, European family firms with an urge to grow have done so through reinvestment of their high earnings. In the new Europe, however, profits are being squeezed, so that now, when cash is most urgently needed for reinvestment, it is hardest to get. Investment banks, the other traditional source of long-term capital, have traditionally extracted a steep price for their help. All too often turning to them for capital has meant turning over company control. Except in Britain, stock markets are not a well-developed source of capital (and are dominated by the investment banks). One common response to the times has been a wave of mergers between family companies and of sellouts to U.S. or other foreign companies searching for footholds in various national markets. In any event, the pre-eminence of the family-run concern is fading. A long era is passing.

In Europe, as previously in America, the corner store and family company are being bypassed, left behind. The portent and impact of this change are much greater than in the United States, because in Europe these businesses have been much more firmly rooted in the social order. "It sounds a bit Marxist, or 1840s, but over here you've got to think in terms of the *haute bourgeoisie*, who run and own big business and the banks; the *bourgeoisie*, who man the professions and government departments; and the *petite bourgeoisie*, who run the small shops," says a U.S. marketing man working in Belgium, France, and Germany. "These are the 'respectable' people who between them have pretty much run Europe." And he adds, as we have heard before: "Each group has its own customs and codes and an unwritten rule not to interfere with the other, not to rock the boat."

As symbols (and agents) of the new order evolving in Europe, American companies serve as emotional lightning rods. They draw political heat and emotional blame for the discomforts of change. But the main agents of change are purely European. Some, in fact, are bastions of the old order. The groups which have thus far been activated most and changed least by this passing of an era and the development of a new Europe, for instance, are the banks, which are thriving. In Europe, banking means more than it does in the United States. It is less a handmaiden to industry than its rich and demanding spouse. Traditionally, European banking has called the tune for European industry. To a great degree, as we will see, it still does. Banking is a key factor in the changing European milieu.

CHAPTER 4

OF BANKS AND BUSINESSMEN IN EUROPE

THE BANKERS' HOUR

In America, banks are banks; they lend money to businesses and individuals. Investment brokers are investment brokers; they garner capital through stock issues and dabble in the arcane ebb and flow of the stock market. By U.S. law, the two activities are kept separate.

In Europe, banks are banks all right, and investment brokers are just what the name implies, but the distinction between these two is nonexistent or blurred. In Germany, for instance, commercial banks are a principal source of short- and medium-term credit to business and are only beginning to discover and actively woo the individual bank depositor or customer, as in America. But commercial banks are also heavy investors in company stocks; through their trust departments they hold—and usually vote—the shares of individual clients. The banks between them have voting control of the major part of German industry.

Explains a foreign banker, "In Germany stocks are for the wealthy. They are held in big blocks." He notes that mutual funds, which started in Munich in 1950, are slowly changing this by attracting small investors. The government is encouraging mutual funds (which have lower loading charges, or management fees, than those in the U.S.). But the top banks all have mutual funds too. They are not losing position.

Continues this Frankfurt-based banker, "There is tremendous power concentrated in the banks. A banker can sit on as many as twenty company boards; after that he must get government permission. The head of the Deutsche Bank, Herman Abs, is on close to forty boards, usually as chairman. These bankers have large staffs who watch the companies for them. The top-echelon business people here stick together. There is much consensus on industry decisions, and the banks are the chairmen of the Club."

In Belgium commercial banking and investment banking, as in the U.S., are by law separate activities conducted by separate companies. However, since the boards of directors of many commercial banks are identical with the active boards of related investment banks, the separation is one of form rather than fact. In France commercial banks (the four dominant banks are government-owned) can hold only 10 percent of their deposits in corporate stocks. Insurance companies must invest 90 percent in government bonds, and savings associations must hold 50 percent of their funds in government bonds. However, numbers of private commercial banks, as in Belgium, are closely associated with active investment banks, aptly called *banques d'affaires*.

"In France," explains a New York investment banker, "everybody is into everyone else; suppliers do their best to own a piece of their main customers, and customers figure it's good insurance to have a piece of the supplier. With secrecy, side arrangements, and complications an everyday part of life, suppliers, and competitors too, like to be in a position of knowing what's going on. So they buy each other's shares, sit on each other's boards, set up joint ventures right and left. The ownership charts for an industry look like an intertwining tangle of spaghetti. But somewhere in the middle of it all you'll usually find a couple of *banques d'affaires*."

These *banques d'affaires* are the wheeler-dealers of European business. They raise capital by floating stock and bond issues, make loans, invest in companies directly, sometimes take over moribund companies, pump new life into them, and sell them off again. Europe has been booming and therefore capital-hungry, and these gentlemen have been busy, profitably.

Because they possess scarce capital or the means of raising it, and because they charge stiff prices for its usage, *banques d'affaires* are both feared and disliked by capital-starved small- and medium-sized concerns. "Their embrace is too close and too long-lasting," says a tight-lipped French executive. An American financier, describing a new venture arranged with a French machine company, remembers, "We were all set up and almost ready to go with an issue when the company president said he would want to talk the deal over with his bank to keep them in touch. This made sense and we agreed. The bank people came, looked over the proposition, agreed it looked good, then announced, 'We will take a 20 percent participation.' Bang, just like that they cut themselves in on a piece of the action. The company president gulped, but nobody said boo. We had to let them in."

The sophisticated bankers, for their part, have little sympathy for client-company executives, or partners, who can't keep up to or ahead of the game. "We do not run a charity here," explains one. A French consultant: "The banks are always rigorously legal, but you should keep in mind possible irons they have in other fires that they could as easily heat in your own. These men like to make money on an investment from several angles. They like to make money right now, and also tomorrow, but especially right now."

Numbers of *banques d'affaires* have been deeply involved in several popular supermarket ventures in France and, as one participant admiringly describes it, "They make money when everybody else does—and when nobody else does." Here's an example of how sweet-and-sour a non-arm's-length transaction can turn when a bank plays the multiple role of lender, spender, underwriter, promoter, investor, and landlord. One bank made money by purchasing real estate sites which it then profitably leased to a supermarket group for which it was the underwriter. The bank raised stock for the new company at a high fee. The bank participated in the offering and, as supermarkets were then glamorous stocks, it made even more money selling off a number of its shares. Months later, operating and overhead costs of the supermarket group had spiraled much higher than anticipated and the company was still in the red (though the general investing public had no way of knowing this). Disappointed in the lack of profits from its remaining stocks, the bank, in its role of landlord, raised the rent it was charging for use of land and buildings. (A clause permitting this was in the rental contract which the bank, in its influential role as underwriter and stockholder, had previously approved.) Other major stockholders could only fume or shrug resignedly. In Europe, banks still call the tune.

Long before the Common Market was dreamed of, Europe's banks had a well-established network of international alliances and exchanges which they have since greatly extended and intensified. Swiss and French, Belgian and English and Dutch, German and Italian (and American) banks have all been joining each other in new underwritings and joint-venture companies. For instance, the Nederlandsche Handel-Mij, one of Holland's big-four banks acquired 25 percent interest in Bank Jordaan of Paris. N. M. Rothschild of London established a formal financial link with De Rothschild Frères of Paris. Hope & Co. of Amsterdam and R. Mees Zoonen of Rotterdam joined with Morgan Guaranty International Finance Corp. to create a new *banque d'affaires*, Morgan & Cie. Barclays of England, the Deutsche Bank of Germany, an Italian bank, two French banks, and one U.S. bank joined with two major Spanish banks to create a new Spanish investment bank—and so it goes.

American commercial banks such as Chase Manhattan, First National City, and the Bank of America are active in Europe, especially the first two, which have gone through metamorphoses. Until quite recently, American banks in Europe were largely diplomatic and social outposts for the home concern. They evolved in the early 1900s as courtesy stations where rich aunts could get their checks cashed or have a trust officer help keep an eye on investments. Their nephews and nieces on European tours used the bank, and so did a few vacationing businessmen. Even during a short flurry of business activity in the 1920s a faint aura of afternoon tea and evening dinner-jacket languor clung to these way stations. It did not completely disperse till well into the 1950s. Towards the end of that decade, as American companies swarmed overseas, the soft sleep ended; the banks added staff, new services, and a new dynamism.

Since the greater part of U.S. bankers' European business is with U.S. companies, local national banks do not particularly resent the American bankers' presence. As one U.S. bank reports, "In the U.K. our branches have a gentleman's agreement; we don't seek British accounts. In France the ground rules differ, and over half our business is with French companies." But this business usually involves French companies with important business in the U.S. or other countries where the U.S. banks can be especially useful. Few fingers are actually dipped in other people's national pies. First National City Bank has been the most aggressively expansive U.S. bank. It now has branches in England, France, Germany, Italy, Belgium, Switzerland, and Holland. Other American banks in Europe, which tend to work through local correspondent banks in most countries and cities, shake their heads over National City's aggressiveness. "We're going to pick up business from European banks that are angry at National City," predicts one U.S. banker. But National City doubts that there will be enough such attrition to really hurt.

"The crest of U.S. investment in Europe is past and it's hard to pick up local business, but we needed offices in these important European industrial and financial areas to round out our network," says a member of National City. And even in Switzerland, First National City is evidently not too worried about Swiss banks cutting their U.S. deposits in a pique. For one thing, a great portion of the foreign deposits National City receives are specified by customers on letters of credit for deposit with it. Then too, through its extensive U.S. and Latin American connections, the American bank feels it can be useful to European banks and businesses. Comments a National City officer, "We don't expect to pick up too many Swiss accounts, but we may draw some Middle Eastern and South American business to Geneva, and we set up shop there because it pays to have offices in New York, London, and Switzerland; that's the way the international gold flows."

American money men are welcome in Europe because they perform a vital function. They can supply the financial and technical strength for floating joint Euro-American issues and loans in capital-hungry Europe. U.S. financial institutions will back ventures European investors scorn as too modest in payout; the Americans fill a vacuum. The Atlantic financial community, in effect, already exists, and Wall Street firms such as Lazard Frères and Dillon, Read are re-

spectively reinforcing and reinstating old European relationships. But of all the American financial firms in Europe,
Morgan Guaranty Trust's International Finance Corp. is the
most solidly established and comfortably acclimatized.

"Ah, but Morgan is virtually a French bank; they even
stayed here during the war," says a French banker approvingly. Quiescent for a number of years, Morgan has lately
become extremely active in Europe. In 1963 it was rumored
to have picked up 40 percent participation in Neckermann
Stores, the Sears, Roebuck of Germany, and has been involved in numerous other investments. Its senior executives
are a mixture of Europeans and well-adapted Americans.
Some of the Americans at Morgan and some with one or
two other financial groups in Paris are second-generation
Americans in Europe. They are sons of members of the
"old American community," an American enclave that
preceded and survived the famous Left Bank literary expatriates of the 1920s. It is a nostalgic Toynbee-esque fossil
community, an Episcopal-Church-centered, delicately preserved shard of a genteel, turn-of-the-century America. The
community's older members sigh for a France and Paris that
possibly never existed; its younger members are well connected and attuned to the one that does. They travel and
work in the U.S. and Europe with almost equal ease. Almost, but not quite, natives on either shore, they are highly
useful on both.

Moreover, even if only a few minutes by telephone, a
few hours by plane, and dozens of cross-alliances separate
the financial capitals of Europe, there are also hundreds of
years of history and war between them. The Americans
provide an emotional neutrality to inter-European arrangements which is valuable. It is a function previously per-
formed only by the Swiss, Europe's professional neutrals.

Swiss banks are famous for their numbered accounts, secret accounts identified by number instead of name, to which nervous dictators, politicians of various stripes, and tax-conscious citizens of all nations are addicted.[1] Beyond that, however, Swiss banks are a major source of European investment capital. Their banking laws are lenient, and the handful of major commercial banks in that country can, and sometimes do, indulge in anything the *banques d'affaires* may in the form of stock floating or portfolio investment, but they concentrate on commercial-credit transactions. The private banks, for their part, have equal leeway but stick largely to portfolio investments. The Swiss have a reputation in Europe of investing cautiously and for the highest possible return. "They are not necessarily such sharp investors; they are at one remove from the actual investment situations. They are a safe and expensive place to keep your money (one pays for the privilege of a numbered account), and that's that," says an American investment banker. But it was largely Swiss (and American) money which fueled Italy's recent economic boom, and which would likely energize any Spanish economic awakening.

[1] A respectable amount of Russian and satellite money also makes its official and unofficial way to Swiss banks. And, if numerous British, Danish, and West German businessmen who do business behind the Iron Curtain are to be believed, no major contract with Communist purchasing groups is likely to be consummated unless important amounts of cash change hands under the table. Sometimes the exchange is quite open and blatant. At other times money in envelopes or cigar boxes is turned over to persons on street corners or in corner stores, after proper Alfred Hitchcock-style exchange of signals and identification.

Whether this is just one more technique by which Communist countries build up Western currencies or whether it is cached away for future individualistic purchases of Western goodies is hard to say. "But you don't do business in East Europe without 'gifts.' In that sense, nothing has changed in fifty years," says a German businessman.

"We couldn't get any money out of the Swiss but they put us in touch with important German sources," says a Brunswick Corp. manager whose company is heavily involved in real estate acquisition for bowling alleys. In peace as in war the Swiss are knowledgeable, practiced intermediaries, and long practice is important here because communications channels in Europe differ from country to country and from the United States.

INFORMATION PLEASE

As developed and used in European financial and social circles, information is much more than a tool; it is coin of the realm. By mutual agreement and artificial scarcity, the price of information, like the price of diamonds, is kept high. It is kept in the hands of the initiated, who manipulate it to advance or maintain their position in the established order.

An American investment man many years in Paris: "The grapevine is different here. In New York I used to call up friends in business; we'd exchange news and comment. If a story was making the rounds I'd call uptown to let friends know, to get confirmation or comment. We had a continuous flow of accurate information moving across professional and industry channels. Paris swarms with rumors, but they are only one-half 'hard' information fleshed out with highly biased interpretation—and people keep in touch through rigid channels. If I call up a lawyer friend to check on a story, he may not have heard of it, or has a different version, but he says, 'Wait, I'll find out.' Then he'll call another lawyer! It is not a grapevine, it is a channeling system of professionals, or schoolmates.

"When I first came to town, and several times since, I asked French friends to advise me which were the more important or useful clubs and associations to join. They all mentioned clubs or groups—but only the clubs or groups to which they belonged. They hardly seemed to know the others existed or were also important. Things are compartmentalized here."

As foreigners, especially as *American* foreigners, U.S. businessmen escape precise classification in a country's social hierarchy. They can deal easily across class lines, are excused from parts of the social ritual, can develop broader contacts than most Europeans. However, as foreigners they are also excluded from many forms of contact. These are close-knit societies. In Denmark, for example, an attractive and ambitious Norwegian, married to a Danish girl from a well-established business family, says, "Last week I was invited to go hunting with some senior business people here. I have been waiting five years for such an invitation. It means that people I could not have successfully approached before will very soon do business with me. It means I will have information on developments and opportunities in time to do something about them. But even with the help of my wife's family it took five years."

Another thing Americans in Europe soon discover is that Continental bookkeeping is a highly original form of abstract art, represented by specific national schools. In Germany treasurers have a mania for tucking bits of money away in literally dozens of "reserve" accounts. In Switzerland companies brush off millions of dollars in tangible assets such as buildings and equipment by putting them on the books at $1.00 (the way some U.S. companies write up an intangible such as good will). It is a safe bet that a Continental company's operating statement has only the faintest connection with actual profits and little relationship to its cash flow. Professional investors (and this includes numbers of banks) buy stocks on general estimates of industry trends, as acts of faith, on the basis of inevitable and often dubious "inside tips," or scant interviews with company executives. That's why it was front-page news in early 1963 when five major European and a number of American investment groups announced joint formation of a Paris-based investment analysis company, Eurofinance.

Because of the financial importance of its member companies, Eurofinance will gain entree to an increasing number of European companies. Once on the premises, Eurofinance analysts delve deep into company books, hold detailed talks with company executives, come out with standardized U.S.-style investment reports. "We'll finally be able to compare company operations in different countries," says Eurofinance's president.

It is highly indicative of European business life, though, that Eurofinance was in successful operation for a year before its "creation" was announced. And the institutions which Eurofinance represents will, of course, keep any information they receive strictly within their own top executive ranks. So, while a need for capital is removing the veil of secrecy from some European companies, the veil is removed only in select company. It is strictly a private show.

Most European businessmen admit that it would be a good thing if financial and industry information were as easily available in Europe as in the U.S. In the meantime, however, they much prefer things as they are. Any real changes in this situation will have to come from government action. Governments play a vital role in European economies, but a different one than in the United States. Governments are the third major institutional factor affecting the changing milieu in Europe.

CHAPTER 5

OF GOVERNMENTS AND BUSINESSMEN IN EUROPE

In Washington, D.C., where intensive lobbying is an accepted adjunct of the U.S. system of government, it behooves foreign powers to engage from time to time in discreet lobbying (through other than their embassy personnel). Foreign business groups may do likewise. "Public relations" advisers carry on such programs for foreign groups, at times quite effectively. But the structure of power and the application of influence in America are more decentralized and diffuse than in most countries. Europeans, for instance, are accustomed to power systems where members of a more or less identifiable elite have direct and easy access to, and influence on, decision centers. They are accustomed to seeing many important decisions and concessions made privately, *in camera,* by key officials and their confidants. They assume such a system exists, to the same degree, in the U.S. As a result, Europeans dealing with Washington are sometimes taken in by lobbyists who report optimistically on (and bill them for) contacts with shadowy "influential persons" who may have little real influence on legislation or in government.

Similarly, Americans in Europe can be sharply taken aback when they assume too many similarities between the way things are done in Europe and the U.S. An American company, Lockheed Aircraft Corp., for instance, by energetic lobbying in the German Bundestag (Congress), convinced the legislators to call for formal consideration of a Lockheed transport plane for the German Air Force. Lockheed was successful—that is, until a furious German Minister of Defense, incensed at what he considered heavyhanded and unethical pressure from a mere contractor, wrathfully tossed out the U.S. program, publicly denounced the "upstart" company, and threatened to rescind a prior Lockheed program in Germany. In Europe, the ground rules are indeed different.

American executives working their way through Europe find that governments play an ambiguous role. On the one hand, they enforce or directly dispense a variety of social services: sick leave, medication, hospitalization, baby bonuses, discharge benefits, Christmas bonuses (a month's pay in Italy). Governments oversee fringes that can come to 50 percent and more of a nation's labor bill. But governments do not act as nominal arbitrators, referees, or policemen between business groups or between labor and business; they are more likely to take sides. In Switzerland, for instance, government and law (and some think, God) are on the side of cartels. In France, the government, as a main source of medium- and long-term credit, directly and indirectly decides which firms and which industries will get funds for expansion. And governments often directly compete with private industry. Renault, the biggest manufacturer in France, is government-owned and -run. In Italy two government holding companies, E.N.I. and I.R.I., Ente Nazionale Idrocarburi and Institutuo Ricostruzione Industria, compete briskly and sometimes brusquely with private national and foreign companies.

As spark-plugged by the late Enrico Mattei, E.N.I., which owns and runs a complex of oil, gas, and chemical companies, became not only an economic but a political power. It was owned by the government but "owned" a portion of its owners; the company directly subsidized numbers of politicians and political newspapers for its own ends. Its cousin, I.R.I., is a government holding company born of depression. When a series of major banks which held the defaulted bonds of many companies folded in the 1920s, the government took over the banks and, through the banks, the companies. Today I.R.I. owns or controls almost one hundred companies in the steel, shipping, shipbuilding, auto, electronic, and metal fabricating industries. Some I.R.I. companies are completely government-owned. Others are part government-, part privately owned. Some I.R.I. companies may in turn own joint companies with other government or with private company partners. In Italy there is no way of telling where private industry ends and government industry begins. Sharply defined American concepts of government vs. private ownership do not apply.[1]

A good example of government involvement in European industry is the famous and impressive French "Plan" for economic development. The Plan is a nationwide incentive

---

[1] Actually, the line between government and private business in America is not as sharp as it once was or as many Americans like to think it still is. Our giant defense contractor—government-financed companies, for instance—are "privately" owned and managed. But whether these companies have enough business for full employment is an important and constant political and economic consideration. When the officers and directors of the private companies hold policy meetings, key government officials, while not physically present, are in virtual attendance; the government's thoughts, plans, and wishes are constantly in mind. Occasionally, dissatisfied government administrators will quietly see to it that the management of a key contractor is reinforced or changed outright. A few companies, such as the famous Rand Corp., a high-level "think factory" of military scientists, are wholly effectively government-owned corporations.

The vital differences between Europe and America are often differences of degree rather than of kind.

and co-ordinating system. After a government consultative body, in co-ordination with industry, determines what national growth goals are feasible, it breaks these down into wide industry groups and indicates what percentage of the needed investment the government can supply in the form of attractive low-cost loans and what percentages will have to come from industry. Representatives of individual industries then join to determine what they can do to meet these goals and how they will split the government-supplied loans. As the plans progress, industry groups get a sound idea of what others are up to and how this will affect their business—and act accordingly in finishing up their own projects. The Plan is, in effect, a multi-industry cartel through which markets are split and industry plans laid for expansion. It offers credit for investment, an idea of how big the markets are likely to be over a period of years, and (privately among industry members) an understanding of who gets roughly what share of the market.

Private companies can ignore The Plan and go their own way, but find it is much more pleasant to go along. Since the French Government owns the railroads, coal mines, gas companies, and electrical system of the country, it has direct control of how these industries handle their investments. The government controls or has veto power over the bulk of medium- and long-term credit available in France. Through quotas, restrictions, and a thousand and one minor regulations it can make life uncomfortable for firms that kick over the traces, and France has a long tradition of direct government intervention in industry. When Remington Rand moved to close down a French typewriter plant it had built with government assistance, the decision created a political uproar. Shortly after this, while dodging through Paris auto traffic on his way to lunch, a French company president (like many French executives, he was an ex-official of the

Finance Ministry) said, "I have just now come from visiting friends in the Ministry. They are trying to decide what they will do to Remington Rand about this thing."

But Remington Rand, which had decided to move its typewriter production from Common Market France to Common Market Italy, was more of a symptom than a special case. In 1962 and 1963, the Plan was running into difficulties. As Common Market tariffs dropped, it was becoming obvious that international competition could disrupt any "co-ordination" which involved only French industries. This was especially evident in the appliance field and in the tractor industry (where one third of the market was taken by imported models). The French response has been to promote a form of *Le Plan* throughout the Common Market. Whether the French Plan would be acceptable, or could work, in a multicountry economy is questionable, but there is little doubt some form of economic "co-ordination" for Europe is in the cards.

The above will be especially true if Europe's socialist parties continue to gain in strength. In the new Europe, however, the socialist parties, the "other half" of European democracy, are themselves in transition.

THE SOCIALIST TWIST

Perhaps through dogma-affected misreading of their socio-economic systems, possibly because of their lack of political power, maybe because their own ideology has blinded them to anything but the replacement of capitalism—or, more likely, for all these and other reasons—a generation of socialists, to American eyes, seem to have been indignantly and repeatedly clambering aboard the wrong bus. They have fought for and received series after series of government-supervised social benefits for workers, but they have left the essence of the old capitalist systems, though shrunken in extent, otherwise untouched. Rather than reform Europe's business systems, they have concentrated on trying to live with them prior to "eliminating" them.

British and French socialists have long been the most doctrinaire exponents of thunder and expropriation in Europe. Gripped tight in the righteousness of class war, many of them reject any action that hints of acceptance of private ownership as a form of class treason. But socialism is changing. In Britain the late Hugh Gaitskell, leader of the Labor party, tried (although unsuccessfully) to renounce the doctrine of the ultimate socialist takeover of industry. Younger union men, especially on the Continent, no longer talk like the older labor leaders. ("And a lot of the older fellows only talk the way they do out of habit," says a U.S. labor specialist.) Instead of the bitter righteousness of the "oppressed," a labor leader in the new Europe talks with the calm precision of a technician laying out a program. Socialists are becoming aware of, and a part of, the new Europe. They have seen theoretical socialism applied in various countries around the world and are not particularly proud of the results. They have noted that the professed magic of nationalizing major industries in their own countries has not automatically put workers on a par with managers. They have, however, seen that increased prosperity and rising labor wages can eliminate the material differences between classes. A few of the more sophisticated have begun to grasp and to quietly expound a number of other points:

• *First*: socialism, which started out as a means towards an end, the breaking of class barriers and the creation of equal opportunities for all, may have been sidetracked into becoming so much of a magic formula and an end in itself that its exponents lost sight of their original goals.

• *Second*: As a modern socialist puts it, "There is no point in going around trying to nationalize industries if we can get what we need through government credit-and-planning controls." The speaker, W. T. Rodgers, a brainy British Labor party member of Parliament holds a minority but influential position in his party. Younger socialists, rather than turn their countries into vast proletariats, see the possibility of elevating the working class up to the level of the middle class.

• *Third:* Education may be a key. Gradually, more and more socialists are concluding that a thorough reform of educational systems will be one of the most effective means of opening up their societies.

Meanwhile they are beginning to think not of recasting but of reforming their national industrial systems. They speak of a guided capitalism or co-ordinated capitalism to describe something very much like the mixed private-government economies most of Europe already has. As they get more realistic and conservative—or middle class—Europe's socialist parties also tend to get more votes, and this could be a self-reinforcing trend. Socialism no longer means exactly what it used to. But just as socialism is the other half of European democracy, so unions are the heart and other half of European socialism. Most socialist voters are from the working classes. Workers tend to organize in unions, and in the new Europe the old unions, too, are not the same as before.

CHAPTER 6

OF UNIONS AND BUSINESSMEN IN EUROPE

Historically, European labor unions have tended to count on quickie walkouts and slowdowns as an economic weapon against management. Unable to institute a check-off system by which union dues are automatically (and relatively painlessly) taken out of members paychecks by employers, they were seldom able to build up the financial muscle, or war chests, with which to conduct long strikes. What's more, unlike unions in America, European unions evolved in chronically labor-surplus countries and in tightly organized societies where the panoply of tradition, authority, and laws of government were marshaled against the organizing of labor. Unable to effectively confront management on the economic front, the unions turned to politics and the ballot box for legal recognition and for correction of grim nineteenth-century and turn-of-the-century working conditions.

But many European unions, which have traditionally tried to deal with business largely through political action in socialist parties, are now doing an about-face. In the new Europe they are turning from political to lunch-bucket issues, are swinging away from concentration on regional or nation-wide bargaining with employer federations to in-plant bargaining with individual companies *à l'américain*. (Ironically, this shift is taking place at a time when, for equally sound reasons, some U.S. unions are turning more and more to industrywide bargaining.)

This is a momentous shift with many implications. Greatly oversimplified, it means larger, more efficient companies will have to pay more than the national minimums presently set for manufacturing federations by their most inefficient members. This is not an easy course for unions; it means acceptance, in the long run, of plant shutdowns at the inefficient end of the spectrum. This in turn means social trauma. European labor is not mobile. Job layoffs in historically labor-surplus areas are a fiercely resented sin. Job security is sacred. Yet the unions opt for this change. Strong new socio-economic forces are obviously at work in the once stable hierarchical societies of Europe.

A number of American and international unions, through exchange programs and training assistance for union leaders, do what they can to abet this change. To Americans a trend toward equalization of U.S.-European pay scales will mean less worry about export or import markets. In Europe it will mean, at first, more industry emphasis on productivity. Eventually, as more productive workers receive better pay, it will mean a new rise in mass consumer markets.

The transition will not be smooth. Pay rises will leapfrog productivity increases. Governments will lecture labor on the national need for low costs. There will be more strikes. But it is a rare management that, without the grim, usually combined pressures of competititon and labor, voluntarily invests money and, most important, energy and brain power in new systems and equipment. In the prosperous new Europe, more and more labor groups, out for more of the good things of life for their members—right now—have been applying increasing wage pressure since 1962. Partly, this pressure is a matter of union membership roles, which are shrinking, and of union survival. At a time when, say, German workers are not particularly interested in politics or socialism, but are highly interested in Volkswagen 1500s, or in the new Opel autos, or in TV sets, the unions must respond by getting better wages for their members. Also, in Germany, there is a strong sense of "rightness" in, or righteousness about, wage increases for labor. Says Dr. Gunter Friedrichs of the Metal Industry Trade Union, in Frankfurt, "After the war German labor carried the nation on its back. We held back on pay demands so the nation could rebuild." Most wage rises in postwar Germany have arisen from scarcity of labor rather than union pressures, German labor men believe. But now, they say, Germany is on its feet, and so many phenomenal profits have been made that it is time for labor to begin to get more of the cake. Looking ahead to the time when the bloom might fade from the boom in ebullient Europe, the unions want to extract key concessions during a labor-short period. Dues check-off, for instance, though spurned by German unions, are a prime goal in Italy and in France.

Meanwhile, the degree to which European unions will co-operate with managers to achieve greater work efficiency in order to provide more "cake" for workers to share, varies greatly. High pay-and-productivity oriented Swedish unions, for example, will prod union members—and management— for higher output. Tradition-cramped British engineering or machinist unions, however, will argue for months or call workers out on strike "rather than," as one union organizer puts it, "allow any Tom, Dick, or Harry to step in and do the work that's the prerogative of a skilled mechanic." Italian unions, on the other hand, have been amenable (or indifferent) to work changes or equipment installations which managements introduce to increase efficiency. French unions sometimes oppose in principal, but are generally too weak to effectively resist, modernizing work changes. German unions tend to go along readily with productivity improvements. In fact, with an eye on automation, and attendant technological unemployment already visible in America, the powerful German Metal Workers' Union has been actively pushing reluctant management groups to make changes in the classical German system for training machinists. Since machinist trainees, during their long apprenticeship, are a source of cheap, trained labor, however, many companies resist.

Meanwhile, the unions have trouble in their own ranks. Traditionalists in the movement bitterly resist anything that smacks of an amicable working relationship with managements as a sellout of the working class. On the Continent, in France and Italy, for instance, the largest unions are communist-dominated; the anticommunist unions break into rival Catholic and socialist groups; and management federations (while making appropriate, pious, anticommunist noises) play one union group off against the others.

But now throughout Europe key unions, usually spearheaded by the Metal Workers, are shifting tactics. Instead of merely confronting a federations of companies with across-the-board demands, the unions are also zeroing in on particular companies with specifically tailored demands. The union thinking here is that, while they do not have the strength for a successful all-out struggle with a whole industry, they do have the resources to square off with a few companies. They estimate that, once a few key companies give way to union demands, the pattern will be set; most others will follow suit. What's more (and this is a key point), in the new Europe, where competition is becoming a reality, the unions are betting that many companies, fearful of losing markets to competitors through long strikes, will be much more willing to settle with unions than they would have been in the carefully cartelized, heavily protected old Europe. In other words, what's happening is that parts of the basic structure of business in Europe are changing—and one change (intercountry competition) reinforces the other (in-plant bargaining), which in turn augments the first.

It happens that in this developing labor climate, "foreign" American firms might not get much effective popular, government, or industry support in a tussle with native unions. Also, U.S. companies are accustomed, at home, to give-and-take bargaining with unions. For these reasons, U.S. companies in Europe seem tempting union targets for in-plant bargaining drives. Should U.S. companies receive increased union attention, it will be a change from the pre-1960s.

LES AMERICAINS

Through late 1962, if one were to ask an American plant manager in Europe about unions, he would be likely to hear the reply, "What unions?" Sometimes this would be said facetiously, with a grin. At other times, a manager caught by surprise at unions even being mentioned, would pop it out as a genuine question. Except in Britain, where a particular form of local anarchy can keep plant managers constantly aware of a restive labor force, most American companies (their wage rates set and their bargaining carried on by industry federations) hardly realized that Europe's quiescent workers were unionized.

In the new Europe, however, numerous American companies are going to become much better acquainted with their union organizations. But the Americans do possess built-in advantages. Britain, like every other country in Europe, presents a special case in labor relations, but it does serve to point up some of these peculiar American strengths.

YANKEE EYES ON BRITISH UNIONS

One of the first things newly arrived American plant managers discover in Britain is that contracts between employees and employers are not strictly enforceable by law. From this flows much more. So much more, that a Midwestern, Detroit-trained plant manager says, with enough approving nostalgia to make any American union man start with surprise: "Back home, every couple of years, we have bargaining and a lulu of a strike that shuts the plant down for a month or two. But when it is settled, it is settled; everybody goes back to work—for a couple of more years. Over here you are never through bargaining. One trade-union group or another is after you about one nit-picking thing after another—all the time."

Part of what bothers this man is that the British trade-union movement tends to be all heart and very little head. British unions are rich with emotion and are among the most humane and optimistic, but they are also the most petty and backward in Europe. Union officials at all levels tend to be dedicated, scrupulously honest, overworked, underpaid men with no authority. British workers, who fear that their union chiefs, if well paid, would no longer be "working class," resist increases in salary or staff for their unions or more than a few pennies-per-week dues for themselves. This parsimony keeps the mystique of the British labor movement unsullied, but it also means that in newly prosperous parts of Britain ambitious young workers shy away from union posts. It also means that the union economists, time-motion engineers, and bargaining specialists, who play such a vital part in modern union-management negotiations, are not available or are spread too thin to be effective in Britain. The British union movement is a grass-roots affair. The real power rests with the locals. The top leadership can impress and persuade, but only gently direct and rarely coerce, their locals.

Reflecting all this, British union discipline, report Americans there, is at once tight and amazingly slack. That is, if one small group of workers decides to pull a walkout, other laborers invariably lay down their tools in sympathy—usually without even asking what the strike is about. "Och now, a man's got to stick by his mates, you know," says a Glasgow machinist in explanation of this instant unanimity. Workmen who do not join in such walkouts are "sent to Coventry" (i.e., given the silent treatment) by their fellows. There is class solidarity at all levels in Britain.

But since British national unions have little economic or legal, and only passing moral, control over their locals, unauthorized, or "wildcat," strikes (as the British, taking up the American phrase, now call them) are common. In Scotland, where over fifty U.S. companies have set up plants, the head of a U.S. heavy-equipment manufacturing company, notes: "The main trouble is these unions are too democratic for their own good. The nationals have no real power, and the shop stewards are errand boys." He goes on to explain that in the U.S. top and local union representatives will bargain with management over wages or fringe benefits, usually come to some agreement, then go back to the work force to *announce* what they have achieved. Once a contract is signed, the work force accepts, by and large, what its representatives agreed to.

British shop stewards, however, will talk with management, make demands, receive a counter offer, leave, call a meeting with their constituents, get new orders from their mates, then march back to confront management once more. This is real democracy and it brings drama into workers lives. Undoubtedly it also brings a sense of participating in important affairs, of controlling one's destiny, to numberless laborers at the bottom of the social pyramid. But the system is cumbersome, time-consuming and, most important, ineffective. The next real or imagined grievance suffered by discontents on the shop floor is the signal to kick off the whole process once again.

But chip-on-shoulder balkiness is no monoply of labor. British management has its fair share. For an extreme example, take Rip Van Winkle-like Scottish industry, just now rousing itself into the twentieth century. In Scotland, a characteristically Gaelic intransigeance combined with a fierce faithfulness to the causes of yesteryear has kept management and labor locked tight in a struggle from another century. Says a U.S. manager in Glasgow, "It's a stalemated class war left over from I don't know when. Both sides assumed fixed positions a couple of generations ago, and nobody has budged since."

Asked about their local opposite numbers, American plant managers in Scotland are enthusiastic. They find Scottish fellow industrial chiefs blunt-spoken, friendly, and warmly hospitable. But about their hosts' attitudes towards productivity and labor, most Americans there have deep reservations. Between a haughty resistance to new methods and technologies, a seemingly ingrained inability to come to new terms with equally obdurate unions—and a shift in world economies—Scotland's once great shipbuilding and heavy industries have been fading since the 1930s. Uneconomic coal mines have been closed. Unemployment is rife. Scotland is in depression. With intelligent government and local industrial assistance, new light industries are evolving, but they have to live with, and have yet to overcome, the bitter, generations-old legacy of the older industries. Newcomers to Scotland report a labor force that is almost pathetically eager to work, and pathologically suspicious of any management moves outside established patterns. New work methods, pay systems, or training schemes must be carefully explained, and thoroughly presold, to labor or they fail.

In their 1890 aspects, however, such parts of Scotland are only a few years behind many other parts of manufacturing Britain. There is real and deep estrangement between much of British labor and many managements, which few British managers seem able or willing to bridge. Instead, they make do with, or use of, the situation as it is.

For instance, in winter beclouded and smoke-wrapped northern England a large American equipment manufacturer was knocking off the end wall of its factory in order to expand the plant. On an inspection tour the U.S. chief of this American subsidiary noted that the bone-chilling, winter damp was sweeping into the factory through the partly opened wall. "Hadn't you better get some tarpaulins up over there?" he asked the British plant manager.

"Oh, indeed no. That would never do," replied his manufacturing manager. "If we do that before the men complain, they will claim it is insufficient. We really must wait till they raise a growl. Just you wait a bit. You'll see."

Within a short time a delegation of shop stewards came up to complain bitterly of management's disregard of the workers' health. They demanded that the company put up some tarps over gaping holes in the end wall. Management acquiesced. The tarps went up. Everyone—the plant manager, the shop stewards, and the workers—was pleased with himself. They had all proved something and gotten something, especially the plant manager and the shop stewards. The manager, who did not really want to keep his men working in the cold, proved to his chief that he knew his men—and got them warmed up at minimum trouble and expense. The shop stewards proved, to themselves and the men, that they would not take harsh treatment from management lying down; they got the tarp put up.

Months later, the American company chief, in approvingly recounting this tale of predictable Pavlovian reactions and his English plant manager's effective technique for dealing with workers across a gulf of suspicion, continued to overlook one point. This episode was one more sign to workers that the management really didn't care at all about them—but they could get their due anyway by calling on their stewards. The company was doing nothing to break the old patterns of suspicion. Instead, it was reinforcing a generations-old feeling of *us* against *them*. By coincidence, this U.S. company happens to have had a history of poor labor relations in Britain.

Slapping the arm of his chair for emphasis, the chief of this same bedeviled American company says, "I swear, sometimes I think that all these fellows are really looking for is attention!" He is right. Not fifteen miles away two other American managers have created the grievance machinery and a communications system with their work force that gives them excellent labor relations and increasing productivity.

They are proving that American companies in Europe, if they manage to avoid falling into the feudal practices and attitudes of the most backward members of national manufacturing associations, can get along well with local labor groups. Americans, because they are not emotionally committed to or (in the eyes of labor) tainted by the labor systems of old Europe, have some advantages. They can start fresh. This does not mean that Americans can bluffly behave as if they were in the U.S. The American habit of laying off workers during slack periods, for instance, although hardly popular at home, is bitterly resented in Europe. European work forces, however, are particularly susceptible to "Boulwarism," the General Electric Co.-evolved forms of solicitude for workers' needs and personal dignity—with a minimum of paternalism.

Americans also have a reputation, sometimes deserved, of being willing to sit down for face-to-face confrontations and straightforward negotiations with labor groups. From some wellspring of European folklore flows the continuing belief that Americans, once effectively confronted, will give labor a square deal. "The Americans work their men, but they are fair," says a British labor organizer of U.S. plants in his area. Though British managers at the Ford Motor Company plant at Dagenham, England, were plagued for years by sour labor relations and hundreds of strikes and walkouts, General Motors' Vauxhall plant maintained continuous production. Settled among the friendly but prickly Scots, the Euclid Truck Company and Cummins Engine Company were able to introduce new production systems and techniques and to maintain excellent labor relations for many years. I.B.M. has a reputation throughout the Continent as a good employer. At its Fawley refinery site on the English coast, Esso, by patient negotiation, explanation, and sounding out of its work force, was able to introduce changes in labor-saving work procedures and improved pay systems that made headline news when announced in Britain.

In the new Europe, when union lightning strikes, those American companies which show a little imagination will be able, without being patsies, to strike up the kinds of agreements that benefit management *and* labor.

Meanwhile, what is important to Europeans is not that a few American companies are likely to be getting special attention from European unions or setting pacemaking new agreements with them. What is important is:

• That unions in Europe are turning to in-plant bargaining and lunch-bucket issues.

• That in doing so they make it easier for socialist parties to withdraw partway from dogma and to re-establish new goals more appropriate to the times.

• That Europe's influential banking and financial systems, in leading the move towards the new Europe, will also be changed by it.

PART II

AMERICAN MANUFACTURERS AND AMERICAN MARKETING IN EUROPE

It is a strange tiger Europe's people ride toward the consumer society. It is a creature with transistor whiskers, television eyes, and consumer-credit claws. It devours nineteenth-century unionists, socialists, and capitalists with equal and impartial gusto. As we will see, it is equally adept at chewing up unwary or over confident Americans.

CHAPTER 7

AMERICAN MANUFACTURING IN EUROPE

"The Americans are everywhere; they swooped down here like birds on a field," says a still startled German businessman. By 1963 there were more than 850 U.S. firms of one type or another in West Germany, nursing assets of close to $2 billion. Some 3000 U.S. companies in Western Europe sell everything from soup (Heinz) to radar sets (Raytheon), from thermostats (Minneapolis-Honeywell) to trucks (Euclid), from dog food (Pet Foods) to mining machinery (Joy Mfg.), from toothpaste (Colgate) to bowling alleys (American Machine & Foundry). These companies establish plants in Europe for mixed reasons: because of profit and growth opportunities, to get under a tariff wall, because if they don't somebody else will, because they see a smart competitor doing so, because an important customer moves—and supplies a market.

It is characteristic of American business that several years after a few major, bellwether companies take and prove out a given course, the competitive (and fashion) aspects of U.S. industry impel hundreds of other companies to rush hard on their heels. Since the Korean War, there have been sudden and overlapping five- to six-year cycles of U.S.-industry excitement and investment in: capital equipment, management development, electronic computers, research and development programs, automation, and, most recently,

European markets. After a certain point, such movements take on a momentum and logic of their own; by 1960 almost no major self-respecting, "forward-looking" company was willing to face its stockholders without some sort of international operation in hand or in mind.

The American involvement in Europe, however, promises to be a double-barreled, one-two process. Once settled in the growth markets of Europe, U.S. companies have begun to look beyond Europe to an Atlantic Market with cross-competition of goods and services within this 500-million-person area. And in the next decade, as the mass markets of Europe continue to develop, more and more European companies will begin to recognize what a few of them know and are acting on: America is already a mass market, a highly developed one. More and more large and medium-size European firms will set up sales, assembly, and manufacturing facilities in America. As this happens (sometime in the 1970s), Americans will have the wry pleasure of seeing the other side of a familiar coin. They will see Europeans, who do not necessarily speak good English and who have no feel for local mores, come over to supervise subsidiaries in the U.S. Many of these Europeans will be quite competent. Not a few will be impressive. Many will also seem poor mixers, a bit naïve, definitely inept at picking the right kind of American to run their company, and somewhat slow-moving.

But that is for the future. At present it is largely the American companies that are settling in Europe, creating impact after impact that one does not read about in the newspapers.

In America, during World War II, thousands of U.S. companies went through a rush course in high-volume, high-tolerance production techniques. The McCreary Machine Works, a small, 25-man, textile machinery company in upstate New York, for instance, became a producer, first of machine-gun barrels, then of aircraft parts. It learned how to work with new materials at new speeds. Prodded by engineer-teacher troubleshooters from major contractors, it switched from small-scale, one-at-a-time production of machines with tolerances of a few hundredths or thousandths of an inch to high-speed turnout of thousands of parts with tolerances in the hundredths of thousandths of an inch. By the end of the war this company, like others, possessed a manufacturing competence its managers had never before envisioned. "And that is what we expected American companies in Holland to do for Dutch industry," says a member of the Dutch Ministry of Economics.

Densely populated Holland, once a largely agricultural country, is turning to industrialization to quicken its economy. The careful Dutch feel that their best opportunity in the new Europe lies in developing small, light industries. They especially welcome U.S. manufacturers into the country, because the Americans have the subcontracting habit.

Most larger European companies, through tradition and habit developed over years of shortages, are highly integrated. Many a European manufacturing chief will proudly explain that even the hardware, the nuts and bolts that go into his products, "are made right here in our plant." By contrast, U.S. companies are on a continuous buying bender. With variations between companies and industries, 30 to 60 percent of the value of any fairly complicated U.S. product is attributable to purchased parts. The Dutch Government is betting that U.S. companies, in their search for parts and components, will help create new and quicken old industries wherever they settle.

Take I.B.M.-Holland's Amsterdam plant, where I.B.M.-International a few years ago decided to make its 772 selectomatic typewriter, the one with the silvered ball that whirls across the page. The first production units were assembled from precision parts shipped from the U.S., but company engineers began developing European suppliers as quickly as possible. By late 1962, I.B.M.-Holland had 200 manufacturing subcontractors making parts for the new typewriter; one hundred suppliers were Dutch, and the company hoped to double and possibly triple the number of Dutch suppliers by 1965. Some I.B.M. parts were too complex for local Dutch companies to produce. A number of small, specially shaped elements, for instance, are made of compressed powdered iron, which is then sintered (baked, as bricks are) in an oven. Uniform porosity and a specific gravity close to that of iron are needed; and only after trying Holland, Germany, and Italy did I.B.M. find a supplier in Britain (as it turned out, the supplier was a subsidiary of an American company which used the process at home). Similarly, most of I.B.M.-Holland's screw-machine parts come from Switzerland. (The Swiss beat the Dutch out on tolerances and prices.) But the minute a Dutch producer begins to get close to Swiss capabilities he will find a willing and high-volume customer in I.B.M.—and company engineers who will help him eliminate production bugs.

Not far from I.B.M. another U.S. firm, Tokheim Corp., turns out gas-station pumps. This 130-employee, 100-percent assembly operation draws on 80 Dutch subcontractors and has a group of engineers and inspectors who devote their time to helping suppliers keep up to tolerance and up with delivery schedules. A mile or so away another U.S. company, Royal McBee (typewriters), has several thousand assembly employees and 250 subcontractors, 75 of them in Holland. This company gets its type face from Switzerland and its typewriter keys from Germany. "Most of our subs are in Germany, where the technology is high, but anytime we can develop a secondary source here we nurse him along to maximum volume," says a company official. In counting on

U.S. companies to subcontract, the Dutch Government has a safe bet.

All over Europe other U.S. firms try to develop subcontractors. If a U.S. subsidiary's plant manager is European he is more likely to be inactive at subcontracting. "I believe in doing all we can right here," says the British manager at a U.S. office-machine company in a statement of Old World philosophy.

But a few miles away the American production chief of a competitor says: "If suppliers can beat my own manufacturing price and guarantee delivery, they can save me money and headaches. I'll buy outside." As they scour the breadth of Europe to find suppliers, American companies are often a small European manufacturer's first pleasant taste of business with another country. As competition in the new Europe becomes meaningful, and cost accounting more precise, more and more large European companies are deciding that cost savings outweigh the psychic advantages of production "integrity." Subcontracting *à l'américain* is spreading.

Meanwhile, U.S. companies are exerting another kind of technical impact: through introduction of new products. The greatest number of U.S. firms in Europe are industrial concerns whose products, if seen, are seldom recognized by ordinary, "civilian" consumers. For instance, when Anna Halsman, our typical German housewife of Chapter 2, strolls through the new supermarket near her home, she is lured by dozens of attractively packaged products. Some of the plastics, the brightly colored inks that print on plastic, the paper, the aluminum, even the glues that hold a package together but allow easy opening—may be American. If she buys skinless sausages, it is possibly by courtesy of Tee-Pak International, a U.S. firm. Certainly some of the machines that print on the aluminum foil around her frozen-food packages were American. The paper in some of her packages was made by high-speed Beloit (of Wisconsin) paper machines. Many packages were formed by American Machine & Foundry Corp. equipment. Such consumer-serving products would have evolved and are evolving in Europe, but they already existed in America and were easily adapted. "There's no point in their reinventing the wheel; we can get it for them wholesale," grins an American machinery salesman in Zurich.

Many U.S. companies find a market in Europe because of particular design or patent advantages. Cessna Aircraft has a subsidiary that makes hydraulic equipment in Britain. It moved abroad when a major international customer, dissatisfied with available English equipment offered the company enough of a market to get started. Fairchild Camera Co. deals in electronic engraving equipment in Holland and transistors in Italy. Reed Roller Bit and a number of other oil-equipment specialists dominate the European oil-equipment business. Brook Instrument Co. produces flow meters; Hewlett-Packard, the world-famous electronic measuring instrument company, has a plant in Germany. A full dozen American process and electronic production-control companies hang their hats in various parts of Europe, and so do as many pharmaceutical houses, strengthened by years of extensive U.S. and European research.

"These American companies, they should not come here," complains a German businessman in Bonn. "They should be working in the underdeveloped countries." He does, however, think it would be fine for Americans to license some of their advanced technical or consumer products to European companies, as some U.S. appliance companies have done. It is only since "Tecumseh"-licensed manufacturers began turning out thousands of that U.S. firm's low-cost refrigerator compressors that a stream of inexpensive refrigerators started to flow through stores to homes and apartments all over Europe. (Because of this, supermarkets are doing more business and the frozen-food industry is growing.) Most American companies, however, prefer to export technology through their own subsidiaries or joint ventures in Europe. Licensing is easy money (it involves no investment or risk), "but it ties you up hand and foot, and cuts you out of basic growth in an area," says an appliance-company executive who feels that companies which do not establish themselves in both Europe and America will in the long run be left behind by those that do.

Another American export consists of management techniques: advanced American planning, production control, and accounting systems. As European companies get larger, as markets and suppliers grow more competitive, precise knowledge and control of costs becomes crucial. The American way with paperwork can be a source of money-saving techniques. But these planning systems demand platoons of competent middle managers. Executive training programs are starting to blossom, and management ranks are beginning to swell in the new Europe. Ironically, while U.S. companies work to cut overhead—"to get slim like the European mills," as a Connecticut Valley machinery executive puts it—many European firms are adding services and staff, like the Americans, in order to survive.

SOME WORDS FROM THE WISE

At the working level in Europe, U.S. companies concentrate on the business of turning out products and making a profit. For newcomers to Europe, the U.S. companies already there are the best possible source of local information. A man willing to listen can hear and make use of tales and advice from predecessors who have been through the wringer.

About 1960, for instance, on the theory that transistor

technology in the U.S. was three years ahead of Europe, an American electronics company opened a British subsidiary, using secondhand equipment then being replaced at its Los Angeles plant. The new subsidiary began well, captured 16 percent of its transistor market, then stalled. Other U.S. and European electronics companies, moving in with the latest low-cost equipment, had forged ahead, bringing prices down and keeping the new subsidiary's books in the red. By 1963 the subsidiary's British engineers, bitter at their colonial status, were still trying to convince the American head office that it might pay to install up-to-date, high-volume equipment.

U.S. companies moving to Europe with the latest equipment sometimes find they can beat the U.S. productivity rate. "We use the newest equipment and do 15 percent better than the home plant," boasts the European chief of a Johnson & Johnson subsidiary. The reason: incentive pay rates in the home plant are loose because, as the new equipment was developed, each modification led to tough bargaining and inevitable accommodation with the U.S. unions on incentive rates. In Europe, where it is starting fresh, the company knows what the late-model equipment is capable of and sets rates accordingly.

Generally, U.S. companies in Europe that employ women assembly workers seem to have minimum labor difficulty and least trouble getting close to, or ahead of, U.S. production rates. But women employees are often scarce. In labor-tight Germany, 40 percent of the women are already working. In much of the Continent there is strong prejudice against working women. In Holland, for instance, when Philips, the giant Dutch electrical company (the General Electric of Europe) built a new plant in an agricultural region, it had to conduct a series of public-relations campaigns and hold an extensive open house before it could persuade suspicious farmers to let their buxom daughters leave home and kitchen for work in a factory.

U.S. companies that try to instill U.S. systems and pace in a European plant find it best to never let the traditional European systems take root—but this means hiring young men, starting small, building gradually. Most U.S. companies are in a hurry. Another technique is to take a number of European production personnel, train them on actual production in the U.S. for months, then send them back to Europe with a running start.

The benefits of such visits are especially strong amongst technical and administrative middle and upper managers. A small electronics subsidiary, after dithering with indecision for six months, screwed up its budgetary courage and sent three engineers to the parent company's laboratories and main plant for five weeks. After the team got back, efficiency on the production line increased 20 percent. Morale among the entire technical staff also rose. "You've got to be sure the senior people get over first, and you have to be sure enough men get over together so that when they come back they have an impact," says a European plant manager, who notes that, aside from prestige, morale, and technical gains, European engineers and their opposite numbers in the U.S. now communicate with each other more freely and effectively; they know each other as people rather than as signatures at the bottom of letters.

At I.B.M.-International a senior manufacturing official says, "We like to shift people around. New products account for lots of trips. European program managers and production and assembly engineers go over to train at the same time as their U.S. counterparts; so European plants can go into production almost as soon as the U.S. plants do. These assignments vary from three weeks to nine months in duration, and in any one year the company might have 200 people in the U.S. on such projects."

Aside from the manufacturing groups. I.B.M. has swarms of general-management marketing and research people moving back and forth across the Atlantic and throughout Western Europe, training, "keeping in touch," conducting joint studies.

National Cash Register's technical staff shuttle across the Atlantic and around Europe co-ordinating production, development, and research programs. Raytheon-Europe similarly sends transatlantic commuters to and fro in chase of technology. It is largely companies in advanced technologies that keep European and U.S. management, production, and development people in close personal contact. They report basic benefits and wonder why other U.S. companies don't do more of the same.

CHANGES OF PACE

Meanwhile, an American businessman in Europe keeps running into surprises, big and little. He may find his supervisory people less interested in a raise than in the privilege of coming to work half an hour after the rest of the staff. He may find that labor contracts are legally unenforceable or that his plant is on strike because he tried to cut back on a tea break. He may discover the illegality of using premiums and giveaways for product promotion. He may find the government "suggesting" it would not be wise to expand in a given field or, on the contrary, pressuring him to build certain kinds of equipment.

In Holland he will discover that overtime work is restricted by law, that not only are there the usual legal minimum wages—but legal maximum wages. Employment is full in much of Europe, and German managers will sadly explain that German workmen don't work as feverishly as they used to, that only the immigrant Italian laborers willingly put in long hours. But in Italy itself overtime is restricted by law. In Britain workmen like overtime; in fact, some insist on overtime as their due—on any day except Saturday. "We almost had a mutiny when we tried to work the men on Saturday. . . . Saturday is football-watching day," says a U.S. plant manager of his British work force.

From personal experience or long-term observation, American manufacturers in Europe warn of:

Low wages. American companies that move into a country and try to get away with paying the minimum going wage are asking for low productivity and continuous labor trouble. Smart companies pay at or near the top of local rates.

Tax incentives. "If there is a tax incentive, it is to help make up for other faults, and you had better know beforehand what they are," warns a veteran Minneapolis-Honeywell executive in Britain. A number of companies, blinded to existing economic flaws by tax and low labor-cost aspects of some regions, have never made enough money to take full advantage of the tax deductions.

Regional development schemes. American companies coming into a country are usually much more amenable than local companies to co-operation with governments in establishing plants in far-out development districts. Sometimes they are quite pleased at the results. "But once the government gets you out on the edge of someplace, they are likely to ignore your problems and needs and let you hang for yourself," says the head of a Minneapolis-Honeywell plant in one of these areas.

Hiring and firing. In the U.S. it is standard practice to lay workmen off during slack periods, to hire and fire as the needs of the business fluctuate. (Our unemployment compensation systems are in part designed to facilitate this process.) In Europe, however, hiring is more permanent. Firing is expensive (it can cost from three to nine months' severance pay and more to let a man go), and there is a strong emotional reaction against this "heartless American practice." A number of companies such as Remington Rand have had costly strikes or tiffs with governments over layoffs.

Unions. They are just beginning to get restive and active in new ways in Europe. It is not wise to ignore them.

Employer federations. In some countries you have to join them, in others it is optional. The federations handle national and regional union bargaining for their members and can be useful. "But don't forget," says a General Motors manager in Europe, "the fellows who run these federations usually represent the more numerous small and backward companies. While the federation is saying one thing, the biggest and smartest companies may be doing something else. You have to be careful about how much you let them direct your policy."

Governments. They can interpret their own regulations any one of six different ways. It is important to keep in touch with government officials, both to find out about shifts in ministerial sentiment and to keep ministries in touch with company plans. This way no one gets any unpleasant surprises.

TRANSPLANTING TECHNOLOGY

As more and more new European plants continue to turn out new products, some interesting technological relationships are coming to light. For instance, there seems to be very little technological leapfrogging going on in Europe. Evidently, at the working level, technology and techniques must be created or assimilated step by step. Countries and industries that are technologically behind do not seem to be able to study the very latest advancement, improve it, then leap ahead of the pack.

"The North Italians are catching up in a number of fields very quickly and may move ahead of the pack, but they are not missing any of the evolutionary steps, they just go through them faster," hazards a New England industrial engineer, impressed by the Italian penchant for modernization and fast write-offs of equipment. Throughout Europe, NATO'S multicountry production of the highly complicated F-104 aircraft and weapons system may be a case in point. The F-104 is a Lockheed aircraft chosen by a number of NATO countries for air defense, its systems to be built largely in Europe. Many European defense and industry officials admitted that they looked on the F-104 as a technique for buying advanced technology in one quick and easy contract. It proved to be neither quick nor easy. Aside from a number of international and intranational political and business squabbles, the program ran into serious technical difficulties.

A U.S. engineer involved in one of the subsystems going into the aircraft notes, "we need standard parts to a millionth-of-an-inch tolerance for this unit. These people in Europe have fine tools and equipment, they can make parts to tolerance; but for them—up till now—it has been a laboratory stunt. They make one part; we are making them by the thousands. But it took us ten years to learn how. The Europeans can learn how, too, but it will take a couple of years."

Various national engineers, touchy about accepting advice from U.S. original-equipment developers, refused to call them into full or early consultation. With costs rising and the projects behind schedule, more components than were originally planned for had to be supplied from the U.S. This sent project costs up even further and drove European contractors into genuine fits of rage. By 1963 the program seemed to have generated at least as much ill will as technology.

From their side of the fence European managers working for American companies have comments of their own. Almost to a man, European managers feel that Americans try to hurry too much, do too much, worry too much—about too little. "Is all that extra fuss and energy worth the little bit of extra result that comes out?" asks one Briton. Many Europeans wonder if those extensive and expensive U.S. accounting and control systems give true value for the money they cost. Some European plant managers feel they do not have enough authority. "If someone in the States really wants to know why parts A, B, and C cost 30 percent more this quarter than last," says one manager, "let him come over here for a week and talk about it face-to-face. Otherwise, he should keep an eye on quarterly profits and, as long as they are good, leave us alone."

Both European and American plant managers feel they have too many visitors from the U.S. who don't stay long enough. "We see them often enough, but it's for an afternoon as they are passing through on their way to Belgium or Germany or where have you. There is no real opportunity to discuss problems. They run away before we can force them to learn anything," complains a plant manager apropos visiting "experts" from the home plant.

Finally, summing up the essence of five years' experience in Europe, an American production chief warns U.S. headquarters personnel and all newcomers: "In Europe, everything takes longer."

CHAPTER 8

THE UNCOMMON MARKET [I]
Europe's Uncommon Consumers

AMERICA ON THE CONTINENT

Tired tourists craving the reassurance of the familiar in strange Europe need only look and go shopping. The railroad station in Milan, for instance, may be blazoned with ads for Coricidin cold tablets. In nearby cafés waiters serve Coca-Cola—in goblets. Customers at adjoining tables smoke Kent, Chesterfield, Pall Mall, or other American cigarettes. The handsome young women tastefully do their eyes with U.S. mascara. When they deign to use lipstick, it is Revlon, Helena Rubenstein, or a rival American brand.

A visitor turning the corner near Beethoven Strasse, Amsterdam, finds packages of Aunt Jemima Pancake Mix, Uncle Ben's, and Minute Rice beckoning through foodstore windows. Aside from such oddities (to Americans) as canned potato salad and treacle pudding (in England), a survey of major foodstores almost anywhere in Europe finds Heinz Tomato Ketchup, Del Monte vegetables, various co-op-pack California fruit, and Maxwell House coffee on loaded shelves. An aisle-and-escalator tour of Europe's department stores is a trip through Memory Lane. Copper-rivet, form-shrink blue jeans. Sea & Ski suntan lotion, Remington razors, Gillette blue blades, Duco household cement, Camay and Palmolive soap, Seaforth shaving lotion—any one of these and more familiar products pop up to greet the passing eye.

Every year, in counter design, layout of departments, and choice of goods, Europe's and America's major stores look more and more alike. The Scandinavian furniture one admired in San Francisco or Chicago is sold in Munich, Germany. Italian silks that caught milady's eye in Macy's, New York, are sold by Jones of London. The china, brass and glass bric-a-brac, ashtrays, ice buckets, and wall pieces with which some ladies delight in gifting themselves and their friends are the same from Atlanta to Copenhagen. The illusion of Main Street on the Boulevards is sometimes so powerful that, deep in the happy haze of shopping, an American woman in Brussels turns to the clerk and absent-mindedly asks in English, "Do you have these scarves in blue?" Met by uncomprehending silence, the American woman laughs, apologizes, and asks her question again in French.

The illusion is short-lived. In Germany, though the shelves may proclaim America, a second look at the color and cut of clothes quickly reminds one of time and place. In Italy, similar illusions are quickly dispelled by blue-smocked counter girls. These dark-eyed, young office-hour nuns (of the Mercantile Order) are so numerous they make any store seem full. (Americans find service is no faster, but there is much more of it.)

American marketing men in Europe experience something like the short-lived illusion that shoppers do. But a number of U.S. consumer companies have found out, painfully, how different European markets can be. The most common American marketing error (obvious yet almost unconscious) is the blind and bland assumption that, if a product goes over well in the United States, it will be enthusiastically grabbed up by goods-starved Europeans. Actually, European sales successes are not automatic. European consumers are not "like the folks back home." Cases in point:

• Betty Crocker cake mixes. Betty Crocker came over to the United Kingdom with a loud fanfare of advertising. "Betty Crocker is here," said the portrait ads of this American personage. Alas, nobody seemed to know or care who the handsome gray-haired American intruder was. After four years, Betty's hair turned whiter.

• Green Giant premium vegetables made a similar Atlantic transplant, but soon found its overseas operation turning sallow due to "No Sale."

• Campbell Soup poured out millions of dollars buying into old markets and creating new ones in Europe—with mixed success.

• General Mills, to provide the British with the advantages of U.S. cereals, tested four brands, including best-selling Cheerios. After about a year it withdrew these offerings. The British went on stolidly munching their familiar Corn Flakes, the prewar and postwar standard breakfast food.

• Meade Johnson's Metrecal, a runaway success in the U.S. and Canada, is something else again in the U.K., where it was introduced as Metercal. In fact, Chas. Pfizer, another U.S. company, took away the bulk of the market Metercal built up at some cost. Americans, who are weight-conscious and malt-drinks-indoctrinated, took to Metrecal quickly and easily. The British responded slowly. But when Pfizer introduced a Metrecal-type product, Limmits, in *tea-biscuit* form, the British chewed them down.

Tea and biscuits are a factor in the cake-mix business, too. A British advertising man in the cake-mix field explains, "The British eat a good bit of cake, but we also have a thing called tea. Cake, to us, is something served with tea. This cake is dry. You eat it with your fingers, tea cup in one hand, cake or bread in the other . . . just like the Mad Hatter in *Alice in Wonderland*. In America, cakes are for dessert. They are rich, fancy, frosting-covered cakes: good, but a bit messy with tea."

When the National Biscuit Company came to Britain in 1956, it arranged for 500 housewives to bake their favorite cake. Most of them turned out a spongelike tea-cake affair, and Nabisco, moving to market with a similar mix, eventually got 30 percent of the market. In 1959, proudly flaunting the Stars and Stripes, Betty Crocker brought American-style cake mixes to Britain. By dint of extensive advertising, Betty was eventually able to take 10 percent of the cake-mix market (16 percent in the London area). Competitors, however, firmly contend that Betty hardly dented the big dry-cake market, but created a new, fancy-cake market amongst upper-middle-class housewives. In 1963 a discouraged Betty packed up her bags and went home.

The Campbell Soup Company's case is especially interesting because it is still unfinished business. Campbell came to Britain in 1959 with appropriate fanfare: the slogan "The Campbells Are Coming" and a ten-year plan for capturing the bulk of the soup market. Heinz, which came to Britain in 1905, had long had the lion's share of the British soup market. Since the end of the war this had been a seller's market; there was more demand for soup than local companies were producing. It was also a ready-to-serve, liquid soup market; all one did was open up a can, heat it, and serve it. Campbell changed this. It brought in new production and introduced U.S.-type condensed soup which one dilutes with water. Heavy advertising and promotion have since marked the industry. In 1962, Campbell gave away 4,000,000 cans of soup; Heinz offered 57 Mini-Minor autos with a free can of soup to 900,000 contest entrants. In 1963 promotions, Heinz offered 57 holidays (for Heinz's 57 varieties); Crosse & Blackwell offered a new home and car and a shopping spree; and Campbell offered free groceries for life. Campbell, which shouldered its way in aggressively, became number-three soup seller, taking 15 percent of the British market, but won no crown. Heinz maintained its market share (60 percent). Crosse & Blackwell, owned by Nestle, kept 18 percent of the market. It was the numerous smaller fry who were virtually squeezed out of business. Also, condensed soups, a product new to Europe, have met greater resistance than anticipated. After four years the Campbell operation still depended on dollar inflow from the parent company.

Campbell's European venture was actually a two-pronged effort. Shortly after setting up in Britain, the company opened a factory in Italy and a European headquarters in Geneva to tackle Continental markets. They did well in Sweden, but elsewhere the vagaries of national taste and the difficulties of promoting new products took their toll. In 1962 Campbell pulled in its horns, transferring control of European operations to Britain. At the two-fifths point of its ten-year program, Campbell is behind schedule. But Campbell is a big ($600-million sales per year) company, and it is in Europe for keeps.

Other U.S. companies in Europe have other difficulties and make other mistakes. "What would we do differently if we could do it over again? Well, we'd make our marketing studies before instead of after building a factory," says a rueful sales manager from one U.S. food company. And his is not the only major firm to make the elementary mistake of confusing Westphalia, West Germany, with West Virginia, U.S.A.

Even if they make no basic errors of judgment and nuance, U.S. companies still find markets hard to crack and schedules originated in the U.S. impossible to maintain. At home, veteran companies develop regular patterns and rhythms for the introduction of new products. The P & G formula gets a product launched and established in eighteen months. But there is little room in Europe for the free-swinging promotion U.S. companies use to back up new products at home. TV spots are limited and must be bought up anywhere from three months to a year ahead of time, depending on the country. Channels of distribution in Europe are crowded, slow-moving, and unwilling or unable to take on the load of new products European and American companies push onto the market. There is a wholly different pace and a lower order of intensity in European marketing. A product-launching that takes eighteen months in the U.S. can take three years in Europe. Though nervous tension on the part of individual Americans does little to change this European tempo, many Americans keep trying. "We're not here to adapt; we're here to change things," says an American marketing manager in Geneva. Thus far, though, his company has spent several million dollars and made no profits in Europe. Most U.S. companies in Europe are less stubborn, more realistic, and more profitable. The smartest organizations, which begin by studying Europe's consumers, soon find them more variegated—and undergoing more change—than those in America.

EUROPE'S CONSUMMATE CONSUMERS

A good way to begin to think of European consumers is by remembering or conjuring U.S. consumers of decades past. The consumer and industrial goods sold in Europe today are modern. Europe's plastic products, transistor radios, TV sets, washing machines, and autos are of the 1960s; but its wage scales (and distribution systems) are like America's of the 1920s and 1930s.

European workmen and office employees earn between $25 and $40 per week. They buy their food and household items from neighborhood stores. Most Europeans are apartment dwellers. They are paid weekly in cash rather than by check. The men control the money, doling it out to their womenfolk as needed. The great bulk of a working man's money (36–40 percent, depending on the country) is spent on food. Of thirty items a housewife buys during the week in North Britain, possibly three may be discretionary items. This does not leave much leeway for experiments with new products, but even so, there are seeming inconsistencies in consumer spending patterns.

The south of England, for instance—partly because retired and well-off, middle-class people choose to settle there —has a higher income and educational level than the industrial Midlands. However, it is the dingy apartment dwellers in the sooty manufacturing cities who make the best market for new products, especially convenience items. "The well-to-do in the South save their money for the children's education or for a trip to the Continent. Industrial workers with a few shillings in hand are happy to try something to brighten up their lives right now," explains a Briton. Similarly, consumer companies in Germany find it is not the taste leaders of the upper and middle classes, but working mothers, who, pressed for time and with a little extra income available, will try the exotic, brightly wrapped convenience items such as frozen foods—from new, U.S.-style, open-display cabinets.

Americans in Europe soon discover a complex mixture of regional and national tastes and habits. Just as Boston housewives prefer and pay a premium for brown eggs while New York matrons insist on white eggs, so German *fraus* in North Germany buy vitreous porcelain white sinks for their homes while their sisters in the South want enameled steel. Italians take happily to colored refrigerators; the Dutch still prefer antiseptic white. German women like dehydrated, packaged soups. Italian and Swiss women like packaged soups too, but are especially partial to bouillon cubes. The Dutch are hearty pastry eaters, yet a cake-mix company would face a tough uphill battle in Holland. Dutch women don't bake; over 95 percent of their pastries are purchased! There is a bakery or pastry store on virtually every block in Rotterdam. France has the lowest per capita consumption of toilet soap in Europe, though cosmetics do well.

But for all their differences, Europe's consumers do have areas of agreement that are broadening. Styles in clothes for one. Different fashions and styles, some of them subtle and elusive, some obvious, color the European scene. You can spot German women by their high-crowned mannish hats. Strolling through Hamburg's most fashionable shopping district, they need only a stout stick and a dog to look as if they had just come in from a ten-mile country trudge. This basic hat style has not changed in over thirty years. Dutch ladies have their own distinctive headgear: variations of a high, short-brimmed muffin or pillbox affair that sit Tower-of-Pisa-like atop the head. Older German men like baggy pants. Frenchmen wear strangely angular suits with peaked lapels. Sartorial Italians affect such tightly tailored clothes one expects to see them mince when they walk, and a few do. But almost everywhere there is change. A sleek New York woman who moved to Holland says, "The Dutch women are actually turning stylish. That tailored, boxy look is disappearing." Especially among younger women, the fashion magazines, now international in taste, are having an effect. This change filters through to the men. Frenchmen are discovering English tailoring. Italian suits (modified) and even the slope-shouldered, Ivy League styles are finding their way around the Continent. The Italian style is on the streets of the U.S. too.

In the new Europe a sense of form is also getting through

to industry, whose products must now compete in looks as well as price with other goods. France's engineer-dominated companies have by and large managed to resist esthetics in favor of stiff lines, simple moldings and castings. The Germans try hard to give a light and airy look to lamps, radios, and tables, but somehow don't quite make it. There the object sits foursquare on the ground. The British have a Design Institute that wages guerrilla war to improve the international appeal of stodgy British goods. It is the Scandinavians and Italians who, through clean lines and form in their designs, appeal to the international eye. But it is the Scandinavians and Italians who are more and more copied, or who are commissioned to design the autos, radios, toys, and household gadgets people buy in the new Europe. There is an important growing together. Consumers *are* getting more alike. Italian refrigerators sell in France and Belgium. German radios do well in Britain and Italy and are moving into France. There seem to be more and more American goods everywhere. The department stores look more and more alike.

An American advertising executive in Frankfurt (whose main client happens to hold a similar premise) says, "I don't believe in this business of special differences between countries. People have basic needs and drives for security, sex, power, and status, which are similar the world around. These are what we appeal to in selling a product." Procter & Gamble sells soap and detergents successfully the world over. Mostly it sells soap designed to help people get their clothes clean. Its advertising is directed to this straightforward proposition.

However, to pretend that German, French, Italian, and British people do not have important differences in taste, values, and reactions would be to deny a thousand years of history and the facts of modern life. Consumers in various countries are the products of their own particular conditioning, and dozens of U.S. companies in Europe bear the financial scars to prove it.

It is impossible to pin down (or even to know) all the nuances or factors that shape a market—but we can get some of the essential facts and flavor. Take Germany, which because of its recent history and present situation is especially fascinating. Like an anatomist's figure drawings which dramatically show the knotted, vivid muscles that are barely suggested under the body's covering of skin, Germany displays, in sharp detail, changes that are far less obvious in other countries of Europe.

GERMANY: THE UNCERTAIN PHOENIX

Wrecked by war and racked by change, this country of fifty million energetic and easily organized people is the richest single market in Europe. Twice, in two generations, a threat, and then a sharply defeated, outcast, disoriented nation, Germany has now emerged from ashes and ruin to an equally disorienting neon-and-chrome consumer economy. Germany's class lines, first loosened by chaos, are now being slipped by prosperity. New men are rising in industry, and the working class is being transformed. In the sociologists' A–B–C–D divisions of the social pyramid into upper, upper-middle, middle, and lower classes, the fastest movement in newly rich Germany has been from D (lower class) to C (middle class). This is the social jump in which Theodore and Anna Halsman, mentioned in Chapter 2, are involved. This shift and more than fifty years of turbulent German history (including post World Wars I and II inflation that wiped out many savings) help explain the kinds of things the German mass market buys. They like modern, but they also want baroque, heavy, turn-of-the-century forms and frills which to them spell the stability and emotional security of another era.

"In America you have consumers. Here in Germany we have them also, but in Europe you should also try to understand the concept of the burgher," says Dr. F. Hebert of Contest Gmbh., Frankfurt, a motivations-research organization. "He is a man who wants to possess things, not to consume them." The Germans are people who lost everything in the past, some of them twice. Now they are prosperous, money-and-possessions-conscious. They want to pick up life where they left off; tradition has an important appeal. "But they try to forget the late 1920s and '30s, so there are great gaps," say Hebert. This taste nostalgia shows up most clearly among the lower class as it makes the jump from D to C. This class shift makes them unsure of their taste, and they try to pick up the *bürgherlich* ideas of twenty-five years ago (which were a reflection of a *bürgherlich* world of twenty-five years before that). In Neckermann's, the mail order store, catalogue, for instance, the furniture is something out of the past, with modern touches: pieces of brass and polyester, floor and wall lamps formed in Teutonic curlicues. There is a particular affinity for brass. All this is an attempt to recreate, through visual "echoes," parts of an older atmosphere, Hebert feels. "Their taste is in their feet," said an American professional of German designers, but the designers have been giving the customers what the customers wanted. German mass taste (a problem that never confronted Europe before) is improving. At least one German appliance company, Braun Gmbh., turns out what many competitors feel are some of the best-looking products in Europe.

Meanwhile, with labor scarce and prices high, a do-it-yourself boom reminiscent of the American 1940s and '50s is building.

Since 1945 Germany has been exposed to extensive American influence. Among the working class in Germany you see various forms of what a German marketer calls "primitive Americanism": Levis, cowboy boots, G.I. haircuts, civilian versions of Air Force windbreakers, Elvis Presley and country music. But the more one's products aim at the mass C and D markets in Germany, the less they should flaunt obviously American names, say German marketing men. The upper level A and B markets are more sophisticated, eager to take up fashionable products from any source. The C and D groups are trying to learn and want to be modern; but, unsure of themselves, they cling to *bürgherlich* for comfort.

An example of this polarity of aspiration in working and lower-middle-class Germany is Germany's largest circulation magazine, *Hörzu* (Listen), a larger, more varied version of America's *TV Guide*. On the outside, the periodical is a replica of the "old" *Saturday Evening Post*. (In fact, one of *Hörzu's* favorite cover artists is an old time *Post* contributor.) *Hörzu* covers usually depict modern people doing "modern" things: painting the living room, fussing with appliances, playing with dogs or children, choosing furniture. This art work is crammed with detail (e.g., in a paint-the-living-room scene: paint-stiff brushes lying beside cans of kerosene, paint spots on clothes or faces). The pleasant, pleased-with-life couples on the cover are young; the wife is chic; the husband is usually an amiable Dagwood. The atmosphere is one of "mother knows best."

This is a caricature of the "young Germany." On the inside, however, the magazine is a *bürgherisch* refuge complete with humorous animal pictures, reports on African tribal habits, doll collections, and homey trivia of the genre.

The novelists, who tend to do such things more incisively than sociologists, who must wait for facts, have depicted Germany as a country groping for values, worshiping then

discarding various ethics. The more muted discoveries of the
social and market researchers support this view and point to
likely developments and problems. A few findings:

• German attitudes toward authority are changing, but
only slightly and slowly. Papa, or *der Alte,* still represents
security. People don't try to step out of place too often.

• However, in business the whole structure of the corporation and of authority patterns in the corporation are changing. The organization man is replacing the automaton. As a
result, the traditional father role in Germany is under pressure.

• The woman's role is also changing. Forty percent of the
women in West Germany now work, bring in money, have
a feeling of independence.

• Latchkey children (those whose working parents give
them their own house keys so they can get into the home
after school) are increasing in number. Escaping the close
supervision of parents, these children are just a little wilder,
a bit more unruly, not so awed by authority, and more independent than many of their schoolfellows.

Predicts a German psychologist, "We'll have trouble with
our kids just like you in America. Mother will become more
the center of the family. Meanwhile, there will be much
stress and strain." That he and other Germans can make
such points calmly is a sign that walls have already crumbled.
And some of the most obvious cracks in the still massive social structure are those between generations.

Americans in Germany and Germans themselves are quick
to note that differences between the generations there are
sharply defined. At the top are the men in their sixties and
late fifties who run business and government in Germany
today. These are the old Germans, those whose thought
patterns were set in the 1920s and '30s. Behind them and a
little to one side, their once youthful ranks greatly thinned

by the war, are the men in their forties and late thirties, the workhorses of the reconstruction. Between these two groups there are differences, but much understanding. Then there are the men in their late twenties and early thirties just now coming up in business. These are the first postwar generation and represent a different kind of person. Maturing in the years of the postwar debacle, they received no indoctrination (from any source) that their own experience did not quickly discount. Cheerfully cynical, alert—above all, realistic—they are among the most engaging and independent persons in Europe.[1] Over the next ten years this particular age group will begin taking over the control posts in much of German industry.

German youngsters in their late teens and early twenties are something else again. Uninvolved with the war, brought up in increasing prosperity, these are a golden youth. Their fathers and elder brothers report of them, with mixed pride and puzzlement, that they are different, not as dedicated. "They are more international-minded. They think about Europe rather than Germany," reports a university professor. A German-American, a former Wehrmacht soldier and U.S. prisoner of war who went to school in the U.S., married there and became an American citizen, but who now works in Europe, says: "My wife and I still like to jitterbug, so every once in a while in Germany we'll go someplace where there is a good band. Usually the place is full of youngsters. They are pretty relaxed and a lot more open and independent than we were. I'm hopeful for them."

At the A (upper class) and B (upper-middle class) levels of the social pyramid, among those in their twenties and

---

[1] Psychological marketing note: Members of the older generation still smoke prewar-type Turkish tobaccos, while younger men smoke postwar-introduced Virginia blends.

early thirties, there seem to be two attractive "idea" forces at work. These forces tend to be represented as American-influenced and European- or, possibly, French-oriented. Among technicians and university graduates in process of making the twofold jump from D (lower class) to B (upper-middle class) the "American" outlook tends to predominate. (They have more to gain in renouncing old class values.) Among people from established university families a more defensive Francophilia has also been developing. These "idea" influences are not mutually exclusive; they exist together in one person's concepts; they are always mixed. Where preponderances are evident, however, they tend to be as described. The "new" Germany, about which all Europe worries and wonders, is still in the formative period.

Consumers in Germany, whose metamorphosis presages some of the changes due in the rest of Europe, bear few resemblances to their neighbors. For example, the ebullient Italians.

FRIENDS, ROMANS, FELLOW CONSUMERS

Italy, across the Alps, is a different country with a different set of values, and a much different air than earnest Germany. If in Britain tea and its attendant rituals are still a key to parts of the market, and if in Germany *bürgherlich* indicates the way to the mass market's heart; then in Italy, *la bella figura* is the open sesame—to everything. *La bella figura* (the closest English equivalent would be "cutting a fine figure") means more than a petty keeping up with the Joneses. It connotes a special Italian sense of style, of the moment, and of life. It is something very Renaissance, and possibly older. The prideful courtiers posing around a fifteenth-century duke and the present-day, TV-conscious dignitaries, retainers, and ladies photographed at an Italian ship launching are much alike—every person reveling in a moment of carefully preened self-esteem, playing a part before admiring relatives, friends, and the world, each actor at center stage.

La bella figura may mean eating pasta for six months in order to rent an appropriate villa at Lake Lucerne during the worst of the summer heat. This, not in order to be as good as someone else, but to be worthy of one's self. *La bella figura* can mean hiring footmen for the night to serve behind each chair when an American businessman and his wife come to dinner. It means buying a hand-assembled Alfa Romeo, or a Fiat, or a Vespa scooter—but, in any event, getting the best and loveliest thing that one's money or credit can buy. To cut the fine figure, Italians, especially the North Italians, work hard and spend big, with a flourish, and when possible, with flair. The flair is important.

This is a market where appearance and form are paramount. The important thing is that the product—whether sewing machine, refrigerator, or vacuum cleaner—be lovely, shiny and spanking new. This is a market where a clean-lined, softly colored typewriter takes markets away from its bulkier, possibly more durable, office-gray competitors. This is a market where a typewriter with a hairline scratch or a barely perceptible shading of its paint will be returned to the store. This is also a market where two years hence a new product will sweep away the old. It is a consumers' market.

Italians have a zest for trying new products, few doubts or compunctions about entering all the way into a consumer society. "If they had the money, Italian producers and consumers would go all-American on consumer items, promotion, and advertising tomorrow," says an American advertising man in Rome. And yet, Italian consumers, too, are quite different from those in the U.S.

For example, though there is no retail price maintenance in Italy, appliance discounters have not evolved. This, because competition keeps appliance dealers slicing their own margins, leaving little marketing fat for discounters. More important, Italian customers like the assurance of buying from an official dealer. "Rinascente, the department store, tried selling television sets a few years ago, then dropped it," reports Daniel Lee, Jr., of Philco Italiana. The reason: most purchasers in Italy today are first- or second-time buyers of products no one in their families has ever owned before. To these apprentice-consumers, buying an appliance means discussions, comparisons, delicious indecision—and anticipation. Price is important, but special features, the opinion of the neighbors, and, above all, the assuring technical jargon of the "authorized" specialist dealer are necessary. This is part of a buyer's euphoria, which jaded American consumers can remember but no longer recapture.

THE BIG CHANGE

American businessmen in Europe face the continuous process of adjusting to all the above and the dozens of other national differences that make business in Europe both more difficult and more interesting than at home. They have to know, or learn, when to adapt and when to hold fast to U.S. techniques. As foreigners unfamiliar with local customs, Americans are handicapped, but as foreigners they also have advantages. The outside viewpoint is useful. For instance, when European marketing men truthfully but ominously warn that many consumers in Britain, Switzerland, or Germany resent products sold at a discount, an American can agree with the fact but not with the conclusion that discount goods won't sell in Europe. They do sell. Many middle-class European consumers (and businessmen) are accustomed to price systems wherein much of the so-called "value" of products (like the "value" of diamonds) lies in the great profit margins tacked onto these goods and in their relative scarcity. Discounting destroys these economic and social-value bench marks. In the consumer society, washing machines, as they become commonplace, lose prestige value, autos *almost* become mere autos instead of caste marks. It is not low price, but loss of old "value" measures that disturbs conservative consumers. The burghers feel that their own deeply cherished possessions are made less valuable. This same disquiet appeared in much milder form in the U.S. during 1948–50. But price cuts do open up new markets. Consumers everywhere show a remarkable record of recovery from the shock of lowered prices. Discounts in Europe are a prevalent and healthy sign that distribution systems there are finally beginning to crack and change.

CHAPTER 9

THE UNCOMMON MARKET [II]— DISTRIBUTION

Caution! Revolution at Work!

"Maybe in 25 years, after it's all over, we'll have some idea of what's really happened."

A CHAIN STORE EXECUTIVE IN LONDON

The key countries of Europe are in Stage Two of an evolution into consumer economies. Stage One was the postwar reconstruction boom that shot their economies to new prosperity and the beginnings of mass markets. It was a fairly simple investment and manufacturing stage. Stage Two, a selling stage, is more difficult and complex, for Europe's distribution systems are a part of the social structure of its countries. During the Middle Ages a guild-and-city-fathers-controlled pattern of manufacturing and retailing evolved in Europe's cities. The social hierarchy and attitudes of these stratified burgher communities were built on this business pattern. These economic and social patterns (adapted to and expanded by the Industrial Revolution) still hold sway in Europe.

But, growing too fast to be contained, elements of the new Europe are supplanting the medieval and nineteenth-century underpinnings of the old. The old social structure and attitudes remain in being (as have Europe's largely bypassed nobility), but new relationships and structures rise beside and sometimes within the old ones. What is happening is somewhat akin to what happens as a thriving city grows away from its crowded, ancient center. The old city remains in place but becomes only one part of the metropolis rather than its heart and essence. In this respect Europe has been undergoing a building boom.

Meanwhile, Europe moves towards a marketing economy. We can see something of what this developing economy is like, how it works and where it is going.

SOMETHING OLD

By Detroit or Dallas standards, salaries are low but prices are high in Europe. A can of Campbell's (or equivalent) soup selling for $.15 in the U.S. cost $.35 (U.S.) in France. Kleenex costs $1.00 in Spain. A chocolate bar costs $.25 in Switzerland (more than double the U.S. price). A major cause of these high prices is high-cost distribution. Says a U.S. food company manager in Geneva, "German supermarkets get a 30 percent total mark up (vs. 18–20 percent in the U.S.)." In France retailer groups get up to 30 percent, and the wholesaler's markup is between 15 and 20 percent. Ask a wholesaler what he gets and he'll say 12.5 percent (as against 5 percent in the U.S.); but add up the bonuses, rebates, quantity discounts, and deals at the end of the year and he'll have anywhere from 15 to 20 percent. Appliances, clothes, and furniture have similar markups. Generally the cost of distribution (of getting one's goods on retailers' shelves) is two, three, or more times what it is in the U.S. There is fat in Europe's retail systems. Change is long overdue.

In France, for instance, distribution of fruits and vegetables is a ritual out of the Middle Ages with Napoleonic embellishments. Through a strange logic of centralization, vegetables grown in Normandy are shipped to Paris, put through various paper and warehouse transactions, and shipped out again—some coming back to be sold in Normandy. The vegetables are travel-worn, and the farmer producers and final consumers are mulcted. Another indicator: in the early 1960s there were thirty food chains in France, but they did only 10–15 percent of the food business, the rest going through local stores via wholesalers of various types and sizes. A chain operation is no guarantee of efficiency or low price. In France, traditional chains pay local store managers a flat 6 percent of sales. The store managers (of what are usually one-room establishments) make their own decisions on who to hire (usually members of their family), how to stock, how to decorate the store. If they wish to add a vegetable or meat counter to the basic line of groceries, it is their own lookout. The chain owners are really wholesalers with control of prices.

Moreover, most food chains in Europe, especially in Germany, where price maintenance is upheld, are owned and run by wholesale groups. There are some 185,000 food and dairy stores in West Germany. These stores are serviced by some 14,000 wholesalers, of whom 3500 do 85 percent of the business.[1] EDEKA, the largest grouping, consists of some 230 wholesalers who service 43,000 stores selling nearly $1 billion of food per year. This makes for a close-knit system. In West Germany, Kraft Foods, the American dairy products company, tried to bypass the established wholesale setup by building a sales force and dealing with retailers and retail groups directly. After a few years the Americans came

[1] The hand of European management is often concealed, but Unilever, the largest food company in Europe, has solved at least part of its distribution problems by taking important ownership positions in major chains and store groups throughout Europe.

to terms with major wholesalers, and once more distributed through these established groups.

But it is not just wholesalers and retailers who are anxious to keep the established order intact. Manufacturers, especially in Germany, are militantly conservative. Says an American supermarket operator, who after careful study decided not to set up shop in Germany, "Say you buy up a warehouse full of beer, intending to sell it at a discount. You know that the manufacturer will never sell to you again, but it is worth it to you to break the price and draw people to the store. Well, it's not just that one manufacturer, but all kinds of other manufacturers, will come around to let you know you can't buy from them again. The manufacturers associations can break you—and they will if you try to rock the boat."[2]

SOMETHING NEW

However, when enough people begin to earn enough money to create mass markets—for wall can-openers, electric hairdryers, autos, breakfast foods, and a thousand other items—changes take place, shortcuts develop. In the new

[2] Corporate competitiveness, which in the American milieu is taken for granted—and which Americans in Europe often assume as a cloak of virtue—is not really second nature but something maintained in the U.S. by law and vigilance. At a dinner meeting in New York, when an American marketing consultant discreetly chided representatives of U.S. food companies for their compliance with restrictive trade practices in Europe, he got a curious and bland reply. Yes, said these all too quickly Europeanized executives, they realized it might quicken national economies and in the long run improve their own businesses to aid adventurous retailers' attempts to institute price competition in the food business. However, at the moment they were making nice profits for very little effort. They had no desire to change this pleasant state of affairs.

Europe, for example, self-service variety stores and super-markets are spreading. Producers of some kinds of items, notably electric appliances, are abetting, if not directly aid-ing, discounters. New, combination food-discount-depart-ment stores are evolving. The development of the Common Market speeds things up, too. For example, when German tire manufacturers refused to supply Neckermann's with low-price auto tires, the company had little trouble finding Italian suppliers who would. This cracked the local cartel.

At the moment, retailing in Europe is an amalgam of stiff-jointed distributing and pricing systems—and some hope-ful experiments which may yet make the consumer king. You see this most clearly in Britain, where dynamic changes are underway.

After the Swiss, the British are possibly the world's most compliant customers. Grateful for whatever little attentions they get from their indifferent storekeepers, the good-natured islanders accept queues, incompetent service, inadequate stocks, and shelf-aged goods as part of the national legacy. This holds at all levels of retailing. Not even the famous Harrods department store in London is exempt from these quaint faults; Harrods merely raises them to higher levels.

Harrods is a marvelous store, the epitome of a type. A class rather than a mass store, Harrods is a gothic-baroque, sooty, pink hulk of a building, to the door of which black, giant-headlamped, vintage Rolls-Royces roll. Out of these carefully preserved relics white-haired old lady customers totter or stride (depending on their own state of preserva-tion) to help oil the golden wheels of commerce. For many, a trip to London is a trip to Harrods. On the inside, this national monument is a hushed, high-ceilinged, many-halled enclosure, with carpets and walls gently shaded, aisles wide, counters unobtrusively modern. Handsome, well-dressed people talk, shop, and walk leisurely from room to room. In the music section a lovely mother and her seven-year-old, Breck-Hair-Shampoo-ad son test a piano. Live, life-sized, toy-soldier, off-duty guards officers pose by the glove counter. Not far away, her English complexion accentuated by the light, a young beauty pretends to ignore them. On another floor a middle-aged couple examines dining tables. Careful clerks stand by to give assistance—if called. Throughout the store customers move quietly, relaxed, pleased with the surroundings and with themselves. Harrods supplies that which nervous Dallas ladies most earnestly desire: atmosphere, a sense of luxury, and ego balm.

And yet, behind this effectively bland exterior beats a heart that misses. After ordering a set of steak knives, a customer finds that those on display (scratched) are what the clerk is wrapping. Through some oversight there are none in the stockroom. Getting another set from the manufacturer takes six weeks. Nobody seems surprised. There are other little flaws. Planning to host an important party, one American in London ordered liquor for the event two weeks beforehand, delivery to take place two days before the affair. On the appointed day the goods did not appear. A telephone call turned up no record of the order, but a new order was promised for the next day. Next day, by afternoon, there was still no delivery, but the store told the worried customer that his original order had been found, and had been processed. He would see delivery early next day. By late afternoon next day, the day of the party, the liquor had not arrived. An hour after the affair was underway, on emergency rations, the delivery men wandered up to the door.

Veteran customers take this sort of thing in stride, try to plan accordingly. "He should never have ordered so far in advance. Their memories are really not so very keen at Harrods," says a Londoner. Old-timers also warn newcomers to save sales slips and double-check the bills each month.

Bookkeeping in British stores can be whimsical. The American party-giver, meanwhile, remains a loyal, dissatisfied customer. Other stores, he explains, are no better and sometimes worse.

At the bottom, corner-store level of the retail system there is the same slackness. The surroundings are grimmer. Walk by Wellington Street in Leeds in the industrial North and you see miles of one- and two-story hovels 200 to 250 years old. Cul-de-sac alleys lead off the road. The tiny row houses have no toilet, no yards. There is a shop on every corner for twelve families where "the old girls stand in line in the morning in dirty bathrobes with their hair in curlers to get kippers for breakfast," says a British sales manager who worked in the area.

Further north in smoky Glasgow, an American woman reports, "It took me three hours to get lemons for a lemon pie the other week. None of the stores in the neighborhood had any. 'Today isn't the day for lemons,' they said. If customers want lemons on the wrong day it's just too bad."

Across town a lady who likes a particular kind of oat bread her local store periodically carries has to get there early on Wednesdays or find this popular item sold out. The grocer refuses to stock more. "Och, if they don't buy oat they'll buy rye," he says. But the days of this Marie Antoinette manner are numbered. Possibly there will always be a Harrods in England, but the corner stores are in for trouble. Not only food, but local appliance, furniture, and variety stores are threatened. New kinds of retailers and new kinds of retail systems are evolving an Old Blighty.

One extreme of the type, John Bloom, a cocky cockney out of nowhere, has singlehandedly set the British appliance industry on its ear. In the process he has become both a millionaire and a lively affront to the industry's Colonel Blimps. Bloom's odyssey is instructive.

THE SUPERSALESMAN

A lightly built man in his early thirties, Bloom, who at one time affected a wispy, red chinbeard, looks more like a pseudo-beatnik Greenwich Village coffeehouse waiter than the industrialist he is. Starting in business for himself in 1958, Bloom sold imported Dutch washing machines at $80 less than the cheapest English models. "The product wasn't the best, but it did work," he says. So, too, did Bloom's price and sales strategy. By the end of 1959 he had piled up $80,000 in profits. His technique, still unchanged: advertise in the papers, stressing price; have a mail-in coupon with each ad. By calling on the "live ones," who sent in coupon inquiries, his salesmen were making sales on half their house calls.

Late in 1959, convinced he was on to something, Bloom bought up a fading company with a famous name, Rolls Razor Ltd. Says Bloom, "Ads are the key to this whole business. And Rolls is a prestige name." On taking over the moribund razor company, Bloom called in company engineers and technicians, showed them a model of his washing machine, and said, "Make something like that, but better, or we close down." Ripping ancient cubicles and storage bins apart to lay out a conveyor line, the factory went to work. For capital Bloom scrounged what he could from company resources and borrowed what he could anywhere. "The banks wouldn't talk to me; I paid blood for that money," says Bloom. He raised $560,000. That first year the company turned out 26,000 machines and lost $644,000 (partly made up by $440,000 in profits from the still growing import operation). In 1961, however, Rolls turned out 86,000 machines, made an $840,000 profit, and was on its way. The banks, by 1962, were always pleased to hear from Mr. Bloom. His competitors wish they never had.

Growing with un-British exuberance, Rolls, in early 1962, had 200 hard-eyed, soft-smiled salesmen touting its washers to housewives all over Britain. Pricing his machines at 25–30 percent less than the major producers, Bloom took 10 percent of the washing-machine market. Partly he was creating new markets, partly he was slicing into established producers'. Either way, he was showing the regulars up as incompetent. Trimming overhead, production costs, and dealers' margins, name producers such as Hotpoint and Hoover brought prices down and intensified advertising. "But they'd have to operate at a loss to sell at my price," says Bloom, who doubled washing-machine production to reach for 20 percent of the market by late 1962. Rolls also took over distribution for Prestcold, a major British refrigerator firm, selling refrigerators, again at 25–30 percent below previous prices. Later, in 1964, when it developed that Prestcold could not produce equipment efficiently enough to maintain a low sales price, Bloom dropped Prestcold as a supplier. Meanwhile, spotting a mass market, two large companies, English Electric and Great Universal Stores, have entered the field with washing machines a little above Bloom's top model in price. With the pace quickening, Bloom moved to add vacuum cleaners, photo equipment, and various small appliances to his line of washing machines, refrigerators, dishwashers, and portable heaters.

Sweeping around, and turning the flanks of the appliance industry through direct-selling methods, Bloom has crumpled its price structure and complacency. What fat cats there were in the industry have turned lean and mean—at least in their feelings about Bloom. But Bloom has done them a service. He provided the first dose of the conditioning they need to survive in the new Europe, and his indoctrination course came none too soon. In the spring of 1963, Zanussi, one of the fastest-moving and most aggressive of the Italian appliance companies, invaded the British Isles with a low-cost ($236), fully automatic washing machine. Zanussi is selling its machines by the John Bloom newspaper-ad-and-coupon system. This in turn is forcing Bloom to rush production of his own fully automatic machine. And, as soon as possible, Bloom will want to invade the Continent.

No fly-by-night now, but flying high, wide, and handsome day and night, John Bloom, onetime poor boy, is enthusiastically amassing the joys and travails of the *nouveau riche*. In conversation he quickly manages passing mention of his chauffeur, butler, private manse, and boat. His involvement in an unpleasant London-Riviera scandal made British newspaper headlines for weeks, but Rolls is still selling more of everything it can, everywhere it can.

Bloom may yet trip. He operates a one-man organization and has been expanding very rapidly. If he runs into marketing or financial difficulties, his more conservative and better-heeled rivals would smugly move in to pick up the pieces. But, win or lose, Bloom has usefully made his mark, shown a way to others.

All over Britain retail changes are underway. Other sales-minded manufacturing companies, such as Cyril Lord Carpets Ltd. and Dimplex Ltd. (electric heaters), have, à la John Bloom, hurdled cumbersome retail systems to deal directly with consumers. Through 1963 retail price maintenance, long upheld by the courts, was being eroded in the market place. In foods it had long vanished. In clothes, furniture, and appliances it was more and more honored in the breach. In 1964, an election year, the Tories, after much soul searching, eliminated retail price maintenance in Britain. Meanwhile, private brands have been blossoming. Great Universal Stores, nicknamed "Gussie," a British mail-order-department-store version of Sears, Roebuck, has boomed since the late 1940s. Marks & Spencer, an aggressive variety and clothing chain, has grown by concentrating on acquiring high-quality items for sale at low prices in pleasant, open-counter stores. A sign of the times: Marks & Spencer draws clients from Harrods as well as from the working classes.

Tesco Stores, an aggressive supermarket chain, and numerous rivals such as Grandways, Anthony Jackson Food-fare, and Bordergate Properties, are all busily experimenting with self-service "economy stores" featuring food and a broad range of general items. Even the tire industry, long a cozy, Dunlop Tyre-dominated gentlemen's club (i.e., cartel) is slashing prices, reorganizing distribution systems, and seeking new, large-volume outlets. U.S. trading stamps, meanwhile, have swept British food stores. Britain is undergoing a revolution, and on the Continent similar though slower-paced upheavals are taking place.

In all Europe, however, retail developments, while similar, are also different from those that evolved in the U.S. The best way to see this vital point, though, is by taking a look, first, at European supermarkets, then at a type of conglomerate store that does not yet have a name.

CHAPTER 10

THE UNCOMMON MARKET [III]
New Stores in Old Europe

Travelers return from Europe saying that there are supermarkets everywhere. There are—and there aren't. Supermarkets, the duly accredited signs of the consumer economy,
do indeed seem to be popping up all over Europe. There
are over 1000 such supermarkets in Britain. They are expanding north from the London area and will number 4000
by 1970. Already there are over 2000 supermarkets in Germany. In Holland in 1963 the Dutch Co-operative Society
announced plans to turn 300 of its 850 stores into either
small self-service or supermarket operations. But these statistics are misleading. There is less to European supermarkets
than meets the eye.

Supermarkets in Europe are not, as in the United States
or Canada, big food emporiums girdled with parking lots.
Land costs, building costs, road nets, auto population, and
salary levels make them something else.

The closest U.S. equivalent to a European supermarket
are the tight-packed superstores one finds in crowded mid
Manhattan. Even then, there are great differences. Most
British supermarkets, for instance, are about the size of a
U.S. laundromat (2000 to 4000 square feet). They tend to
be bigger in Germany. But, where the average U.S. super-
market boasts some 6500 items on its shelves, the average
German store in 1963 carried 1500 to 2000 items. There are

other more subtle differences, and some basic contradictions. In Italy, for example, the Rockefeller-financed International Basic Economy Corp. has launched a string of U.S.-style foodstores (real supermarkets) in Genoa and Milan. These stores sell food at an average of 15 percent below local rates, yet are very profitable.

"Maybe they are doing all right," says a major U.S. food company's marketing manager, "but I was in an IBEC store in Milan the other afternoon at three. You could have shot a cannon down the aisles and never hurt a soul." After two and one-half years in Europe this well-paid executive should have known that in Italy, between 12:30 and 3:00 P.M., the world stops for lunch and the Italian siesta. At 4:00 P.M. that store was crowded. On Saturdays the entrance must be closed from time to time to give shoppers a chance to buy and get out before new throngs sweep in.

In order to survive in Europe, however, a store must adapt. A group of executives and technicians from a U.S. supermarket chain surveying Europe, looking at the phenomenally wide aisles in an IBEC store, clucked disapprovingly at the obvious waste of space. "It's crazy," said one. Crazy, maybe, but in Europe wage rates are lower than in the U.S. Refrigerators, if owned, are smaller than in the U.S. Therefore, in Europe, women shop more often (for daily needs) and buy less than in the U.S. This means that more of them crowd into the store. The wide aisles permit them to get around each other, quickly pick up their goods, and get to the checkout counter. Naturally, with more customers making fewer purchases, a store needs more checkout counters and cash registers to get the ladies in and out in minimum time. The essence of supermarkets is high turnover at low overhead. The fact that large parking lots or a set number of cash registers per square footage of store are an aid to this operation in the U.S. does not mean that they are essential in Europe. Even the food carts with which shopping matrons prod each other out of the way in Italy are different from those in the U.S. When it first opened in Italy, IBEC imported the standard groceries-plus-a-small-child-size foodcarts common to U.S. stores. They were hardly used. Most food purchases at IBEC range from $1.50 to $2.80 in value and are often less. Ashamed of being seen bringing one, two, or three items to the checkout counter in big carts, the customers avoided them altogether. When IBEC trimmed the size of the carts down from Cadillac to Fiat size, the carts were taken up happily.

At peak, IBEC stores were selling $13 worth of goods per square foot of floor space each week (compared with $2.69 in the average U.S. supermarket). "The average sale was one third that in the U.S., but we did four times the volume. Seventy thousand people move through a store in one week," says Roland Hood, a company vice-president. IBEC stores sell out their stocks every two weeks. This is the equivalent of selling out everything in the store twenty-five times a year, and this is the open secret of their success. With this kind of turnover it is possible to see why, even if they only make, say, 2 percent average profit on their goods, the stores are prosperous. After all, they make that 2 percent twenty-five times. The emphasis is not just on volume but on high-speed volume, or turnover, on organization for the high-speed sale of goods. It can be done in Europe. By and large, however, it is not being done. And here contradictions appear.

European supermarkets play up the name but not the game, have the form but not the essence of their American prototypes. Except for a handful of loss-leader items (butter, coffee, sweets), most European supermarkets at best operate only a few percentage points below the corner grocer in price (and on some items, at or above him in price). They concentrate on volume but not on high-speed volume. They cling to high markups.

A twin set of reasons for high markups in Europe are that European supermarkets are city rather than suburban phenomena and that supermarkets are still relatively scarce. They draw, not on auto-driving housewives but on nearby pedestrians. Supermarkets five blocks apart hardly affect each other. Each store has a dense natural marketing area, a forest of surrounding apartments off which it lives (much as a feudal baron with his castle and surrounding lands had a demesne). Therefore, except in a number of special locations, few supermarkets in Europe presently compete directly with other supermarkets; most compete only with small stores. The attractive layout, fresh produce, and handy packaging of the supermarkets permits them to draw customers from the small stores without resorting to price cuts; so they don't. Supermarkets can save costs by instituting self-service, bulk buying, processing, and warehousing. They compete with the small store on price as much as they have to, but no more than they must.

The above is an oversimplification but the essential point. There are others. In America the giant food chains took to supermarkets only at the last moment, when forced to by competition. The situation in Europe is not too different. The chains build supermarkets but they don't push the pace, can't quite bring themselves to compete sharply with their own small-store operations. For the time being, secret or open resistance of retailers' and manufacturers' associations, and inertia, are combining to maintain and protect the old and high-cost retail order in new disguise—as supermarkets. (Curiously, some of the fiercest resistance to supermarket operations in Europe has come from consumer co-operatives, the very organizations which in theory would most avidly welcome lower-cost marketing. Consumer co-operatives were created to combat high prices in regular retail stores by supplying products at lower prices or by offering rebates to members. Somehow confusing ends with means, many co-op members, especially in Britain, bitterly resist trimming off inefficient small stores and building of supermarket groups as a betrayal of consumer co-operative ideals and a sellout to modern capitalism.)

Also important: land, building, and capital costs are high in Europe—so high they sometimes turn supermarkets into something else. Land in Paris, for instance, is as costly as in parts of Manhattan. Rental of space in the new Time-Life Building in Paris is $8 per square foot. Building construction is 50 percent slower and up to twice as expensive on the Continent as it is in the U.S. In 1962, it cost 8.5 percent at the prime rate to borrow money in Europe (vs. 4.5 percent in the U.S.). In net, it costs two to three times as much to open the doors of a supermarket in Europe as it does in the U.S. So, even among merchants who understand high-speed, high-volume selling, a different manner of store evolves, a store type that has no name and, as yet, no final form.

Faced with high land and building costs that show up as steep rents, European store operators try to get better margins by selling high-value, high-markup nonfood items. As a result, in profitable stores only 15–25 percent of the space and 40–45 percent of sales are taken up by foods; the rest is given over to general goods. The food, at discount, is used to draw people into what is no longer a food but a food-department store. This mixed, food-"economy" store has been evolving independently in France, Britain, and throughout the rest of Europe. The most glamorous example, the famous Innos chain in Paris, is a combination well-stocked supermarket and discount-department store that sells brand items at 15 percent below list. However, selling food is one kind of business. Selling radios, television sets, washing machines, clothes, and sporting goods are other kinds of business. So merchandising problems mount. Salesmen are needed. The self-service aspects that started the whole thing off begin to fade. An Innos-type operation calls for extensive capital and multiple outlets to carry heavy management and overhead costs.

At a less magnificent level, however, the outstanding merchandisers in Europe today are the French-owned Prisunic chain, which runs several hundred combination variety-store-supermarkets-cum-discount houses throughout the Continent. Prisunic is something of a self-service Grant stores (a cut or three above Woolworth), with a supermarket in the basement and some hot discount items scattered here and there. Low-price private brands are pushed. At least at this stage of Europe's evolution, Prisunic seems a winning combination.

Patrol the streets of Europe's major cities, and you find hundreds of tiny stores crammed with goods—especially appliances. Small-appliance stores (one and sometimes two or three to the block) seem as common as luncheonettes in the U.S. They are a sign of new prosperity, but so many ineffective small units side-by-side are also a sign of high markups and ineffective distribution. The shakeout of marginal retailers has yet to come in Europe but is on its way. When it comes it will be Europe-wide.

Meanwhile, Neckermann Stores (the Sears, Roebuck of Germany) has set up a subsidiary in Austria. Great Universal Stores (the Sears, Roebuck of Britain) has acquired a mail-order house in Holland. Prisunic has 200 stores in Italy. Le Grand Magasin à l'Innovation of Belgium (with which Jewel Tea of the U.S. is associated) owns 51 percent of Innos of Paris. Marks & Spencer, possibly Britain's most efficient retailers, sell goods to Innos and to the largest Italian retail chain, Rinascente UPIM. Associated British Foods (owned by Canadian Garfield Weston) has acquired controlling interest in Entrepôts Dubuffet in France. (Since Weston also owns a German supermarket chain, he may be the first to organize an all-Europe supermarket system.) At the end of 1962 a $250-million bank syndicate, headed by the prestigious Crédite Suisse bank of Zurich, Switzerland, offered its shares on the stock markets. This new firm's purpose: to buy stock in existing companies and to develop new outlets in the retail trade, particularly in the form of shopping centers, supermarkets, and self-service stores. And so it goes. These are individuals and groups intent only on building personal or corporate fortunes and careers. But shuttling back and forth across Europe's countries they carry the threads that can weave the fabric of the new Europe. They *are* the new Europe.

LES AMERICAINS

By early 1963 few American retailers had jumped into Europe with both feet. Safeway, the U.S. supermarket chain, was in Britain, and Gem International, the highly successful discount group, was opening up some British stores. Other firms keep making studies of the market; some will eventually move. Sears, Roebuck's European expansion had been rumored for four years. At one time Sears was reportedly close to an agreement with Neckermann, but was pushed aside by German financial groups. (Morgan Guaranty, the investment bank, reportedly later took an important minority interest in the Neckermann firm.) In parts of Europe a Sears-type operation would be as catalytic and beneficial as Sears' now famous industry-creating and consumer-benefiting activities in Mexico—and Sears in 1964 was getting set to open up stores in Spain.

However, most senior U.S. retail executives can still remember the political pressures and turmoil that swept America when first the chains and then the supermarkets began squeezing out marginal small stores around the country. (The Robinson-Patman Act was born of this era.) In Europe, which is even less acclimated to change than America, equally vast upheavals are just reaching the painful stage. To have American companies leading the surge of change would be like waving a bright red flag before Europe's righteous and politically articulate *petit bourgeois* shopkeepers. There is a certain wisdom in Americans keeping their interests in retailing to an investment and consulting role. But retailing in Europe is such an obvious growth field (for highly competent operators) that more U.S. companies will move across the Atlantic.

CHAPTER 11

THE UNCOMMON MARKET [IV]
Advertising

American advertisers and advertising men in Europe assume a proprietary air. After all, it is they, the originator-developers, who are bringing the U.S.-evolved skills of advertising to Europe. There is enough truth in this smug attitude to keep European advertising men gasping with deep hurt. There is also enough nonsense to keep Americans tripping up.

It is true that American advertising methods have virtually transformed British advertising, are in the process of changing German advertising, and in time will make over the French, Italian, and other Continental ad industries. It is also true that most modern European advertising is a copy of what is done in America. The postured models, the props, and often enough the advertising themes used to pitch European companies' products are lifted directly from the U.S. "But really, these things are quite different than they seem," insists a European ad executive who, along with most of his fellows, loves to lecture on the uniqueness of his national audience and its instinctive rejection of crass, U.S.-style commercialism. In fact, there is a continuous debate going on in Europe over the applicability of U.S. vs. European advertising approaches. Stripped of essential modifiers, conditions, and exceptions, the two positions are as follows: American advertising is designed to sell, to persuade the listener or viewer to buy a

particular product at the first opportunity. Its appeals tend to
be quite direct. (Buy it now. It is better . . . good for
you . . . makes you feel good . . . makes you look good . . .
etc.) European advertising is designed more to amuse, to
titillate the audience and leave them with a good feeling
about a product or company. "Their art work is lovely—but it
doesn't have anything to do with the copy—and the copy
doesn't push the product," complains an American food-prod-
uct manager about his French advertising agency.

European advertisers and agencies are coy because, till
recently, few European firms felt any real need for advertising; they lived in comfortable, often cartelized, sellers' markets. Till very recently, too, there were no mass markets to
speak of in Europe. What little advertising European owner-
managers indulged in tended to be directed at peer groups
of middle- and upper-middle class buyers. Also, in the traditional European milieu (especially noticeable in England
and France) there is a long-standing taboo against *appearing*
commercial. Advertising, by these lights, can be snobbish (or
dignified), it can be amusing—but it should not be pushy.

Lately, as rudimentary competition and mass markets come
into being in Europe, the comfortable old rules of the game
have been changing. Once one company horrifies its friends
and competitors by actually indulging in aggressive advertising, the others find they must follow suit or lose business.
As the catalytic Americans, who advertise as a matter of
course, move into Europe, they accelerate the process. European advertising men and companies cluck at the foolish
amounts of money the Americans waste on ads—but more
and more Europeans find they must do likewise. Often they
turn to U.S. ad agencies for help. Having hopefully (or
glumly) followed their U.S. clients abroad, a dozen U.S.
agencies now range Europe. J. Walter Thompson, McCann-
Erickson, BBD&O, Ted Bates, Young & Rubicam, Foote,

Cone & Belding—the roster is lengthening yearly. No self-respecting major agency would be caught without a European office or, at least, a series of European affiliates. These American ad agencies in Europe strain to build up local accounts (it becomes a partial measure of their prestige and "acceptance"), and so the americanization process goes on. But when European ad men warn that their national markets are unique and can't be treated like U.S. markets they have a point, a point which too many Americans insist on learning by trial and error.

TRIAL AND ERROR, AMERICAN STYLE

"Coca-Cola refreshes you best" is a phrase that travels well. In English, French, Spanish or Italian this simple theme helps sell one of the world's most successful products. As noted in Chapter 9, a detergent company's advertising promise to get clothes "dazzling white" or "shiny bright" or "cleaner than any soap" can also make the trip across the ocean with little trouble. Other products and other slogans, however, don't always do as well, not even in Britain, where the language is similar.

The British, in fact, provide a fine example of how different basically similar cultures can be. Cultural differences are hard to qualify, but consider the matter of attitudes toward children. The British love their children and stuff them with sweets till their little teeth fall out, but the British concept of what a child is, or should be, is entirely different from that of their American cousins. One sees this in various ways. The Chelsea and Kensington areas of London proper, for instance, are blessed with numerous schools, and at almost anytime of the morning one can stumble across double files of eight- to eleven-year-old boys or girls standing stoic on the sidewalks or being marched along to some educational rendezvous arranged by their elders and betters.

Now, whether at the halt or on the move, a gaggle of American kids on an educational outing is one of the more awesome forces of nature. It is a writhing, jabbing, jabbering, elongated packet of colored shirts, caps, shoes, sneakers, and energy that continuously breaks into roughhousing, gum-chewing fragments. The critical mass for one of these waist-high, wide-eyed riots is about nine children, beyond which it takes two high-decibel, low-boiling-point teachers to keep the group moving (or still). Even then, individual high-energy particles keep looping in and out of the central mass.

In its own way, however, a group of school-uniformed (short pants, knee socks) English schoolchildren is every bit as awesome as the American phenomenon. At the halt, the lone teacher-guardian lounges several paces away ignoring his charges. Two-dozen longish-haired youngsters may stand side by side. A few may look curiously about them. Most of them are not talking to their neighbors, but waiting only for the word to move off. (As their stoic fathers did on 1940 Dunkirk beaches.) To the American hurrying by, the silence of these groups of youngsters is something somehow trouble-some and a bit unsettling. To an Englishman it is only right and normal. In the British view, there is a world of children and a world of adults, and where the two worlds impinge the children are expected to respectfully and quietly give way. (By the same token, adults do not try to intrude or "pal" their way into the world of children.) There are brash and brassy British children but, by and large, these young-sters conform to the dictum that children should be seen and not heard. British society is not child-centered. Few British children, for instance, have any say (as yet) in what foods do or do not go into the family larder. Further, the present role of the child in English society is one which the British cherish and are determined to keep pretty much as it is.[1]

All the above is by way of background to the remark of a London ad man: "So you can imagine the average British parent's reaction to a box of breakfast food showing a freckled, red-haired, crew-cut, bow-tied U.S. child leering out saying, 'Gee, kids, it's great!'" Yet, in its ill-fated first efforts to sell breakfast foods in Britain, the General Mills Co. did attempt a direct transplant of such an all-American package—with little success.

Since the men who guide U.S. companies into error overseas are intelligent U.S.-market veterans, one begins to suspect that there may be American aberrations or blind spots at play here. There are. American marketing men tend to think of the world as the United States in embryo. Even when they know that European habits, assumptions, and reactions are different, they remain unconsciously convinced that, once presented with U.S.-style products and situations, most Europeans will react like American consumers. Americans are certain that what Americans want and like, others will also. Moreover, this assumption (which holds true to a surprising degree) in turns leans upon another. This is the unconscious belief that European consumers have been through (or don't need) the advertising indoctrination Americans have been exposed to for more than a generation. It is when they do not verify these joint assumptions that Americans overseas get into trouble. Cases in point:

[1]The youngsters themselves, however (mostly among the lower class), seem to be breaking away on strange paths of their own. In the spring of 1964 in a scene right out of Marlon Brando's *The Wild Ones* a destructive herd of close to 1000 British juveniles took over the small resort town of Clacton to loot stores and carry on a series of factional fights among themselves.

When Salem cigarettes, the top-selling menthol brand in the U.S., moved to Germany the name was changed to Reyno (because the Salem name was already taken up by another product). However, only the name was changed. The proven successful (successful in the U.S., that is) green-tinted, boy-girl, and water under the trees pictures and theme were carefully carried over to the new German market. Nonetheless, Reyno did poorly—for several reasons. Salem's mild menthol cigarettes, an instant success in the U.S., actually leaped to success and prominence on the yeoman efforts to Kool cigarettes, which for a generation had been selling Americans the idea and taste of a menthol smoke. But in Germany, where menthol cigarettes were something new, Reynos were on their own. Hitting the market cold, they found that it stayed that way. Second, the green-tinted, boy-girl photo ads did not merely spell cool refreshment. To Germans they also spelled: (A) menthol, i.e., a noncigarette, and (B) youth, i.e., inexperience. Reyno's image was that of a beginner's, a woman's, or an effeminate man's cigarette, not a real smoker's cigarette. After realizing this, Reyno started playing down the green tint, playing up warmer orange tints in its ads. Then it took to showing photos of a cigarette split open to reveal the superabundance of rich, brown, "real" tobacco in its cigarettes. Gradually, sales began to climb.

Again, Gleem toothpaste, the toothpaste for people who can't brush after every meal, ran into difficulties when test-marketed in Europe. Unblessed by years of earnest dental-association reminders or by pious, man-in-white-smock exhortations to clean their teeth at least three times a day, Europeans are not so sure it's a good idea to clean one's teeth at all. The majority feel that a perfunctory polishing up every day or two is quite sufficient. The guilt-edged Gleem slogan, cleverly designed to ride on a generation of three-times-a-day hygienic indoctrination, did well in America. To Europeans the slogan was meaningless, it relieved no guilt. It did little for sales.

Simple national pride (and prejudice) can also trouble a company abroad. When Maxwell House, "America's Favorite Breakfast Coffee," moved to Europe, its proud "American" slogan raised at least as many consumers' hackles as it did curiosity or desire to buy. Firmly convinced that their own coffee is the world's best, few Dutch, Germans, French, or Swiss feel the need for taste-coaching from foreigners. (Actually, Maxwell's European blend is different, darker, than its U.S. product.) Rebounding neatly from its original *gaffe*, however, highly successful Maxwell now bills itself as an international coffee—with host-nation overtones. In one European film strip, for instance, a young man just back from a trip abroad has coffee with welcoming relatives. The sense of the sequence goes:

> "Uhm, that's good coffee."
> "It is Maxwell House coffee."
> "Oh, yes? They have that in America, too."

Kleenex tissues, a volume seller and household name in the U.S., first came to Germany touted as a handy hanky. But the Germans already know about paper handkerchiefs; they have a large, durable, four-ply affair on the market. "And if you blow your nose too hard on a Kleenex you wind up with a wet hand," admits a Kleenex representative. Kleenex then tried billing itself as an all-purpose hanky with multiple uses—but this only confused potential users all the more. Finally, and successfully, Kleenex began announcing itself as a lady's complexion tissue—which, significantly, is precisely how it got going in the U.S. about a generation ago.

As the above examples show, American advertisers'

assumptions about Europe tend to be based on their assumptions about modern America, but these incidents also show that American businessmen in Europe do learn from their mistakes. Moreover, a number of these instances, such as the case of Kleenex (which reverted to its original U.S. appeal of the 1930s), also hint at a lesson: by mining their own backlog of experience in the U.S. markets of twenty and thirty years ago, Americans can draw useful analogies for the mixed old-new markets (and distribution systems) of present-day Europe. What's happening in Europe is that literally millions of new, untried, and unsure consumers—and the businesses that serve them—are learning and adapting simultaneously. Here the Americans, who have lived and worked in the U.S. consumer economy, have some slight advantages. Before they can effectively implement any advantages, however, the Americans also have much to learn.

LESSONS FOR YANKEES

Most U.S. ad-agency men in Europe are recent arrivals who are learning about Europe along with, or only a short jump ahead of, their clients.[2] Since part of their job is to sell expertise, including knowledge of markets and consumers, agency men in Europe have to scramble to note, understand, and try to assimilate the many differences between these markets. In Italy, for example, English-language names and directions on appliances boost sales. In France, English-language markings hurt sales. In southern England housewives habitually buy their cakes ready-baked from local stores. In the north-border country of Yorkshire the women

[2] Even when firms have been overseas many years, transfer and turnover of personnel account for the fact that American staffs are often new to the country.

are enthusiastic mixers and bakers of breads and cakes. It is only in London and the industrial Midlands that ready-mix cakes do well. McCann-Erickson found that in Sicily men do the bulk of the food buying for their families. "Walk into the grocery stores and there the men are with their string bags, picking up the family groceries," says a McCann executive. In Italy proper the head of another American agency doubts that this could really be so or feels that the story is, at least, highly exaggerated. A North Italian advertising man who seldom leaves Milan is equally dubious, "After all, buying food is woman's work," he explains. But in southern Spain (Spain, like Sicily, was once dominated by the Arab culture) an Andalusian businessman finds the idea perfectly natural. "Until my father died, it was he who used to buy the principal groceries in our home," says this señor. And in 1830s America, says Russel Lynnes in his book *The Domesticated Americans*,[3] it was the men who went to the markets. "Ladies" did not go to such rough places.

U.S. ad men find that suburbia, which has done so much to shape U.S. living and buying patterns, hardly exists in Europe. Europe's people are apartment dwellers; European marketing is city-centered. The growing concentrations of people in Europe's cities are an obvious and concentrated market—with contradictions. In Belgium's cities, for example, there are more, smaller, and, presumably, less efficient stores per capita than in the country. And all over Europe the countryside is booming. France's farmers are buying appliances, autos, ready-made clothing—and farm equipment like credit-happy American suburbanites. In Holland auto registrations, which used to be concentrated 70 percent in the urban areas, are now evenly distributed between town

[3] Harper & Row.

and city. (In other words, the greatest growth has been in the country!) Philco Corp., expanding its appliance line in Italy, looks for its principal growth markets in the newly prosperous country towns.

It is only when they learn to spot and explain these and other trends in national markets that agency men in Europe begin to get clients' and businessmen's respect. Then their real frustrations begin. The ways, means, and rules of advertising in Europe, while quite reasonable to Europeans, can seem wildly improbable to Americans.

SOME EUROPEAN RULES OF THE ROAD

What troubles American ad men is how difficult particular groups of customers are to pinpoint and to reach through existing media and under government regulations. Movies, for instance, are relatively popular in Europe and an important advertising media; during intermissions TV-type commercials and stills are flashed on the screen. But in Italy relatively few women go to the movies, and only men, as a rule, read newspapers. Except in Sicily, where the men shop, it would do no good to advertise supermarket and department store sales in local newspapers, because the ladies would never see the ads. This means that products purchased by the ladies must be advertised in women's magazines. Since the women's magazines are national rather than regional, this in turn makes local market-testing in Italy difficult. What's more, all over Europe newspapers and magazines are relatively inflexible in format and hard to deal with. In the U.S. most newspaper and magazine publishers will happily tack on extra pages of editorial material to accommodate advertisers who suddenly show up with important new business. In Europe, especially in Germany and Spain, they will more likely turn down new business rather than expand an issue beyond its original regular size.[4]

Of course, for the really aggressive marketer there is always television. In Europe, as in the U.S., TV has become the most effective salesman in history. But, again, there are difficulties. There is regional television in Britain. There is also regional television of a sort in Germany (a residue of three-power occupation zones); but in Italy and Spain television coverage is nationwide—another stumbling block for companies interested in local test-marketing. In France there is no advertising on TV. Generally in Europe, TV advertising is closely controlled or limited. U.S. companies, accustomed to the easy luxury of one- and two-minute commercials in the middle or before the dramatic end of a program, find that European TV spots are 15-, 30-, and 45-second affairs. Often these spots are jammed willy-nilly at the end of a program. Advertisers do not sponsor and in no way control programs or content! All the advertiser buys is time—and he has to get in line for that. In Britain, BBD &O, the ad agency, reports that it must schedule its TV spots a minimum of three to four months ahead of time, with prime hours scheduled even further ahead than that. In Germany, Young & Rubicam books its TV time a full year ahead. In Italy, TV spots are doled out six months to a full year ahead of time according to a company's size, previous usage of TV (i.e., its seniority as a customer), and its deftness in

---

[4] What keeps local U.S. newspapers fat are local ads by merchants and numerous national consumer-product manufacturers making a pitch to housewives, the principal spend-alls in our consumer economy. These newspapers are business ventures, which have political leanings. But in Italy, for example, most newpapers are political ventures, subsidized by political parties. The monetary incentive for new business exists, but in diluted form.

developing influential "contracts," with government administrators.

Meanwhile numbers of European governments, anxious to avoid what they feel are the excesses, the signboard jungles, blaring commercials, and possibly misleading, if legally permissible, claims that "enliven" U.S. advertising, clamp strict rules on promotion. As a result, many of the freewheeling promotions U.S. marketing men use to keep their products moving are illegal in Europe. For example, in a booklet Young & Rubicam uses to prepare its U.S. clients for the facts of life in Germany:

Very broadly speaking, the legal principles are these: Advertising claims must be true. They must not refer to competitors, either directly or indirectly, in a way that might interfere with the latter's competitive chances.

That advertising claims must be true refers to all statements, whether in words or pictures, pertaining to the qualities, origin, manufacture, and price of goods or services. And no misleading statements must be made that give the average, superficial reader or viewer the impression of a more favorable offer than is virtually given.

Omissions, ambiguous statements, or partly true statements are also considered misleading. Even an objectively true statement may (subjectively) have a misleading effect upon the public. Example: Advertising for a Steinhäger (schnapps) claiming this brand is 'twice distilled.' This is true, but a misleading claim, since under German law every Steinhäger must be distilled twice.

Advertisments must not refer to competitors, either directly or indirectly, in a way that might interfere with their competitive chances. It is illegal, for instance, to promote one's products, services, etc. by comparing them to competing products. Comparisons cannot be banned completely from advertising. Therefore, German law permits a comparison of *new methods and 'systems'*— which are a result of scientific or technical progress—with existing methods or systems. Comparisons of *products,* however, are only permissible under exceptional circumstances: firstly, in order to defend one's product against a direct attack by a competitor; secondly, if it is unavoidable to explain a technical advance. The courts apply a very strict interpretation to this exception.

Claims of unique excellence—often expressed by superlatives like "best," "finest," etc.—must be demonstrably true. They are not considered true, for instance, if the qualities claimed are in fact also shared by competing products. Superlatives which are obviously not serious, and can be recognized at once as gross exaggerations, are harmless from a legal point of view. But in no case must these claims insinuate that competing products are inferior. They would be considered 'comparative' and therefore illegal. Testimonials by professionals (doctors, dentists, scientists) containing a comparison and evaluation of competing products must not be used in advertising.

"Fairness" of promotion is watched. Promotional measures must be justifiable from a viewpoint of economic soundness, and must not interfere with competitors' legitimate business interests. This applies particularly to such promotional means as discounts, special sales premiums, free samples, etc.

Price maintenance is legal. The stipulation between producer and purchaser to maintain certain prices in the resale of goods is in principle permitted as far as branded goods are concerned. Such stipulations, when reported to the Federal Cartel Authority, are valid in the whole Federal Republic.

Premiums are forbidden in principle. However, exceptions are made for small articles of insignificant value, or for inexpensive articles which are marked visibly and indelibly with the name of the advertiser so that they do not have a market value. The idea is that premiums must not represent such a value in themselves that they are a real, serious buying incentive for the article with which they are offered. This also goes for self-liquidating offers, if the money saving for the consumer is of a more than insignificant value.

Free samples are also restricted.

Prize contests are permissible within the following limitations:

The purchase of the merchandise must not be a condition for the participation. "Buying compulsion" makes a contest illegal; therefore, the advertiser cannot demand box tops, labels, etc. to be sent in with the solution. The participant in a prize contest must not be misled in any way as to his chances. The contest must not require a financial investment, except in the form of putting postage on a letter. A contest may even be illegal if potential participants have to get their entry forms in the store, office, etc. of the advertiser running the contest. This is considered a "psychological buying compulsion," because many people are thought to be too shy to enter a shop without buying there. All of which means that contests cannot be used as a means to directly stimulate sales, but rather as an advertising device.

These multiple regulations perform a dual function: (1) they protect customers from many of the more obvious aspects of U.S consumer society; (2) more important, to business groups they are a bulwark of the status quo. They make it easier for established products and companies to keep their place in the market, and difficult for new products and companies to splash into the front ranks.

As a result, American companies accustomed to high speed, high-pressure marketing approaches are nonplussed. Says a senior official of A. C. Nielsen Co., the market-research firm whose retail surveys many American companies use: "When they can't spend 30 percent of their budget on promotions and free-sample deals, some of the U.S. managers we've met say, 'All right, cut the budget 30 percent.'" But this, he says, is to ignore one of the principal factors in European advertising.

The one constant and salient feature in U.S. ad men's comments about Europe is how difficult Europe's consumers are to find and to reach with an advertising message or promotion deal. But, if in many cases the customers seem to be hiding under a rock, they are responsive when advertising does reach them. They come out from under to buy. This is why American and European companies are willing to line up a year ahead of time for limited numbers of too brief TV spots. In Europe advertising pays—and in Europe advertising is a growth industry.

Europeans spent just under $5 billion for advertising in 1962 and an estimated $6 billion in 1964 (compared with $13 billion in America in 1962). The national advertising expenditure in Italy in 1962 was some $4.50 per person per year versus $65.00 per person in the U.S. Advertising expenditures were $24.00 per person in the U.K., $16.00 in Germany, and $9.00 in France. All over Europe, though, these figures are on the rise at close to 10 percent per year, and in the new Europe American manufacturing companies, almost by instinct, and their major European competitors, by quelling inherited instincts, are thinking, acting, and advertising Europe-wide. While not ignoring differences in national markets, bellwether auto, applicance, and food firms such as Renault, Philips and Nestle (or Ford, Hoover, and Heinz) try to capitalize on Europe-wide distribution. International Tel & Tel, a solidly established telephonic, electronic, and appliance producer (no relation to American Tel & Tel), is straining to co-ordinate production—and marketing—of its varied German, English, French, and Italian appliance items. Similarly, Singer, once purely in sewing machines, is now hustling thousands of Singer-brand refrigerators, washing machines, and vacuum cleaners through its extensive European dealer network. Ad agencies that can sell these multicountry companies on well-run, well-co-ordinated multicountry offices and services will take the largest and most important ad accounts in burgeoning Europe. The U.S. ad agencies have the organization, the financing, and the desire for Europe-wide operations. They will capture much of this European business.

So while semisecluded, hard-to-reach consumers are one major aspect of advertising in Europe, the "Americanization" of this advertising is another. "Americanization," in this sense, has two overlapping meanings. Not only American-developed methods, but American-directed companies are sweeping the ad business in Europe.

But it is an uphill fight. In countries where effective advertising services do not exist, major companies, of necessity, have developed their own. In Spain, when the president of McEvoy International, a small, newly established U.S. agency, called on the local Nestle subsidiary, he was courteously received and proudly escorted through an extensive, fully manned and well-equipped ad department that functioned as a captive agency. What, asked the Nestle manager, could the Americans do for him that his own people (with advice from the parent company) could not do as well and less expensively. In Italy in 1964 relative giants such as Fiat (autos), Olivetti (office machines), and Montecatini (chemicals) had their own house agencies and were yet to be convinced that an outside agency had more to offer. Also, these potential clients boggle at the 15 percent service charge U.S. agencies normally take from the media. And in Italy the media, refusing to play or pay the American way, will not refund U.S. agencies their "standard" 15 percent fee. They give 5 percent, 6 percent, or 10 percent, depending on local practice.

"Most medium-sized and many large European companies are family-owned, and most of their advertising is handled by sons or cousins the companies have set up in business," says a Paris-based agency head. What he means is that in Europe many so-called ad agencies are nothing more than small, low-overhead media brokers who arrange for space in newspapers and magazines. Indifferent art and copy preparation is done by the client or contracted out to other small specialists. In France, which one major agency head dubs "the graveyard of U.S. advertising agencies," some 1500 to 2000 such small "agencies" split the bulk of the national $360-million plus ad business. Publicis, the second biggest French agency, reportedly grosses only in the $16-million to $20-million range. The biggest agency in France, Havas, (it is partially government owned) billed $28 million in 1963. U.S. ad men in Germany report that agencies there break down into three types: advertising counselors or consultants; a handful of U.S.-type, full-service agencies; and the inevitable slew of media brokers.

Meanwhile, the marketing services and talent on which the new ad agencies and their clients depend are still evolving. A. C. Nielsen of the U.S. and Joseph Atwood Ltd. of Britain offer widespread Continental offices and market survey work to a variety of clients. Dozens of local firms have sprung up or been adapted to do multiple forms of consumer and market research. Figures are hard to develop in Europe, and much of what passes for market research there is a sophisticated form of shooting from the hip. There is a real danger that field men will sit at home and draw on their fertile imaginations for "research" findings. But with agencies riding herd on, spot-checking, and incidentally training these groups, the quality and depth of their research is steadily improving.

Within the agencies, copywriters are scarce. "Copywriting is new in Germany. It was never looked on as a field in itself," explains a Foote, Cone & Belding executive. U.S. agency heads find they have to push fundamentals such as getting copy and art people to work together. "It is hard to get European artists to subordinate themselves to the job," says a McCann man. But advertising is an interesting, well-paid business, and yearly it also becomes a socially more accepted, even admired career.

A British account executive with a U.S. ad agency in London: "I've been here ten years. Advertising used to be ever so slightly disreputable. For some years I was the only public-school man in our group. Now the field is full of smart young men from public schools. Possibly word is out that it is more amusing than working at Lloyd's [Lloyd's is the Establishment-manned insurance group]. Maybe the bright young men started coming into this business because the Harvard and Yale boys do it. At any rate, we now have quite a pick of men from Oxford and Cambridge."

On the Continent the same evolutions are underway. Advertising in Europe will always remain distinct from advertising in the U.S. National tastes and prejudices will demand different approaches in different countries. Compared to their U.S. counterparts, European consumers will still be hard to reach with a repetitive sales message. In fact, the unapproachability of so many European consumers points up the special virtues of a technique of which U.S. companies are highly conscious at home but which they, like most European companies, largely ignore in Europe—namely, public relations. But that is another story.

PART III

SOME "TYPICAL" AMERICAN DEVELOPMENTS

Like the latticework fingers of ice that grow across the surface of a quiet winter pond to eventually interlock in a solid sheet, each new product, company, or service that develops in Europe's forming consumer economy provides a surface and starting point for others.

As parts of Europe's economies develop nearer to the American model, it becomes possible to successfully transplant more and more U.S. products and services to Europe. These in turn help create conditions which speed the evolution of similar (though not always identical) European products and activities.

Often, the transplanting of "typical" American activities to Europe accentuates American European differences as well as evolving similarities. Take, for instance, the delicate business of corporate acquisitions:

CHAPTER 12

HAVE MONEY, WILL BUY

U. S. Corporate Acquisitors in Europe

In the field of company acquisitions U.S. companies in Europe play the ambivalent role of catalyst and bogeyman. Just as the bogeyman is used by mothers and nurses to frighten youngsters into desired (i.e., good) behavior, so various European business and government groups may use the American presence to frighten industrial groups into good (i.e., desired) behavior. American auto-tire producers were originally welcomed into France because the government felt that market-dominating Michelin could do with home-based competition. Food-processing companies that could help lower the costs of consumer items (by more efficient manufacture or distribution) have similarly been welcomed. But the American bogeyman is such a convincing (or useful) myth that numbers of business and government groups have played on the fears it arouses to try to curtail U.S. investment in Europe.

Meanwhile, American and European businessmen go on with the sometimes intricate and always fascinating business of acquiring or merging businesses.

THE AMERICAN EXPERIENCE

Though the essentials of corporate acquisitions may be the same the world over, there are important differences in approach. The business of buying or merging a business, in Europe, for instance, can be as carefully staged and studiously stylized as an Old World seduction. But the consensus in Europe is that in acquisition negotiations the Americans lack *délicatesse;* they come on too strong and too soon. A European merger specialist complains that after a few minutes' conversation with a prospective acquiree his callous American clients are all too likely to brusquely say, "Okay, now let's take a look at your company books."

To owners and managers, especially to owner-managers, the turning over of a company to a second concern can be an emotion-laden affair. It is a situation that calls, at the least, for a certain protocol and careful guarding of sensibilities. Yet, even when Europeans take the initiative in negotiations and take the lead in setting the proper tone for a parley, Americans can display a (to Europeans) distressing lack of finesse. The management of a respected French manufacturing company, using bankers as intermediaries, approached the head of an American machinery company about discussing a possible *rapprochement* between the two companies. After hardly a minute's thought or hesitation the American said, "Sure, what kind of *rapprochement* do they want?" When the banking John Aldens brought back this reply, the French managers were nonplussed. These executives had been looking forward to a delightful series of delicate soundings, the gradual development of an entente. But here were the Americans ready to take a brisk dive into propositions and details before even the basics of an understanding had been established.

After a few Europeans have sputtered like wet fuses or actually exploded themselves out of negotiations on being summarily asked to produce their books, Americans in Europe begin to realize that there is a cultural-economic difference of viewpoint here. Part of the difference is that in America, land of the publicly held corporation, the Securities and Exchange Commission, and certified public accountants, parts of most large and medium-sized companies' books are a matter of public record. In America, asking for a look at profit-and-loss and balance sheets early in company negotiations is a cursory commonplace, a clearing of the decks for serious talks. In Europe, however, a continent of privately owned or closely held companies and often capricious tax collectors (where some companies keep three sets of books), to ask a company president for a look at the figures is a bit like asking a conservative Arab to unveil his daughters. The books are a treasure that may eventually be revealed, but not to passing strangers.

Actually, it doesn't take Americans in Europe too long to learn that (depending on the country and industry in which they are involved) company books are not the source of accurate information Americans assume. For instance, a French banker explains, "We find that well-run private companies make ten to twelve times their reported profits." If fortunate, the American in Europe may discover painlessly that bookkeeping there is a form of sleight of hand. A consultant who conducted acquisition studies for an American electronics company, for example, did very well in cultivating the co-operation and interest of a promising Italian company. At the proper moment, and evidently in the proper way, the American asked for and was ceremoniously presented with copies of the company's profit-and-loss and balance sheets. After looking over these figures, the consultant regretfully informed his Italian friend that he did not believe his client could go on with negotiations; neither profits nor parts of the balance sheet met the client's requirements. "Oh, we can easily repair that," said the company president. "Just tell me what your client would not like in the books and I will change them."

THE MARRIAGE BROKERS

American companies establishing themselves in Europe have a choice of starting fresh with a new, wholly owned subsidiary; joining forces with an established company on a joint-venture basis; or acquiring a going concern outright. In theory, acquisition of a going concern is the simplest and fastest way of getting into a market, and the Americans, always in a hurry, lean to acquisitions. By making an acquisition in a new market a company may hope to gain production facilities, skilled labor, sales people, and market outlets, plus skilled management, an accepted brand name and, perhaps, membership in the local industry "club." Sometimes a company gains all these prizes; occasionally it gets none. Americans have learned, the hard way, that it pays to take time to learn what manner of people they are dealing with and exactly what they are or are not getting from an acquisition. A highly diversified American industrial-manufacturing concern, one of the top 200 U.S. companies, discovered a few years after acquiring a Belgian subsidiary that the company president, who came with the property, was funneling great amounts of company money into his own pockets. After a too quick, wheeler-dealer tour on the Continent in the late 1950s the then head of I. J. Case acquired a French tractor manufacturing concern that over a period of years cost Case some $10 million in losses. But, popular horror stories and rumors to the contrary, most American companies in Europe are fairly careful in their studies and assessments of possible acquisitions. And they find that, as they were warned, things are not like home.

For instance, U.S. company acquisitors in Europe, almost immediately, discover Europe's ubiquitous banks. In America commercial banks can be useful intermediaries for arranging introductions or making suggestions to clients about possible merger partners. For these good offices the banks charge no fee, hope instead to gain new accounts. American investment banks, the Wall Street houses, also get into merger and acquisition deals, but seldom too actively. Most U.S. corporations arrange their own mergers and acquisitions.

In Europe, however, where banks may wear triple hats as commercial lenders, underwriters, and investors, it is another story. Corporation stocks in Europe, especially on the Continent, are usually held by a relatively few wealthy individuals and by the investment banks. Anyone who wishes to acquire a good-sized, publicly held company invariably finds himself dealing with bankers as owners. These banks charge a percentage (5 percent or less as the size of the deal increases) for their help in arranging an acquisition. They tack on other charges where possible.

Some banks will spend large amounts of money and time in concocting acquisitions. One group of French and Swiss banks operates a Geneva-based consulting company (which is really a stalking horse in the acquisitions field) for its owners. Any active bank will have ten to twenty deals cooking at one time and be on the lookout for more.

"It is good to deal with a *banque d'affaires,* because they know their way around," says a French consultant. But he also advises clients to examine all the strings in any deal. These strings, he notes, are not necessarily placed to the disadvantage of a bank's client or partner, but neither are they necessarily to his advantage.

Here is a minor example of the close-in dealing of European banks. A large American company interested in acquiring a German equipment manufacturer whose stock was at that time quite low, approached one of the largest German banks. This bank, on its own account, was a major stockholder in the company and held more shares in trust for clients. When the Americans offered a price well above the then market price of the stock, the bank happily agreed to unload its shares. But in order to turn the company around, the Americans wanted at least two thirds of the outstanding stock. The bank undertook to arrange this. Secretly approaching selected major stockholders, the bank let them in on this special above-the-market deal. One day the company's employees and one third of its owners woke up to find themselves with a new majority owner. There were no public offerings, no proxy fights, no sudden jumps in company stock prices. Everything was arranged quietly and profitably within the "club."

PROBLEMS OF SIZE

U.S. corporations on a buying spree in Europe find plenty of companies available. Increased competition and problems in raising expansion capital put properties on the market. Besides, a great many family-held companies in Europe are in that critical third-generation stage of family management where business-bored heirs, if they could, would be only too happy to sell off the business. And yet, there is a real dearth of advantageous buys. In prosperous Europe, choice, good-sized companies that might have been readily available in 1957 are doing well enough to turn down offers of foreign cash. And, in a variety of ways, size is a key factor in the American desirability-availability equation. It is another instance of basic differences in American and European environments.

First, take the matter of size of markets. America is, for many of its producers, one great, continent-wide market. Acquisition of a medium-sized or even of a smallish American company almost automatically gives one entree to this great market or to giant regions within it. Europe, on the other hand, consists of over a dozen relatively small national markets. In spite of the creation of the six-country Common Market, acquisition, even of a sizable European company, seldom provides immediate access to more than one or two national markets. It takes numerous acquisitions to cover the European market.

Then there is the matter of size of available companies. U.S. companies' problems in Europe are much like those confronting college football coaches in the U.S. A large state university can field a heavier, more powerful team than a neighboring junior college simply because the university has a much bigger body of students to draw from. Similarly, a company seeking acquisitions in a given U.S. industry and allied fields may find dozens, if not hundreds, of husky potential candidates. In Europe's much smaller national markets, however, the number of large-sized acquisition possibilities shrinks proportionately.

And here another size factor comes into play. Since the average European company is one tenth the size of its U.S. counterparts, this means that the companies at the bottom third of any European industry are too small to be of any real interest to U.S. buyers. Note the pharmaceutical industry in France. In 1962, when the government lifted controls blocking foreign ownership in this industry, there was a rush of potential acquisitors to Paris, where most French firms headquarter. Some ten American and a double handful of English, German, and Swiss concerns began prowling the industry in search of buys. A French banker involved with several of these hopeful forays:

Now, in the French pharmaceutical industry there are only two or three large, non-family-held companies. These big concerns are closely tied in with particular large French corporate or financial groups. They would be very difficult to acquire. After these big companies are perhaps twenty to thirty of what in France would be medium-sized companies, with sales over $4 million per year. Below these you can discover a ragged group of tiny companies ($1–$2 million a year) in which few U.S. purchasers would have interest. I can assure you, all they would acquire would be some ancient equipment and a few regional salesmen.

So this leaves our group of something over twenty medium-sized companies as a target. I can also assure you, many of these firms are not available, are already tied up with licenses or are not at all desirable. So, finally, for the handful of companies that remain, twenty American and European concerns are now competing. This is like a thin stock market with heavy demand. All that happens is that the price for these companies continues to rise.

This is true not only in pharmaceuticals, but in general. Prices for companies in Europe have started to climb, and for this the Americans can take a great share of the credit or blame. European investors are accustomed to receiving almost double the return on their investments that U.S. investors consider adequate. Since there was no adequate capital market (no stock market) for smaller, family-owned concerns to turn to, established financial groups were able to set the going price for companies at a comfortably low five and six times earnings. Then the Americans, who were accustomed to paying twelve, sixteen, and more times earnings for healthy properties, came to Europe. Even when paying as much as ten times earnings for European companies, the Americans felt they were getting a bargain.

Of course, acquisitors dealing with family companies, especially third- and fourth-generation family companies, where control is divided among family factions, sometimes get more than they bargained for. In dealings with family companies, more than one "knowledgeable" *banque d'affaires* or eager American buyer has been hung up on the family tree. For instance, under the auspices of a well-known *banque d'affaires,* an American manufacturing company met and negotiated with Mr. Y, the controlling shareholder of a Belgian machine company. The Americans spent weeks in negotiations and four thousand dollars for a consultant's analysis of the company. They were about to close a deal with Mr. Y when it turned out that Y was not, after all, in control of the firm. Mr. Y and his loyal cousin, Mr. F, between them, were in control of the company. Moreover, the other relatives, using the consultant's report as a sales tool, had found another American buyer. Using the "loyal" Mr. F's crucial block of stocks, this rebel group sold the company out from under Mr. Y.

The second U.S. company that wound up with a controlling interest then had a contentious Mr. Y on their hands, which is one reason so many U.S. companies demand outright ownership of any properties they deal with.[1]

---

[1] In America, companies seeking acquisitions discover a whole subindustry of specialist acquisition brokers, advisers, and consultants geared to serve them. But in Europe, aside from management consultants, whose role is largely investigatory, and the *banques d'affaires,* only one firm, the New York- and Paris-based Monmouth Lee Corp., has developed a Europe-wide reputation as a company broker and specialist in the acquisitions area. In 1962 Business International, the business services and newsletter organization, formally launched an acquisitions service, however, and others were undoubtedly on the way.

EUROPE FOR THE EUROPEANS
(With U.S. Participation)

U.S. acquisitions, or intrusions, are what one hears most about in Europe, and U.S. acquisitors have established the price range for acquisitions in key industries. But this has not been an all-American show. The winds of change have been stirring up at least three other major merger, amalgamation, and acquisition waves in Europe.

First, in each of Europe's national markets, small independent companies have been rushing into each other's arms. These small family companies, usually those hardest hit by new competition and hardest put to raise new capital for expansion or modernization, join forces to achieve economies no one company could achieve alone. In Britain, for instance, the number of independent breweries reportedly dropped from over 500 to less than 300 between the late 1940s and 1960. Where there used to be 7610 textile companies in France in 1958, there were estimated less than 6000 in 1962. Similarly throughout Europe, local grocery stores, hurt by self-service chains, have been flocking to join co-operative chains.

Second, there has been a rash of intercountry mergers and acquisitions. The larger, more aggressive English, Swedish, German, French, and other European companies (in about that order of activity) are energetically acquiring, or amalgamating with, companies in each other's home markets. In fact, just prior to Britain's expected entry into the Common Market in 1962, the British companies scrambling for business properties on the Continent were even outbidding the Americans. Generally, however, inter-European amalgamations proceed at a deliberate pace. European companies like time to take each other's measure. Europeans have a greater predilection than Americans for business "ententes," trade agreements, joint ventures, and such part-way acquisitions. However, it is through the joining of these strong medium- and large-sized European concerns that the real muscle and bone of the new Europe are gradually being knit.

Finally, in early 1964, the third and most impressive wave of major corporate amalgamations in Europe was still getting underway. In newly competitive Europe, corporate size and financial strength have become increasingly important for survival. Recognizing this, giant Imperial Chemical Industries Ltd. of Britain in 1962 tried hard, but unsuccessfully, to broaden its operations by acquiring Courtauld's, the major British textile and synthetic-fibers producer. That same year in France, the two major French Chemical companies, Pechiney and St. Gobain, with active government encouragement, joined parts of their operations in order to present a more effective front to other giant chemical producers throughout Europe. But these were national-company gird-ings for international competition. Something else is also going on.

Europe's banks, which control so many pieces of so many major companies, are acutely aware of the advantages and economies of size and widespread distribution in Europe's coalescing economies. Since the late 1950s these banks, working as feverishly as masons on piecework, have been strengthening old, and laying out new, credit and invest-ment networks throughout Europe. Within the next ten years we are going to see the fruits of these efforts in the unveiling of a number of new, financially inspired, all-Eu-rope, multinational, business behemoths such as evolved in America at the turn of the century and during the 1920s. (The General Electric Company, General Motors Corp., and R.C.A., for instance, are U.S. giants born of the multiple mergers of another generation.)

Because European governments are directly involved, or silent partners, in so many major European industries, and because these governments are chary of foreign preponderance in "vital" manufacturing industries, some of the first all-Europe amalgamations will likely be in retail distribution or consumer-product fields. Eventually, some inter-European amalgamations will probably include government-owned or partially government-owned member firms. (In Europe, it can be comforting to have governments as active backers or members of one's projects.) But American companies and American capital will also undoubtedly be a part of many of these amalgamations.

America is the principal investment capital market in the world. The U. S. Government, concerned over balance of payments and the outflow of U.S. gold to Europe, moved to place a special tax on European investments raised in America.[2] However, large sums of American money are already invested or available in Europe. And international investment money does have a way of filtering around most obstacles. Meanwhile, merger-interested U.S. companies, such as Singer, are exploring systems for joining international groupings, with no loss of U.S. gold through mutual exchanges of stock with foreign partners. The American economic involvement in Europe can be slowed, but it could hardly be stopped.

[2] If the U.S. gold drain is stemmed or if restrictions on U.S. investment in Europe are lifted, extensive American participation in major European concerns would help speed Continental Europe's shift from an inward-looking, protective marketing block to an outward-looking member of the Atlantic Community.

CHAPTER 13

AT YOUR SERVICE, FOR A FEE

American Accounting, Consulting, Recruiting
and Other Services in Europe

KEEPING TRACK OF THE BOOKS

American companies have a compulsion for uniform (i.e., comparable) bookkeeping systems. American companies also like to have the same firm of certified public accountants review the books for all their branches and subsidiaries. To satisfy both these wants major U.S. accounting firms such as Price Waterhouse & Co., Peat, Marwick, Mitchell & Co., Haskins & Sells, and Arthur Young & Co. have set up operations throughout Europe.[1]

To the degree that they do not indulge in the European businessman's favorite sport of tax dodging, U.S. companies on the Continent point up for European governments how much valuable income normally escapes the tax collector. European tax authorities (if they care to make the comparison) can hardly fail to note that American companies seem to pay larger taxes than comparable European firms. In time these discrepancies may lead to a tightening up of European tax procedures (a start was made in this direction in France under De Gaulle). However, the major impact of American

---

[1] The certified public accountant (or Chartered Accountant) is a British-American development. Since American accountants are relatively expensive, many C.P.A.s working with U.S. accounting firms on the Continent are English or Scottish.

accounting practice is in another field and for different reasons.

Many European executives, who feel that anyone foolish enough to report all taxable income deserves to pay for it, do not want any nosy tax-bookkeeping help from the C.P.A.s, but they are interested in U.S.-style cost accounting. Of his European competition an American chemical company executive in Zurich says, "Ask them what their minimum-size profitable order is and they won't know." In sellers' markets detailed analysis may not matter, but in competitive markets, both for purposes of pricing and cost control, detailed analysis is vital. Recognizing this, European companies turn to U.S. accountants for help which the accountants are only too happy to provide. However, the accountants supply most of this sort of assistance through special management-services divisions. These activities lap over into management consulting—and management consulting is a fascinating field in and of itself.

There are all kinds of specialized, generalized, imported, homebred, and hybrid consultants in Europe. Since big-league management consulting, like advertising, is virtually an American invention, the top practitioners are Americans.

THE MANAGEMENT CONSULTANTS

The relationship of business consultants to companies is a curious, almost symbiotic one not unlike that famous one of remora pilot fish, which attach themselves to and cruise first with one then another of various species of giant sharks patrolling the world's oceans. Though pilot fish depend upon their massive friends for existence, sharks can get along without pilot fish. Nonetheless, the pilot fish do have their uses as guides and investigators. Along with their hosts, they thrive.

Similarly, there are an estimated 3000 management consultants of one kind or another in the U.S. If, through some strange stroke of fate, these consultants were to vanish tomorrow, American industry would not falter for one perceptible instant from the path towards which it is heading. But within ten years there would be as many consultants on hand as ever. Consultants, a phenomenon and symptom of the present corporate era of business, play a useful role in corporate society. They are, in effect, an industrial-communications device.

Consultants got their start in American factories in the early 1900s. At that time the country's burgeoning corporations were discovering, and scrambling to gain, the advantages of mass production. Engineering-oriented efficiency experts who could introduce time-motion studies and efficient production techniques began to blossom. Later, as the emphasis in many companies spread from production to marketing and distribution, these service specialists, now styled "management consultants," expanded their role to include these new techniques. By the mid-1950s, in an America adjusting to the economics of a consumer society, hundreds of growth-swollen U.S. companies found themselves concentrating on (1) finding ways to co-ordinate their management-heavy ranks and (2) on long-range planning in this new environment. For help and up-to-date information on these areas may companies turned to consultants.

The result has been a substantial upgrading of consulting. The top level of American consultants have moved out of the factory and into the boardrooms of their clients. This is not to say that all consultants deal only with larger matters of organization and of policy. In fact, only a few consultants do so and only from time to time. Most U.S. consultants, however, work at several levels in a client company. And the thrust of development (and prestige) in consulting has

been towards involvement in long-term planning and decision making.

In moving from the factory and the measurable world of
things to the executive suite and the less predictable world
of people, consultants have developed new skills. A large
modern corporation, more than an economic organization, is
a stratified nine-to-five subsociety with value systems and
taboos and sometimes byzantine politics of its own. Consultants must be corporate courtiers. Like court attendants of
old, though they wield no direct power, consultants can have
much to do with the apportionment and flow of power in
a client company, especially a company under reorganization.
Like courtiers of old, one of the principal assets of modern
consultants is that they have direct access to, and can easily
communicate with, a variety of individuals and groups in a
client company's management ranks.

In essence, their analytic skills aside, consultants are a
selective and highly sensitive communications device! They
transmit technology between companies and within the
management ranks of a given client company. In fact, their
prime fuction is helping the managers of a company communicate with each other. A large part of the "technology"
they introduce has to do with the organization of corporate
hierarchies.

IN EUROPE IT IS DIFFERENT, MAYBE

In Europe consulting has until recently remained in a
production-oriented, 1920s stage of development. The prevalence of small family-owned companies, the lack of mass
markets (and lack of competition for markets), Europe's
postwar emphasis on rebuilding manufacturing capacity and,
through the early 1960s, the prevalence of sellers' markets
—all combined to help keep consultants in their place, that

is, in the factory. Therefore, European managers have traditionally looked upon consultants, not as fellow professionals, but as itinerant engineers, hired hands to be used for a while, then dismissed.

However, in the new Europe the rise of mass markets is leading to the development of large nonowner-managed companies to compete for these markets. These companies are running into Europe-wide co-ordinating problems to which American-style consulting seems particularly applicable.

The fees U.S. consultants charge ($150 to $450 per man per day, depending on the consultant's seniority) frighten away many European executives, but the larger European companies have made increasing use of U.S. consultants. And, under the umbrella of the American fees and approach, a number of European consulting groups have begun to work their way out of the factory and into marketing directors', if not company presidents', offices.

Europe in some ways is a lens which brings American companies and attitudes into sharp focus. For instance, in Europe, even more than in the U.S., it is evident that consulting is a communications or teaching device. European companies do not pay the fantastic (to Europeans) fees American consultants demand in order to bask in the bonny smiles and enjoy the reassuring good manners of their American consultant friends. These European companies pay the Americans to import techniques, and—possibly even more important—to impart and explain some attitudes and points of view (ways of thinking about business) that are increasingly germane in the new Europe.

What's more, even individual American consulting firms become more sharply defined and differentiated from each other when viewed against a European background. In the U.S., members of ACME (the Association of Consulting Management Engineers) self-consciously bill themselves as top-management advisers who deal with top-management problems. And a look at the spectrum of cases these firms might handle in a year, with a generous definition of "top-management," would roughly justify these claims. However, there are nuances. Take Booz Allen & Hamilton, Arthur D. Little Inc., and McKinsey & Co., Inc., three respectable and respected U.S. consulting firms. Booz Allen & Hamilton, with something over 800 professional members on its staff, is the largest member of ACME, has the broadest practice in U.S. industry, and a special reputation in the production and manufacturing area. Arthur D. Little, the management-services branch of the famous scientific research company of the same name, and a relative latecomer to management consulting, built its early reputation in marketing (and was most active at first in chemicals). McKinsey & Co., Inc., the second largest (200 professional members) and the most assiduously and self-consciously top-management-oriented consulting firm of all, actually has a broad multi-level practice. In fact, in the U.S. the practices of these and other firms so overlap that they are difficult to differentiate.

In Europe, in 1962, however:

• Booz Allen & Hamilton, the largest U.S. consulting firm in Europe, had some seventy-five professional people there (75 percent of them U.S. citizens). The bulk of Booz Allen's European engagements were with European clients (60–65 percent), and the greatest part of these were installations of engineering and manufacturing-control systems in the heavy metals, steel, oil, and auto industries. However, Booz was working hard on developing marketing engagements.

• Arthur D. Little, with some thirty professional employees (three of them U.S. citizens, but most of them with U.S. education or work experience), was almost purely a marketing consulting firm with special strengths in the chemical and petrochemical fields. (Some 60 percent of ADL's work in Europe was for U.S. clients.)

• McKinsey & Co., with about fifteen men, most of them with extensive U.S. consulting experience, was working largely for U.S. clients. But McKinsey, more than any other U.S. consulting firm, had cracked the European market via top-level organizational studies with such establishment companies as Dunlop Tyre and Imperial Chemical Industries in Britain and Shell Oil and KLM on the Continent.

Thus, partly by accident and partly through design, the overlapping images these three companies presented in the U.S. were sharply differentiated in Europe. In time, as these and other U.S. consulting firms become better established and build new strengths, their services (and images) will once again begin to overlap.

At this writing it seems that only U.S. consulting firms have penetrated the upper decision levels of European management; but this, too, will change. All over Europe new consulting and marketing groups are evolving. (Numbers of independent American consultants have established themselves in Geneva, Lausanne, Paris, Brussels, and elsewhere.) In Britain, solidly established Urwick Orr & Associates Ltd. is upgrading its services, and on the Continent, SEMCA, a Common-Market-wide, French-controlled firm is moving into upper-echelon consulting—replacing via the all-embracing approach of operations research—a mathematical technique to which its polytechnique-trained French principals would naturally lean.

THE TALENT HUNTERS

Executive recruiting is taking hold in Europe. Spencer Stuart & Associates Inc., a leading U.S. recruiter, is firmly established in Britain and the Continent. Others, such as

Boyden Associates, have also established European offices or liaison with European recruiters. These new forms of executive recruiting, part of a new European revolution which extends beyond business, celebrate the rise and spread of Europe's new manager class and an important change in business mores.

In the old Europe, men joined a company for life. Those men destined to rise in the management of a company, men of a particular family and educational background, knew they were among the anointed even before their careers began. All that was asked of them was that they wait quietly and patiently till their turns came. Other managers, no matter how competent, did not count in the hierarchy. They were valuable employees, but no more. Job mobility was slightly immoral. In the Europe of national cartels and gentlemen's agreements, few companies would be so rude as to hire away each other's managers, or so foolish as to bid up salaries. The man who offered his services to another company toyed with career suicide, and any man of forty who had held as many as three jobs was considered a poor employment risk.

In booming postwar Europe, however, as hundreds of companies grew, expanded their staffs, and created new subsidiaries in each other's home markets, management manpower, previously thinned by war, became scarce. Gradually, the old circumspect, if unwritten, rules on promotion and on pirating of personnel began to give way. Then, as hundreds of U.S. companies swarmed to Europe looking for management talent to help man their new overseas ventures, the old restrictions disappeared.

In the old Europe, what little recruiting was done was handled by personnel firms, which advertised in newspapers, screened the applicants, and sent them on to the client (as a personnel agency in the U.S. handles clerical help). The recent recruiters, influenced by the U.S., make it their business to search through an industry, spot likely candidates, then quietly sound these men out on their availability for a new position. The average "search" takes sixty to ninety days, at the end of which the recruiter presents his client with perhaps three likely candidates. The client meets each of them and makes his choice. U.S. recruiters charge the client a stiff fee, up to 25 percent of the executive's annual salary (sometimes less in Europe), plus out-of-pocket costs. The recruiting industry is booming.

Executive recruiters indicate that European managers are at first taken aback at a recruiter's telephone call suggesting a meeting, but few can resist a meeting. After at first being volubly angry at anyone suggesting that he might even think of leaving his job, one French executive in the metals-fabricating field agreed to meet with a recruiter—"but only out of curiosity," he said. (At a second meeting this man pronounced himself a candidate for the job in question.) Job mobility is greater in Britain than in Germany. "And," says one recruiter, "German executives tend to be very nervous if you telephone them at their offices. They are afraid to have it even suspected that they talked with a recruiter." As a result, the recruiter sometimes first contacts men at their homes, and later meets with them at the airport or at a hotel, or during trips. However, in the new Europe the stigma that attached itself to job changes is giving way to a certain prestige and even glamor.

After using an American executive recruiter to help staff the management, a U.S. company president in Europe can use Manpower Inc., another U.S. firm, to help provide him with clerical staff. When he takes a plane trip he will find Hertz Rent A Car offering to meet him at the airport. With U.S. advertising, accounting, consulting, recruiting, and sundry other services available to him in Europe, it is not surprising that a U.S. executive in Europe will tend to think and act as if he were operating at home. However, beneath the thin new ice of the new Europe, there is more than enough of the old Europe for an American Executive to get in well over his head.

This is one more reason why U.S. companies in Europe cling to their lawyers. In the next chapter we will examine some essential differences, as well as a fading out of differences, between American and European attitudes toward contracts and lawyers.

CHAPTER 14

OF LAW AND DIFFERENCES; AND REASONS WHY

By European lights Americans are strangely addicted to a respect for lawyers and fine print in contracts.

A French banker reports, "One of our French clients recently made a joint-venture agreement with an American appliance company. The two company presidents got along very well. They achieved good understanding. But before signing the contract the Americans sent over no less than three lawyers. These men have now been arguing about this contract for more than three months!"

"The Americans are always playing around with lawyers. Six months after making an agreement they will start fiddling around with the contract," complains a German businessman.

Europeans are genuinely puzzled and often offended by this Micawberish approach to possible partners. "Perhaps," says a Parisian financial consultant wryly, "American company presidents are afraid of being taken in by 'clever' Europeans." A number of American executives agree that there may be an element of truth to this comment. (It is not unheard of, in any country, for newcomers to be hard used by knowledgeable local "partners.") But there is more to the American affinity for lawyers and contracts than overseasmanship. Even in the U.S., few American companies make major moves without the review and acquiescence of their lawyers. If the lawyers do not sit in on key negotiations they are likely to be available in the next room for consultation. Moreover, this reflexlike turning to the lawyers comes not so much from a lack of faith as a love of order. A U.S. corporation lawyer is trained to pose and examine the possibilities, and the combinations and permutations of possibilities, that can arise from an agreement. His job is to make the contract so precise that no disputes on meaning or the mutual obligations of the signers ever arise. That either party should ever turn to the courts is a sign that the lawyers failed their task (or were maldirected by their clients). However—and this is central—in the American business *ambiance,* the courts are recognized referees. It is quite acceptable for a company to take a disputed agreement to court.

The European concept of lawyers and contracts is quite different. And yet, indicatively, in modern Europe the trend is toward something closer to the American pattern. But first, for a look at one of these European-American differences, take the special instance of law in England:

ANGLO-SAXON ATTITUDES

A prime difference between English law and American law is that the Americans have a written constitution. Among lawyers this an old saw—but it still cuts. Perhaps because English is really two languages, a fluid mixture of Latin (with some French) and Germanic (Saxon) tongues, the British have long been wary of the seeming precision of words. Distrustful of words, the British have no written constitution, but a set of hallowed traditions embodying certain principles. They have no great codex of laws, but a vast body of common law. Common law is nothing more than a collection of cases or incidents. In court a white-wigged British jurist concentrates not so much on the language as on the intent of an agreement. What did the two parties agree to and understand each other to agree to? In the case of a dispute an English court tries to determine, in the light of what seems to have been agreed to, a fair, or "just," decision. Justice is viewed as a fairly narrow, almost visible stripe lying somewhere between the positions of the two parties, much as the white divider line on a road marks the left- from the right-hand traffic lane.

Americans put much more emphasis on language. After generations of weaving their way through and around the wording of their constitution (the U.S. Supreme Court's prime function is that of interpreting and reinterpreting the words and phrases of the Constitution), American lawyers are highly conscious of the built-in ambiguities of language. But, unlike the British, who therefore pull away from too close an embrace of language, the American response has been to try to pick and place words in such orderly array that there is little or no doubt as to the meaning of a document.

To American jurists, justice (or law) is not a precise white stripe somewhere between the positions of two or more parties; it is, rather, a broad band that fades from white to deepening shades of gray on either side—and the extent of the gray areas greatly depends on the language in which a law or a document is couched.[1]

---

[1] Here are two examples of American preoccupation with the *language* of documents:

1. *Life* magazine, in an August 9, 1963, story on the Test-Ban Treaty negotiations in Moscow, quoted Averell Harriman, the U.S. "negotiator":

"We spent much time during the official meetings discussing language," said Harriman. "They would table one version of a proposed text. We would table a different one. I would try to find out why they

Another difference between American and English law, notably in the field of business, is that Americans have moved much more directly toward the use of statutes and regulations. In Britain, for instance, the courts have until very recently kept clear of labor-management disputes. A British labor-management agreement was viewed as a private agreement and not a legal contract. Either side may break an agreement with legal impunity.[2] On the other hand, in America, labor contracts are legally binding; much of our labor law has been and is being written in the courts; and we have Taft-Hartley and numerous other acts governing labor relations. Further, aside from numerous antitrust laws, policed by the Justice Department, there are a variety of regulations-armed government agencies such as the Federal Trade Commission, the Interstate Commerce Commission, and the Securities and Exchange Commission, which act as watchdogs, and referees of business groups.

So while American concepts of law are based on English common law, in practice there is a particular American em-

---

were objecting to our *language*. Gromyko would try to understand why we didn't like his. . . .

"The conferences (with Russians) during World War II were so short that sometimes the hastily accepted language simply concealed the differences—papered over the cracks, that is. Perhaps that's one reason those agreements failed to stick. But this time the language we finally agreed upon preserved the understanding of both sides."

2. The New York *Times* in an August 10, 1963, article describing the board of governors of the New York Stock Exchange, said:

"This powerful group runs the Exchange. It is authorized to adopt rules, penalize members, examine their business conduct and to interpret the constitution."

[2] In 1964, however, a court for the first time ruled union leaders to be personally liable for breaches of labor contract and the whole question of law in labor agreements is being reopened in the U.K.

phasis on the language of the law—and business law in America has grown into a mixture of common and statutory law. This English-American "difference" in attitude and practice of law, however, is only one aspect of a broader West European-American "difference."

EUROPEAN THOUGHT PATTERNS

In Continental Europe, where statutory law is common, you might expect to find something closer to the typical American weighing, skirting, and testing of the language of the law. Certainly you might expect an Americanistic preoccupation with the wording of contracts. This has not developed. The reasons have ancient roots, and a look at these roots provides insight not only into American and European legal attitudes but on differences in American and European thought patterns.

It is because Europe's (and Britain's) national business communities are communities—long-established, stable, stratified subsocieties—that they have not needed the precise detailed approach to agreements that is common in America. As Americans in Europe have learned, business communities in Europe operate along the lines of benevolent, protective, fraternal orders. And business in Europe, more than mere business, is an integral part of the social order. Some top banking families in Geneva, for instance, have been in banking, in Geneva, since the 1500s. Generally, European companies are family-owned or -controlled. The *haut bourgeois* financial and industrial families, between them, have long controlled the major companies, and the major companies control industry. In the vaunted French Plan for co-ordinating economic development, for instance, it is the giants, the Big Three (or Four or Five) of an industry, who invariably decide just how the pie of government building-permissions licenses and low-cost loans will be divided by the industry. In return for the quiescent acceptance of this situation by the smaller fry, the industry leaders, the "club" directors, have traditionally provided a protective cost-and-price umbrella under which the small companies could prosper with minimum effort, thought, or reinvestment on their own part.

Few small European companies ever try to challenge the giants in court or in the market place, because (1) there are few laws under which they could effectively charge them; (2) they lack the resources to carry on a long court battle; and (3) most important, in a country of cartels and highly disciplined trade associations the small or medium-sized company that gets too far out of line soon finds suppliers and distributors refusing its business. Such disciplinings, however, are hardly ever necessary. Over the years, co-operation with and within the given order of things has acquired its own moral sanction. And, while the heads of larger companies may have differences among themselves, these, too, are generally settled quietly within the "club." The business communities of Europe are a series of separate, close-knit national societies whose members know each other (and watch after each other) as closely as the gentry of a small town in, say, Minnesota.

AMERICA AND BUSINESS LAW

In America, a quite separate set of practices prevails—again, for historic reasons. America is not just a country, but virtually a continent where, almost from the country's national beginnings, business and industry grew too far, too fast, and in too many places for a cohesive business community to develop. As quickly as self-conscious business communities could begin to organize, they were faced with the rise of parvenu capitalists who saw no point or profit in subscribing to a given group's codes or cartels. Quite early in the game, American businessmen, as they learned to deal with each other and with customers and competitors in "sovereign" American states, began to appreciate the importance of negotiating ironclad contracts that could stand in any court—even against Philadelphia lawyers or their Boston opposite numbers.

In time, through sheer economic pressure as the Industrial Revolution took hold, post-Civil War American industry might have coalesced into something close to the European pattern. There were strong and definite moves in this direction in the late 1800s and early 1900s. However, the development of peculiarly American ideas on monopoly and competition, in the form of various antitrust laws, kept the larger, organized groups of companies from applying the kinds of pressure on prices, suppliers, or distributors to bring nonco-operative companies into line. What happened in America at the turn of the century is that, instead of the then burgeoning financial and major company groups becoming the arbiters and policemen of business (through control of major companies and cartels), the government stepped in as policeman, arbitrator, and official conscience of industry.[3] In doing so, it attempted to freeze and maintain competition in America in terms of the small company

---

[3] Whether by stepping in as arbiter of business quarrels and maintainer of "fair" competition the U. S. Government also blocked the rise of an American *haut bourgeois* owner-financier class, such as that which developed in Europe, is an interesting question but difficult to answer. Certainly the American financiers, the owner-managers of the 1890s, felt they were going the way of, or possibly even leading the way for, their European counterparts and fellow investors. Ironically, as large, publicly held, professionally managed companies evolve in Europe, it may turn out that the Americans did indeed lead the way—partway out a side door.

economy of a previous era. This ideal proved impossible and impractical to reconstruct; but it was then, and is now, the U. S. Government which maintains minimum degrees of competition in certain sectors of American industry.

Since the turn of the century, buttressed by a series of antitrust regulations, small and medium-sized American concerns have been in a position to take each other and the giants to court for infractions of law. The fact that the average U.S. company is ten times the size of its European counterparts means that a medium-sized U.S. concern can well afford the carrying costs of facing even the giants in court. (A Zenith Radio or Philco Corporation, for instance, can readily take on the giant Radio Corporation of America without ruining itself.) An important result of these developments, however, was that, since companies could not easily override competitors by extralegal means, or exhaust them in the courts, there was little incentive to go to court. In fact, with antitrust and regulatory bodies proliferating, America's major companies found them enlarging their legal staffs and leaning more and more on the lawyers' advice for ways of working within the limits of the law—and staying out of court.

Meanwhile, over two generations, America has changed from a land of parvenu capitalists to a country of large, publicly held, and "professionally" managed corporations. As this has happened, stockholders (and the government) have come to demand, and career managers to recognize, a new kind of public morality. The old interlocking directorates and holdings were, for the most part, dismantled. Transactions with other parties have become (at least in theory, and generally in practice) arms-length affairs. It is now a company's acknowledged duty to protect the interests of all stockholders rather than those of a few major owners. And, from time to time, a company may be expected to go to court to prove its devotion to stockholders' interests. For example, shortly after the U. S. Government indicted a group of American electrical-equipment manufacturers for price-fixing and dividing up of markets (something quite legal in Europe), there was a scramble by private-utility-company customers to sue the defendants in court for the triple damages allowable for this offense. Some of these utilities might have gladly settled with the defendants by private arrangement. But if these private utilities had tried to play that kind of a game, says an American corporate lawyer, they would have been laying themselves open to a series of suits by their shareholders. Therefore, the rush to court.

These enviromental factors help explain the (to Europeans) strangely suspicious approach many U.S. companies seem to bring to negotiations and the American habit of continuous consultation with lawyers. In the American *ambiance*, for a variety of reasons, corporations, even when they work closely together, maintain a certain distance, [a mild but definite paranoia], in their relations with other companies.

SHIFTING GROUND RULES

At first glance, in Europe, the only effect of this American practice is that European businessmen are annoyed when dealing with Americans, and a number of European lawyers with U.S. clients find themselves receiving handsome retainers for doing little more than hold their clients' hands. Also, a number of skillful American lawyers are successfully establishing themselves in Europe to serve American clients. And yet, this legalistic "American" approach to intercompany negotiations is going to spread, because of intracompany considerations and for intracountry reasons.

Europe's various business communities resemble each

other in many ways and there is continuous contact between them; but traditionally these have been highly restricted contacts. Few European businessmen are as international in experience and exposure as they like to believe, and in Europe the old national industrial compartments—and the carefully nurtured relationships within these compartments—are breaking down. National corporate giants, who once provided a price umbrella beneath which marginal small producers could shelter, now find that on a Europe-wide or world-wide basis they hardly rank as medium-sized concerns. Some, in fact, are in economic danger. An interregnum, a stimulating period of turmoil, has descended upon European business. New governmental attitudes and regulations about competition in industry are developing. Large, publicly held companies are evolving. In the auto, appliance, electronics, chemical, textile, and dozens of other industries, Italian, French, German, English, Swedish, and other European companies are invading each other's markets, scrambling to develop new subsidiaries, partnerships, amalgamations, and agreements throughout Europe.

Eventually, because of their traditions and inclinations, Europe's business communities will coalesce again into the rudiments of one Europe-wide business community, with a certain amount of "co-ordination" and policing of trade by the commercial leaders of various industries.[4] But the tight,

[4] The Common Market countries are subject to antitrust regulation of a sort, but this regulation has yet to be sorted out or tested and has important loopholes. Since U.S. antitrust regulations extend to cover the activities of U.S. companies overseas, in countries where cartels are legal, (and powerful) U.S. companies face a Hobson's choice: If they co-operate with cartels they are roundly damned; if they resist the cartels they may be doomed. A number of U.S. companies play along with local cartels on the qt. The U. S. Justice Department, thus far, has made few overt moves or investigations in this thorny area.

safe national structures of old will never completely reappear. Meanwhile, in the newly turbulent and competitive European atmosphere, the American insistence on careful wording and spelling out of details in contracts, which once seemed so rude and unnecessary, begins to seem quite urbane and intelligent. In the the new Europe, American-style legalisms are increasingly acceptable.

PART IV

AMERICAN AND EUROPEAN MANAGEMENT AND MANAGERS IN EUROPE

CHAPTER 15

AMERICAN MANAGEMENT IN EUROPE

There are disturbing signs that a significant number of American managers in Europe are neither highly competent nor widely trusted and admired by their home-company superiors. Yet, American companies in Europe, by and large, do well. The fact that so many U.S. companies, though directed by second-string management, are successful is partly due to some U.S. company organization and management characteristics. But first, there is this intriguing matter of the "inept" Americans in Europe.

THE INCOMPETENT AMERICANS?

With thousands of U.S. companies established in Europe, most of them since World War II, European executives have been getting a firsthand look at those famous American managers and American management techniques they have been hearing so much about (largely from Americans) since the 1920s. All too often the Europeans are not impressed. Why?

In Germany, an American special-machinery company took over a respected local concern and sent over a five-man team of experienced U.S. managers to run the shop. The Americans let the core of the existing management go and waded in to run the company "the American way." It has taken this company five painful years to crawl out of the red.

In France, a U.S. appliance producer, for years one of the most prosperous companies in Europe, sold an accepted product at a premium, and boasted the strongest dealer network in the country. With sales on the rise it doubled plant capacity. But with tariffs dropping, Italian and German producers moved into the market, offering comparable or better products at a lower price. They left the U.S. concern operating at 50 percent capacity—and at a loss. "Oh yes, we expected intrusions from other Common Market countries—but not so soon," says a company executive.

Two years after building a modern plant in one Common Market country, an American company changed its mind, decided to centralize all-Europe production in another Common Market country. In formal talks with unions in the first country, the company arranged to close down gradually over a five-month period, guaranteeing wages to its workers for that time. The minute the planned move was announced, however, resentful workers lost all interest in the job, and production swooped down toward the zero point. Five months' wages for over 500 employees began draining the cash box with little to show in return. As a result, the American company feverishly hustled production to the new plant, which was not ready for the influx. The many shifts and changes due to pressures for production in the new plant led to a sudden strike there. The company got into political hot water with the original host government. American employers were once more branded as heartless and fickle employers. European industrialists, while amused, are also amazed at how a company could get itself into such a bind.

As they see these and dozens of other U.S. companies trip on their way to or around the Common Market, European businessmen increasingly voice doubts about vaunted American techniques and American managers. Of course, with over 3000 U.S. companies operating, a few "horrible examples" are bound to appear. Many Europeans realize this. The most perceptive of them, moreover, recognize that ineffective management tends to be marked not so much by sins of commission, by actions taken, as by opportunities ignored and risks avoided. They know that ineffective management is most likely to be marked by a clinging to set procedures ("the way we did it in the States"), by insistence that as many people as possible be brought in on a decision—to share responsibility—or by a general lack of flair or vitality on the part of management. And it is ineffective management, not mere mistakes, with which the more sophisticated European executives charge many of their American competitors or partners. All over Europe, and almost in chorus, alert, self-confident European executives who regularly deal with American managers sing the same refrain: Americans in Europe cannot seem to make decisions on their own, are always on the phone to New York and Chicago, and insist on doing things by the book.

In London a merchant banker, a specialist in acquisitions, who deals therefore with a variety of U.S. companies, joins a visitor for lunch. Over drinks, he hesitates for a bit, then says, "Are the men we see over here truly a sample of top U.S. businessmen?" This man asks a question, but in his own way he is also making a damning statement.

More bluntly, a German executive in the office-equipment field chuckles, "As long as your American companies continue to send over those very nice fellows who won't make a decision or who insist on doing things the American way, I won't worry too much about your famous American competition."

A French trade official wonders out loud why, since it is more difficult to carve out a new market in Europe than in the U.S., American companies send over weak members of management. And in Switzerland, a U.S.-educated engineer in the metalworking field, looks back—and ahead: "During the Marshall Plan days I could understand why the technicians your government sent over often did not know as much as our own; your best men were busy in industry. But now that U.S. companies are coming over themselves we still see second-class people. Why is this so?"

If it were only Europeans who talked in this vein, one could put aside much of this comment as natural bias against foreign competitors. But many American managers operating in Europe say the same thing in one way or another. At his Paris headquarters a U.S. banker, reporting surprise at discovering how many U.S. managers in Europe do not have the full confidence and backing of their top management, feels that this tends to stifle what initiative these men might otherwise show. Throughout Europe, key members of the American business community privately admit that, in a significant number of cases, U.S. managers there are not of the first nor even of the second level of capability in their companies. This lack of talent loses U.S. companies opportunities, profits and esteem.[1] There are powerful reasons why top-notch U.S. managers are relatively rare in Europe.

[1] One minor but indicative example of the lack of authority of U.S. managers in Europe: Switzerland is headquarters for hundreds of U.S. companies operating in Switzerland and throughout Europe. With the blessing—and active promotion—of the U. S. State Department, three leading Swiss newspapers planned a special supplement featuring America and American industry. But when newspaper representatives visited the European headquarters of U.S. companies holding billions of dollars of assets in Europe, they found that only a handful of firms had the authority to invest a few hundred dollars in company ads in this special issue. The majority had to ask U.S. headquarters for special permission. Many American companies seem to treat their European subsidiaries much as they would treat branch plants in a small U.S. town.

WHY IT HAPPENS

The prime reason for the high percentage of second-string management in U.S.-European subsidiaries is indifference at corporate headquarters. A company with $100- or $300- or $500-million annual sales in the U.S. finds it hard to get too excited about a $2-, $4-, or even a $20-million subsidiary in Europe, and this sort of ratio of U.S. to European operations is common. The U.S. company focus (perhaps quite correctly) centers on the U.S. market.

Also, the executive who has the experience, self-confidence, and standing with management to effectively carry out a semi-independent or autonomus operation overseas is usually somewhere between his late forties and mid-fifties in age. This man is expensive. He has proved himself once and his domestic roots go deep. Understandably, he may not be the least bit anxious to set up house in a foreign country, deal with new variables in foreign languages and customs, and maybe fail in a new environment while proving himself again. If he is any kind of a political animal— and most successful executives are—neither does he want to get away from headquarters and the center of power in the company. These well-connected, top-level people can usually find convincing reasons why they should not be sent to cultivate an overseas Siberia.

Younger men in their thirties and forties, whose children are in grade or high school, are perhaps even less anxious to break up family arrangements—and to leave the center of company activity at a crucial point in their careers (every year being a crucial point in an up-and-coming executive's life). These men, too, keep finding reasons and sponsors to keep them at home, for few executives will willingly give up their key aides and protégés for some faraway project.

What happens (unless, through a quirk of personality, a highly competent senior or promising junior man decides to go overseas) is that second- and third-choice men are sent. Where U.S. managers in Europe are inept, the onus lies directly on their company presidents.

To say that all American managers in Europe are several cuts below the best of their fellows back home libels thousands of highly competent, hard-working individuals. Some U.S. executives in Europe are outstandingly able and imaginative. Among U.S. companies, Procter & Gamble and Du Pont, for instance, are two which Europeans and Americans alike single out as being as smart, smooth, and competent overseas as they are at home. Both companies, however, have concentrated special attention on getting particularly able people into overseas posts. And even then, as an American who knows parts of European Du Pont says, "There's a lot more wailing, and much more refusal to recognize, admit, or adapt to special market conditions in Europe than company top brass realize."

Some U.S. long-term residents in Europe think they see a detectable management pattern or cycle in many U.S. companies forays to Europe. It runs as follows:

With investments in Europe having become fashionable, the company president, senior executives, and perhaps key staff people make a flying trip through Europe, study markets and, then or later, pick a site. (One company picked a village in Scotland for its factory because the president's wife, who was with him on a trip, remembered the lovely roses in front of the cottages as a rare bit of sun burst forth.) The company then searches for a man or group of men it can get to go overseas, finds him or them, and ships this "team" over to set things up. Within two or three years the company begins bringing its first exiles back, and casts about for replacements. Such companies will continue to send over a series of hard-working but not always effective managers with few second thoughts, unless losses grow or progress is so delayed that it becomes embarrassing. At this point the company president or a senior officer will hand-pick a key executive. Giving this new man promises of solid support plus some guarantee that he will not be forgotten at headquarters, they send him over to repair the situation.

One such cleanup man says, "So here I sit in an overdesigned, high-cost plant in a poor labor location picked out by someone else. My wife and I live in a drafty, lonely old mansion and I've got a chauffeured Cadillac on my hands because my predecessor (an older vice-president) liked playing the role of British country squire." However, the replacement executive, who is under thirty-five, also has a chance to run a complete plant and to gain administrative, manufacturing, and marketing experience he would never get in the U.S. Also, he knows that if he does well he'll be promoted. (And chauffeured limousines, if a little embarrassing, can still be fun.)

Weak local management may prevent American companies from taking full advantage of opportunities in Europe, but, ironically, this cloud over American management in Europe does have a faint silver (or golden) lining. After all, who would worry about such unprepossessing competitors? Europeans, at first made nervous by U.S. entry into their markets, have taken a look at, or listened to popular tales about, Americans in Europe—and relaxed.

And yet, most American companies do well vis-à-vis their European competition. Some do very well.[2]

---

[2] Here's an indicator of just how successful some companies can be. In Britain the leading soap company is Procter & Gamble. The leading soup company is Heinz. The two leading auto companies are General Motors (Vauxhall) and Ford.

On the Continent, Ford and General Motors (Opel autos) are

If American companies are doing a first-class or at least passable job with "second-class men," how do they do it? The answer lies, at least in part, in organizational techniques as well as several cultural characteristics common to many American companies.

THE AMERICAN PATTERN

In the old Europe (parts of which exist, overlapping and underlying the new Europe), thanks to careful cartels and a series of sellers' markets, most companies had until recently been able to concentrate on production and profits, with little thought or manpower diverted to marketing or control problems. The middle-manager-manned cost-accounting, production, and marketing controls common to U.S. firms are only being introduced, or greatly expanded, throughout European

---

second only to Volkswagen and are moving up on it in total auto sales. Throughout Europe, International Harvester's prime competition in farm tractors comes from Ford and Massey-Ferguson (a Canadian-American company). In computers, Remington Rand, in Europe as in America, is struggling in the number two position well behind I.B.M. One could spot similar leadership struggles between U.S. companies in almost half a dozen fields. In a dozen more, U.S. firms, if not at the top, are hard at work pushing the pace.

All American companies are not so aggressive, and some Rip Van Winkle U.S. companies have been shaken awake by new rivals and new events in the new Europe. Hoover, the leading washing-machine and refrigerator producer in Britain, bruised in soul and pocketbook by newcomers such as John Bloom, is ranging Britain and Europe in search of mass markets. The Singer company, once undisputed top needle in European sewing machines, was jarred out of its slumbers by low-cost postwar producers. Recognizing that sewing machines will soon be produced into a virtually saturated market in much of Europe, Singer is moving into the appliance business with a vengeance.

industry. Meanwhile, even in the larger European companies, management ranks are relatively thin. The management hierarchical pyramid (president, vice-presidents, and on down) is seldom more than two or three levels deep. Staff members are few in number. Most decisions are quickly made by one or a few key men who know their own and each other's minds. A manager is one of the ruling group to whom considerable authority is delegated, or he is a senior clerk permitted no decisions. In Europe the distinction between "officers" and "other ranks" is not a fine line but a gulf.

Because of their own organizational background, European executives who deal with sizable American companies are constantly exasperated at how long it can take them to come to relatively simple decisions. They are incredulous at the legion of cohorts whom American managers "bring into the picture" at one stage or another of a negotiation. This fuzziness of the U.S. decision process compared to their own tight, fast procedure (combined with a poor impression of U.S. managers in Europe) causes these Europeans to discount the effectiveness of what they see going on. Sometimes they are right. But more often they are wrong (or partly wrong) in coming to conventional conclusions.

Americans in Europe tend to brush aside comments about slow or poor decisions by noting the relatively greater size and difficulty of co-ordination in their companies. Europeans similarly explain away seeming American successes in Europe by observing that many U.S. companies are so big that they can afford to buy and bull their way into European markets. Both groups of comments are, to a degree, correct.

In America the bellwether companies that set the tone and tempo of U.S. industry are truly enormous. They are widespread, with tens of thousands of employees, in multi-divisional array. The divisions are often bigger than most European companies. The Pontiac division of General

Motors, for instance, is bigger than Renault of France. The Norge (appliance) division of Borg-Warner is bigger than Zanussi of Italy, one of the major appliance producers in Europe. American companies are staff-heavy. As American management consultants keep profitably proving, most large U.S. companies could take at least a 10 percent staff cut with no loss in efficiency.

But in America, as we saw in the previous chapter, a different economic order prevails than in Europe. In America, effective cartels, because illegal, have proven difficult to maintain, and sellers' markets, in most industries, are a wistful dream of the immediate post-World War II past. Though the fact is sometimes blown up to unrecognizable proportions by business propagandists, there are various forms of competition (sometimes grim) in a good many U.S. industries. That a U.S. company keeps a constant share of the market is no sure sign its competitors are not trying to wrest this market away; it is a sign that the competition are not succeeding. Operating in the U.S. calls for a different kind of company thinking, planning, and organization than in the old-young Europe. At its simplest, baldest—and most extreme—the difference is that sales quotas are not set by plant capacity, as they would be in a sellers' or in a cartelized market. Instead, production quotas are set by sales forecasts. But this in turn calls for careful estimates and studies of the market, tight control of costs, and co-ordination with production. It calls for expenditures on, or investment in, a great many planning and co-ordinating personnel. (In U.S. industry, white-collar personnel have outnumbered blue-collar factory workers since 1955.) And these ubiquitous staff people, insinuating themselves through corporate structures as do vines through a trellis, play an increasing role in more and more company decisions.

This process slows up and dilutes decisions (because so

many people have to be consulted or informed). In American companies line executives spend much time waiting to hear from or co-ordinating plans with (and sharing power with) staff people.

However, in the economic climate in the U.S., which has long been harsher than Europe's, it is also obvious that U.S. companies could not afford the luxury of vast size and proliferating staff groups unless these elements literally paid dividends.

The size, staffing, and conference orientation of U.S. companies slows their reaction time. But these same American companies, evolved in harsher markets than Europe's, bring plebeian habits and disciplines with them to Europe.

Americans in Europe tend to be more numbers-conscious than the Germans, more planning-minded than the French and, after an initial baptism, less dogmatic than either.

Precise marketing or consumer-preference information is scarce in Europe; in the old Europe, companies hardly needed such information. European executives have tended to run things from the seat of their pants, drawing on a combination of intuition, myth, and faith for their market research. It is still common to hear a European executive say, "The mass market here in (France, England, Germany, Holland, or Belgium) will really never accept X." (For X insert almost any convenience item.) In England a clever and experienced marketing man assures all listeners that lower- and middle-class English women will never really go for supermarkets. This man, who is making a small fortune selling to the burgeoning English supermarkets, refuses to accept his own business as evidence. Old myths die hard.

Meanwhile, in Paris, a banker who has had occasion to sit in on a few U.S. company operating meetings in Europe, remarks: "American managers listen, and they ask questions. If company figures are not precise they force their associates to dig up new, precise figures. If statements are based on opinion, they ask for testing and proof. They force decisions out of people—and they set deadlines." In unwitting corroboration, a good many European managers complain that their U.S. bosses delve into details more than is really necessary. Most important of all, however, is the point that Americans have a penchant for setting schedules, quotas, and deadlines, for setting targets, then working hard to meet them.

For instance, Remington Rand's electric razor division (manufacturing plants in Scotland, Germany, France, and Italy) came to Europe in 1952 with what amounts to a high-priced product—and sold it. Its sales force is well trained and well supervised. Salesmen work to a predetermined itinerary. Says a company executive, "At first the sales people screamed about our field-reporting system, claimed they were salesmen, not bookkeepers." But today, thanks largely to controlled push, Remington razors are the leading electric razors in Europe.

Again, Du Pont, has moved to Europe in recent years in a variety of fields. Aside from patent know-how, Du Pont is counting on its expanding technical service group and assiduous attention to customers and customers short- and long-term needs to assure it a place in Europe. Usually Du Pont sells raw materials which go through several steps before reaching the final consumer. But to sell Dacron or some other textile fiber, Du Pont spends time and money advertising to consumers, helping spinners, designers, and clothing manufacturers learn to work with, and develop techniques and styles adapted to, the new materials. At first, unaccustomed to technical missionary sales efforts from suppliers, Du Pont's European customers were upset. They did not want suppliers contacting *their* customers. Then, as the suppliers saw their sales rise and customers' complaints drop, they enthusiastically endorsed this pull-the-product-through-channels Du Pont method.

It is just this sort of organized push and pull at markets that U.S. managers in Europe do well. But to be effective this "American" marketing approach calls for a different sort of management than most Europeans are used to. It calls for specialists and staff people, and—most important—delegation of some kinds of authority quite far down the management ladder. This last is the principal and most important American-European difference in management.

European nationals who head U.S. subsidiaries in Europe, comparing themselves to the chiefs of like-sized European concerns, tend to champ at the bit and try to get a freer hand from their headquarters. But the number-two and -three men among European middle managers in U.S. subsidiaries are often pleased with themselves and their jobs. They are sometimes confused or annoyed by differences in U.S. and European approaches and sensibilities, but they like being expected to show initiative. They may work to a marketing plan, but it is *they* who are asked to design and improve on the plan. At meetings they are asked by a senior official to make suggestions. For European middle managers all this can be heady stuff.

The American marketing chief of a large chemical company headquartered in Geneva says of his European managers, "They like the informality and job directedness here." Europeans interviewed tend to agree. They especially like and appreciate the easing of hierarchical job stratification. As one puts it, "If you know your job, you don't have to worry so much about a superior's or confederate's family or position, and an engineer here does not lose face in taking advice from a foreman." Americans note that European middle managers may get restless and leave a U.S. company, but after a time with a European firm these men usually try to get back with an American company where (within limits) they have more freedom of maneuver and decision.

To the degree that U.S. companies adapt U.S.-developed controls and disciplines to European markets—and to the degree that they can tap middle-management and white-collar technicians' enthusiasm and initiative—U.S. companies do well in Europe. This, if there is one, is the secret of successful U.S. companies in Europe.

CHAPTER 16

EUROPEAN MANAGEMENT
Through American Eyes

What are European managers like? There is a degree of concensus in the reactions of American executives in Europe to their European opposite numbers and associates. The Americans give European management high marks—with reservations. Many say that European managers are as good as or better than their American counterparts. An American staff adviser on manufacturing to an electronics company with subsidiaries throughout Europe says: "Top manufacturing people over here are technically very competent, better than many of our own. They have good theoretical backgrounds." This American notes, however, that European manufacturing chiefs, possibly because they stay aloof from the shop floor, seem to lack production "instinct," the ability to quickly spot and eliminate existing or incipient production flaws. Yet these men delegate little on-the-spot authority to their immediate assistants.

Reflecting this tradition of nondelegation: throughout Europe, Americans find European second-line managers well below the U.S. standards of experience. In their own organizations Americans find it difficult to persuade European second-line managers to display initiative.[1] An American in Scotland sighs, "You can't assume anything will be done unless you give specific orders that it be done."

Of European managers generally, the Americans note that they do not have the American sense of urgency, that Europeans tend to accept market situations as they are rather than try to improve them. All over Europe the Americans report that their European associates favorite, and seemingly automatic, comment to any innovation is, "That might work in America, but it cannot be done here."

Meanwhile, an oil company executive who deals with technical and manufacturing personnel in nine European countries speaks for other Americans when he says he is continuously surprised at how true so many popular generalities about national differences can be. In dealing with individuals this is not so evident, but with groups of Europeans it is. "Take two extremes," he says. "If I'm in Sweden, we all sit back in our chairs and analyze a situation dispassionately; voices are never raised, a mere suggestion is enough to get things moving. But the Italians are something else. They get tempestuous. They have a lot of give-and-take in their talks.

---

[1] An example of second-level management's resistance to delegation. It is standard in many large U.S. corporations to authorize, say, a manufacturing chief to spend up to so-and-so many thousands of dollars without approval from his superiors. What many chiefs do is break down some large projects into smaller components costing less than their maximum authorization. By buying parts piecemeal they stretch their authorizations.

However, when the French president of a fast-growing electronics company decided to delegate spending authority for equipment under 2000 francs to his manufacturing chief, the reverse happened. The production head would save up his various minor needs till they totaled more than 2000 francs. Then he would go to the company president for approval of the package!

In Italy you have to be more open. You have to be prepared to yell and pound the table or they won't believe you are serious."

Following, based on comments of American managers in Europe and interviews with European managers, are a series of British, French, and German management sketches.[2]

BRITAIN'S PROFESSIONAL AMATEURS

In Britain, commerce and industry, with the partial exception of banking, have, until quite recently, developed very little general prestige. Top graduates from the best schools have traditionally sought careers in government (the Foreign Office, the Colonial Service) and in the legal and medical professions. It is still widely assumed that an upper-class Briton gets his principal income from investments and property holdings; he is not expected to bother himself with the countinghouse details of commerce. Persons in business, "in trade," have not been widely admired.

This attitude toward "trade" is partly a hangover from the old aristocracy's view of merchants. Also, it is a reflection of values acquired in Britain's public (i.e., private boarding) schools. British public school education stresses development of "character" in well-rounded, liberal arts-oriented men who, it is assumed, can think their way through to the essentials of any problem, while the technical details are handled by skilled assistants in lesser categories.

At its best this system produces some excellent business

[2] For a detailed, often fascinating account of the social background and orientation of European managers, see *The European Executive* (Doubleday; Anchor Books) by Professor David Granick of the University of Michigan.

chiefs. Top-level British executives, wasting little time with the ambiguities and details that both plague and delight their American and Continental counterparts, can briskly and efficiently whisk through a committee meeting and get on to the golf course before the Americans have definitely decided what it is they are going to talk about.

But the system also has its flaws. For instance, it seems to be bad form in England for men to actually and obviously concentrate great amounts of time and energy on a project, or on its details. Casualness is stressed. Describing his training at the British-manned office of a U.S. agency, a Continental advertising man reports that every time he asked his nominal superiors and advisers any technical or detailed questions on, say, how samples are chosen in market studies, the reply tended to be as follows: "Well, yes . . . ah, you see it's a matter of getting the proper sample size, and that varies between areas. You know, different kinds of families in different regions, that sort of thing. . . . Look here now, why don't we call Jenkins in on this. He's really your man for this; it's not really my line."

As long as there are enough Jenkinses about, the system works. When asked a specific question, senior British managers seem to take a particular delight in drawing on their Jenkinses. Calling the technical man into the office, they repeat the question and glow proudly as he pours forth series of precise-sounding figures from memory. Recitation over, they say, "That will do, Jenkins. Thanks very much." Jenkins happily puts his memory tapes back into storage and returns to his cubbyhole. The Jenkinses, the regulations-and-statistics-steeped sergeants major of British business, are usually non-public-school, lower-middle-class factotums who are well-adjusted to their role. But their sons, who have seen the film and dreamt dreams of "A Room at the Top," are not preparing to take their places. Given an oversupply of detail disdaining chiefs and an insufficiency of Jenkinses, too much studied casualness up and down the management line leads to the sloppy paper work, high costs, and poor deliveries for which small and medium-sized British firms have a certain reputation. The reputation of Harrods as a store which may not come through on time attaches itself to parts of English industry, too. "They always deliver late," sighs a Midwesterner in Britain, speaking of his local suppliers. "And if you ask for something, anything, to be delivered in less than a fortnight they seem shocked. They'll promise it, but it never comes on time." Other Americans sing a similar sad song.

Commenting on the above, a London-based U.S. consultant says, "A lot of Americans come over here and get pretty frustrated at the lackadaisical pace." This man admits it is easy to criticize British managers, but advises newcomers not to sell them short. After five years in the United Kingdom he has acquired respect for his island clients. "These people have lost or given up great chunks of what once were private colonial markets. India, for instance, was a vast private preserve. It was the principal gem in the British crown. But somehow, you'll notice, they have managed to prosper with a minimum change in their way of life."

British managers, many of whom rather like their pleasant-paced way of life (and some of whom feel that winning World War II gave them the right to continue this way of life indefinitely), are astonished by dedicated American men of business who seem to insist on living under the pressure of tight schedules. But British business is changing, too, picking up a new and faster tempo. With the British Empire now a commonwealth of nations, and with Britain's world power status altered, the talented and the restless young men who once went into government service or abroad are discovering the large corporations in Britain—at a time when the large corporation is coming to flower. In ten to twenty years this enrichment of energy, talent, and brains will become increasingly evident in British industry.

THE INTERVIEW

It is a particular pleasure to hear an articulate and competent British executive explain the present situation or problems in a company or industry. First, there is a broad basing or phrasing of the problem, with emphasis on its history and a tracing (and therefore clarifying) of what would otherwise be ambiguities. This is a setting up of context. Then comes an exploration of the present situation, a viewing of alternatives, and a judgment on probable courses of action. Throughout, the listener is kept aware that this is an irrational world and that new factors may well intervene to change the picture, but that within these uncertainties, and for such and such reasons, one or another particular result is planned or foreseen.

At its best the above can be an impressive performance. One can almost see and hear the whir and click of precision, jeweled gears engaging mentally in smooth sequence. The listener is at first awed, then mesmerized and carried along by a sweet, reasoned flow of logic. After a number of such encounters, however, one begins to notice a pattern and even a predictability to the process. In fact, as these gentlemen, who are good at it and who seem to enjoy doing so, talk or think out loud for the benefit of a listener, one hears the echoes of an Oxford, Cambridge, or public-school tutor who did the same for them, saying: "Well now, we've got that more or less in context, haven't we? Of course, there's always the possibility that . . . ," and the tutorial session, sometimes fascinating, occasionally off base, but always coherent, whirs on. As their Continental neighbors like to remark, the British can be highly persuasive. To travel the quicksands of judgment they employ a broad-based approach quite different from their distant French and German cousins.

FRANCE: TECHNICIANS AT WORK, PROCEED WITH CAUTION

In Paris, after school hours, the middle-class sections of the city, compared to other cities, are strangely quiet. A group of school-age children playing or laughing in the streets or parks is cause for comment. Normally they are home cracking the books. Ambitious French parents—and their children—know that the way to get ahead in France is by doing well in school. As *Time* magazine describes it: "Obsessed with cold reason, nimble wit, and ferocious examinations, French education is a series of sieves that let pass an ever smaller number of ever brighter students. The final screening is France's finest filter: the apex academies called the *grandes écoles.*"

From the *grandes écoles* come the *grands hommes* of France, and if in Britain The Compleat Amateur is in control, then in France his antithesis, The Certified Technocrat, rules.

For generations five *grandes écoles,* jointly turning out a little over a thousand graduates a year, have supplied the bright lights as well as the big and medium wheels, the government administrators, who run France. Moreover, since the end of World War II these *écoliers,* after a tour of government service, have been migrating to top jobs in industry. Of the *grandes écoles,* three—the *écoles Polytechnique, Centrale,* and *des Mines*—have been supplying the top echelons of France's great non-family-controlled companies—and are increasingly evident in the management of large family-owned companies as well.

In American terms, this is as if in the U.S.:

• The Government were to own and operate CalTech and M.I.T. (the Massachusetts Institute of Technology), two top engineering schools.

• Many of the U. S. Presidents' cabinet officers—and all cabinet assistants—were CalTech or M.I.T. graduates.

• The top management of 300 of the 500 largest companies in America were sprinkled with CalTech or M.I.T. men, most of whom had worked in top-level government slots for at least ten years before moving over to industry.

• Influential generals and staff officers in the Army, Navy, and Air Force were also CalTech or M.I.T. graduates.

If the U.S. were split by worker and owner-manager class conflicts, and if the U.S. had not two major, but a dozen or more political parties which kept turnstiling each other out of office, then the dedicated, scornful-of-politics cadre of Cal-Tech and M.I.T. graduates might be all that kept the machinery of government from falling apart. They would, by default, have enormous moral and actual influence. They would be a form of state priesthood, which is very much the case in France. The arduous druidic colleges of pre-Roman Gaul are reborn in the *grandes écoles*.

It is vital for U.S. and other foreign businessmen in France to understand the training and frame of reference, or attitudes to the world, of these business and government chiefs who are the prestige-armed, *crème de la crème* of the French educational system. Their motivation, for instance, is not that of the entrepreneur (or his corporate heirs) but that of the nationalist-indoctrinated, government-service-consecrated administrator. This helps explain why mercantilism, the government direction of private business to government ends, is prevalent in France and is assumed there to exist in other countries.[3] French bureaucrats and senior executives often assume, for example, that even U.S. consumer goods companies work hand in glove with the U. S. Government.

Possessed of group *esprit*, like the U. S. Marine Corps, which comes from shared experience and responsibility in school, government, and, lately, business, these "anointed" graduates, after extensive early exposure to the classics, have had intensive training in mathematics and the sciences. They employ a self-consciously "scientific" approach. They have no doubts about their ability to run a government department or a company and, as needed, they can turn to their fellow "professionals" in government or in industry for advice or support. Because of their educational system, French administrators seem obsessed by brains. They speak of their fellows as quite clever, brilliant, or "truly brilliant." The importance of a man's job in government depends on his rank in class, and the *crème de la crème de la crème* become *inspecteurs* in the Finance Ministry. These men, though few in number, set the tone and pace for thousands of their fellows in government and industry.

Americans newly arrived in Europe, and many European

[3] An example of this reportedly occurred in the oil industry. Oil has long been a semidiplomatic business. Since the discovery and development of oil supplies in the African Sahara, the French government, through government-owned or -dominated oil companies, has been, on the one hand, a particularly aggressive marketer of French oil and, on the other, a quite biased regulator of foreign oil concerns in France. As a result, the French president of a U.S. oil company subsidiary in France found himself with such a conflict of duties that he requested to be relieved or, at any rate, superseded in negotiations by an American. In dealing with French negotiators and officials this man found himself subjected to so much "patriotic" pressure that he could not effectively negotiate for his "foreign" company.

critics of the French Plan for centralized economic development, do not recognize that this system is actually a relaxa-
tion of government controls of industry. Before *Le Plan* the
government ran a *dirigiste* controls-, quotas-, and license-
ridden economy. "In fact, the bureaucrats hated to let go, and
they still keep looking for excuses to step into things," complains a resident U.S. businessman. But it is the old-school
affinity of French bureaucrats and business chiefs that permits the liberalizing experiment of the French Plan to go
on.

Meanwhile, though the French educational system has always been competitive, French business life was not. In the
traditional French company, profits are not a prime concern;
at least not at the middle-management level. These men assume that the system and the government will more or less
take care of adequate profits for any company on whose
existence several hundreds or thousands of employees depend. Middle managers worry about keeping the organization
functioning smoothly. Like their cousin *fonctionnaires* the
world over, they go to great lengths to cover up for each
other's weaknesses and errors. French companies do have a
flavor of their own.

OUTSIDER'S VIEW

To many Britons, who offer handshakes sparingly as if unsure whether they will get their hand back, a French office
would seem a particularly dangerous place. Frenchmen, when
they come in to work, go out to lunch, come back from
lunch, meet in the hall, or leave the office at the end of the
day, grasp all hands within reach for at least one quick
bobbing shake. But, once these ritual salutes to the *égalité*
and *fraternité* of the First Republic have been made, the
precise and complex social pecking order of a company re-

establishes itself. The status and perquisites of rank—a giant desk, chauffeured car, and sometimes an apartment and maid for top executives, and lesser goodies for lesser lights—are standard in French concerns. Who must, or who need not, wear a coat in whose presence is a matter of protocol. Senior executives often summon and treat ramrod-stiff assistants with a cold autocracy one normally associates with Prussia, and the senior-junior relationship, even when jovial, is that of headmaster and pupil.

Foreigners have a favorite word for describing business in France: complicated. The Austrian staff chief of a large international company (who is not uncomplicated himself) says of his French associates: "If there are several ways of doing something, I can count on our French company choosing the most complicated."

An American executive notes: "If it is possible to get something from you by indirection, they choose the long way around." And another American says of French partners: "They complicate simple situations just to keep from getting bored." Presented with these comments, a French executive is likely to smile and say, "Ah, but it is simply a matter of looking at various possibilities." Yet, if French executives like complications they also like them with a certain precision; it is part of the famous French logic.

A Spanish advertising man in Madrid, after a training session with a French advertising group, notes that every time he would ask a question he got the same format for replies, which went: "*Un . . . deux . . . trois . . .* (One . . . two . . . three . . .)"—a verbal setting up of postulates from which all else would then "logically" flow.

Thomas Roberts, a U.S. international lawyer, after reviewing a series of graduate theses in law, chuckles, "It's fascinating. Every paper I read came on the same way. One . . . two . . . three . . . four. . . . These fellows block out the universe, then run off their conclusions. That there might be other possibilities or postulates is ignored. Just one, two, three; and, therefore . . ."

A U.S. company treasurer, ten years in France, says of his dealings with officialdom there: "Many have had engineering training. They love formulas. If they can put something into a formula they're just tickled." That the formula might not apply or might even be a hindrance in some cases was beside the point: formulas offer precision.

But American managers note, approvingly, that more than in most countries in Europe, it is important to explain to French managers and workmen why something is being done and what results are expected from it. When carefully briefed, Frenchmen work competently and hard. A number of U.S. companies find their French work force particularly productive. French workers are more responsive to incentives than English and German employees. Americans also note that it sometimes takes pressure to divert French engineers and managers from polishing the minutiae of production or marketing plans in the office in favor of actual testing and adapting of the plan in the factory or market place.

THE INTERVIEW

As a group, however, French executives are possibly the most stimulating and interesting interview subjects in Europe. No sooner have French interviewees made two or three points than they interrupt themselves, saying, "Ah, yes. Obviously that means . . . ," and the listener, a few yards above terra firma now, is confidently led through an orderly superstructure of abstractions toward an announced objective. There is no time for vertigo; any points the listener brings up are included or discarded, depending on their value to the "construction."

Here, again, one hears the echo of the *lycée*, where a bright student striving for marks must assemble facts and present a thesis. In the "universe" of the school what is important are not the ambiguities in some of the facts but the precision and order—again the "logic"—with which they are assembled, and the confidence and surety with which the student handles himself and his material on paper or in debate. Once he is underway, that some of the foundations on which he is building a thesis might shift is something he cannot afford to consider. "*Un . . . deux . . . trois . . .*"— the foundations, if firmly pronounced, are firmly laid.

What keeps a certain percentage of American businessmen in France in a mild state of apprehension is that, when forced to travel these abstract routes, they sometimes cannot help hearing and seeing the assumedly fixed "foundations" over which they move shifting and cracking.

In Germany, Americans don't have this problem.

GERMANY: EUROPE'S DYNAMO

If the Americans go to war as to business or a football game—thinking production and logistics, talking end runs, line bucks, and plunges—then the Germans go to business as to war. Their business literature and conversation is larded with military terminology wherein markets are seized or defended, attacks are launched, intruders repelled, and invasions planned. Americans in Europe find the Germans blunt, straightforward, and, in that sense, easy to do business with. "It's uncomplicated; they get right down to the point," says a Campbell Soup marketing man in Germany. Like the Americans, the Germans are interested in efficiency for efficiency's sake. They are interested in volume. They relish working on large, smooth-running projects.

German business and marketing men, like Americans, are

attuned to numbers and statistics. However, U.S. marketing men in Germany report a mixed reception of their ideas. Says one U.S. ad agency head in Frankfurt: "German marketing men listen to us politely, but I'm not sure how much they hear. You get the impression they are telling themselves they already know all this." It is an accurate observation.

Reflecting the opinions of many of the top German marketing men with whom he deals, Dr. F. Hebert of Contest Gmbh., the Frankfurt-based market and motivations research organization, suspects that U.S. managers' image of themselves as marketing "experts" hobbles them in Europe. "I don't think the Americans realize," says Hebert, "that we have already taken over many of their marketing ideas, adapted them—and improved on them." German consumer-product companies such as Henkel (soaps), Grundig (radios), Braun, or Bosch (appliances) have built up strong marketing organizations. The busy Germans of business Germany are cocky. They regard themselves as the manufacturing power center of the new Europe, and in this they are right. But U.S. managers note that most German companies are production-rather than marketing-minded. They are accustomed to price-controlled sellers' markets and may be forced to learn a good bit more about close competition and consumer vagaries than they really care to know.

More and more German managers are beginning to get some inkling of the above possibility. Accustomed to "orderly" marketing many of these gentlemen really look on intercompany competition as a reprehensible, possibly immoral, and certainly ungentlemanly way of life. The presence of powerful U.S. companies, such as Procter & Gamble and Du Pont, in their home markets makes these German businessmen unhappy. The American is a bogeyman second only to rising labor wages as a disrupter of the righteous euphoria of Germany's prosperous postwar managers. But many successful managers see little need to change their ways of thought and life.

THE OUTSIDE VIEW

Since the end of World War II, when almost everybody in Germany was down and out, some "new" men have risen to economic power and prominence in West Germany. However, the established universities and student clubs, with their faithful alumni looking out for their *bundesbrüder,* still manage now, as in the past, to supply the bulk of the management talent in German companies. German businessmen have little use for formal management-training programs. In 1962 the directors of INSEAD (Institute for Business Administration), in Versailles, a budding, all-Europe graduate business academy (modeled on the Harvard Business School), reported that the only European businessmen who had not contributed materially to the school were the affluent West Germans.

Yet, in Germany, more than almost anywhere else on the Continent, the university honorific "Herr Doktor" before one's name, like a Mercedes in front of one's apartment, is a much sought-after prestige item. The title "Doktor" does not mean that a man has his Ph.D.; it means that he has done graduate work toward his Ph.D. (roughly, the equivalent of a master's degree from a reputable U.S. school). The man who has actually taken a doctorate, who has presented and "defended" his thesis, is entitled to the even more prestigious "Herr Doktor Professor"—whether he actually teaches or not. There is tremendous respect in Germany for the "educated" man; and all educational or other honors the Germans acquire they display.

Since the days when Germany consisted of a series of

minor principalities it has been a status-stratified society wherein the greater nobility, minor nobility, burghers, and tradesmen differentiated themselves from their lessers down the social pyramid by a multiplicity of titles and caste marks. After two generations of war, postwar debacle, inflation, and turmoil, the old differentiators have lost most of their meaning. And yet, partly because of the turmoil of half a century, differentiators, or their modern equivalents, are ever more eagerly sought after. (This is part of the *bürgherlich* syndrome, an attempted, partial return to the comfortable absolutes, tastes, and paraphernalia of the past that market researchers find amongst so many German consumers.)

In Germany, if a man rates a "Herr Doktor," his wife is called "Frau Doktor." A young German girl explains, "It is in bad taste, but many persons do it." And in postwar Germany, where the businessman is king, the perquisites and status marks of business take on a special attraction and luster. When a German product-manager was promoted to marketing director, his wife proudly requested the superintendent of her apartment building to henceforth call her "Frau Direktor."

To her American neighbors in the apartment building this may seem absurdly pretentious, but Americans have little idea of how hard bought and fought for a Herr Direktor's title can be. German companies, in Germany, are not conspicuous for competition against each other. Yet competition (or the elimination of competition) within a German management group can be ruthless, far more so than equivalent struggles for place in the U.S.

If the relationship among near equals and immediate superiors and subordinates in a U.S. corporation resembles a rough republic of a sort, and if in a French concern business life is like that in a precisely regulated but comfortable commune, in a German company it is like a walk through a dangerous forest.

Julius Caesar, writing of the ancient Germans, said: "Every German state takes utmost pride in devastating an area adjacent to its frontier and thereby surrounding itself with the widest possible belt of uninhabited territory. To drive one's neighbor from his land and make it too dangerous for others to settle in the vicinity is considered the essence of greatness as well as a precaution against surprise attack." An American consultant, who has never read Caesar, says of the German executives he has observed at work, "They destroy everything around them to prevent rivals coming up."

A second American, who has a staff job in a largely German concern, notes, "Senior men are headchoppers. If any heads pop up above the mass—off they come. The first thing you learn is never, ever, to know more about something than your boss does."

A Belgian who works for one of the largest German marketing concerns reports that it is standard procedure there for chiefs to assign portions of a project to various assistants without explaining to them what the whole project is about, or what the other men have been assigned. Nor are the assistants encouraged to get together during the project to compare notes. Instead, like compartmented members of a spy ring (or like Manhattan Project researchers), these marketing men make separate reports to their chief, who then assembles the parts. In this way nobody knows as much as, and certainly never knows more than, the project chief.

In Switzerland an international group of four market researchers working for the German marketing chief of a U.S. food company's all-Europe headquarters found their boss applying a similar technique. Since on the organization chart these four men reported to him, his strategy was to keep them from having direct person-to-person contact with the management of subsidiaries in the countries where they were supposed to be doing advisory studies. At one point, for instance, he took his assistants' reports, had them retyped verbatim, and resubmitted them to management under his own name. Three of his assistants rebelled against this ploy. But one, a young German, though unhappy, made no objection. To him this was a normal privilege of rank.

Of those German managers he has observed, Lesley Knight, of Knight Engineering, a U.S. design and consulting firm with much work in Germany, says: "The bosses clamp down tight, and the fastest way an ambitious man can get ahead is by changing jobs." Such statistics and comments as Professor David Granick could develop on German executives corroborate this. The German system produces tough, authoritarian executives who do very little delegating. Whether this is a system that would work well in a large, hard-to-coordinate company—in a competitive situation—is a $64-million question. A number of psychologists and sociologists are beginning to suspect that the need for co-ordination in large organizations is loosening normally strict German authority patterns. A young German manager says, "The old men are still running things here, but just wait ten years, when the postwar generation takes over business. Then you will see innovation and smooth, smart, teamwork."

Meanwhile, the experience of a newly arrived American who took over the top slot in a Frankfurt-headquartered advertising agency throws some further light on superior-subordinate relationships in Germany.

At his first formal meeting with his new staff this American manager, having done his homework, presented his general and specific ideas for an ad campaign and back-up research work for a new U.S. client. After laying out the program and the job assignments it involved, he asked for comments and questions. There was silence. Then a young associate spoke up, suggesting some alterations particularly suitable to the German market. The U.S. president accepted the ideas, incorporated them into the program, made assignments, and thanked the man. The meeting closed.

But one of the older men, catching up with the president in the hall, followed him back to his office saying, "I'm very sorry to bring this up but you just made a serious mistake back there which you should know about." The kindly tutor then explained to the foreigner-American, first, that he had made a mistake in permitting a junior to find fault with his program in open session; second, that he had seriously compounded the error by admitting that his program contained flaws when he then and there incorporated the subordinate's ideas into his own. Only by getting quite angry while explaining, first, that the object of a conference was to uncover ideas and prevent mistakes, and, second, that he expected all members of the firm to contribute ideas at these meetings, did the American regain some of his lost prestige.

Some U.S. managers in Europe feel that they have been betrayed when aides make no strong objections to (or give no specific arguments against) a course of action which they are sure will fail. In the United States a manager will sometimes argue with his assistants to test a thesis. On the basis of this "arguing," he may or may not go ahead with a project —but he has been forewarned. However, most European assistants have been trained never to argue with the boss. Once the boss starts arguing they take this as a signal to shut up. As a result, Americans say of Europeans that a European's favorite comment is, "It can't be done," with no real substantiation of this doubt. And, as a number of Europeans note, the favorite American complaint they hear is, "You're not co-operating!"

In fact, communication, in Germany as everywhere, is a

constant problem for Americans. In Germany the problem has a curious twist. Americans in Europe often like to think and talk of themselves as a simple, straightforward people constantly being surprised and upset by "devious" Europeans. In Germany, however, these roles are reversed. "German is a straightforward, simple language, but English is subtle. It is full of conditions, modifiers, and intonations," says Heinz F. H. Moeller, publisher of *German International,* an English-language German magazine. All too often, feels Moeller, a German will think he has made a firm agreement with an American when it turns out not to have been firm at all, or to have been a quite different agreement than he understood. Something is lost in translation, which the clever Americans can be counted upon to bring to light as needed.

CHAPTER 17

AMERICAN MANAGERS IN EUROPE
Portraits in Monochrome

Europe is a lens which can bring Americans transported there into a degree of focus that would not be possible at home. As a group, Americans in Europe impress, yet strangely sadden, one. The reasons why are varied and diffuse, but like the individually meaningless black, white, and gray specks of a photograph, they combine to form a picture.

A large percentage of American businessmen in Europe are their companies' second-choice men (the first-choice men manage to keep nearer the throne at home). You would not expect these men to dazzle with their brilliance, wit, or energy—and few do. Few Americans in Europe are free-wheeling entrepreneurs. These are company men. Some operate in a continuous, though mild, state of shock—at how the market systems, distribution, and thought patterns they must deal with differ from those in the U.S. Almost all Americans in Europe work in a state of frustration at the different pace of business they meet there. Often they find themselves squeezed between the demands of Europe-innocent superiors at home and the widely differing realities of European markets, where consumers may, or may not, take to a given brand of U.S. soup or cigarettes; where wholesalers may, or may not, accept new products for distribution, or may not accept (or pass on) price discounts; or where piecemeal advertising and promotion programs must be booked on television as much as a year in advance.

Some Americans are not happy in Europe. For personal, family, or career reasons, they would much rather be home. A great many American managers in Europe are men in their late thirties or early forties. This, for those in whom ambition or pride flickers, is a preoccupation and a worry. At make-or-break period in their careers they know they are far from the seats of power. But the managers go where they are sent and, once there, doggedly set about their work. As a group, these men, who are not the *crème de la crème* but something just a few cuts above the U.S. business run-of-the-mill, are impressive.

Where performance figures are available, U.S. companies in Europe, once established, do as well or better than native competitors. Most U.S. managers in Europe are competent because they are realistic: after a time in Europe, if they find that one set of U.S. marketing or management techniques does not seem applicable, they try to find out why and to adapt them accordingly. They keep setting schedules, try hard to meet them, and try (with some success) to instill a sense of urgency, method, and participation among their European associates.

There is a touch of the missionary in most Americans (something on which many Europeans comment), and our American businessmen in Europe are no exception. Convinced that the new consumer societies they are helping to develop in Europe are an improvement on the old, these men are proud of their work. But any fervor, except among newcomers fresh from the U.S., is restrained. In fact, the phrase that most effectively applies to most U.S. managers in Europe is "low key"—which is something that takes most Europeans, and many Americans, by surprise.

THE INSCRUTABLE AMERICANS

Europeans, even quite sophisticated Europeans, cling tightly to a series of cherished American stereotypes based on Hollywood movies, memories or tales of World War II G.I.s, and encounters with camera-toting tourists. This makes the reality all the more puzzling. British businessmen's comments on American businessmen, for instance, come forth as parodies of U.S. 1920s music-hall descriptions of British imperturbability and distance, as in these fragments:

"The Americans are quite polite. Why, they won't even complain about the weather without apologizing first."

"They will talk to you about business as long as you like —but not about anything else."

"They are deadpan. Even their humor is deadpan. It is hard to follow."

"Americans are very friendly, first names and all that . . . , but, you know, they never really do let down the bars."

In Holland a State Department officer notes that the U.S. businessmen he meets there seem to be trying to outdiplomat the diplomats. And in Geneva an American diplomat says of his businessmen countrymen: "They all read and took *The Ugly American* too seriously. I never saw such a cautious, careful bunch."

All of this, of course, is counter to Americans' image of themselves. But the old, shoot-from-the-hip style is out-of-date. In the course of hundreds of interviews—some brief, some lengthy, some amazingly frank, others closely guarded —with American managers in Europe, what filters through, partly in words and partly in silent language, is an underlying sense of pressure and something akin to resignation, a sense of restraint and of conscious self-control. Like lay monks in a medieval religious order, these men are very much in and of this world, but distracted because part of their attention is constantly focused on the internal disciplines and affairs of *their* order, the company. Faint as a wisp of smoke but just as pungent is the sense that these men, replaceable executives who move from slot to slot within their companies, are veterans, long-service legionnaires. One gets the feeling of dealing not only with individuals, but with highly self-conscious, corporate emmissaries. Like diplomats, these Americans in Europe wear a mask, are guarded in their comments, are almost formally correct, try to think and move with measured pace.

They work hard, travel much, but there is no exuberance. "Why should there be?" says one. "The basic operation here is already set up. That excitement is over; now it's just like working in the States, but much harder." True, but it is not that simple either. The Americans who are said to be americanizing Europe strangely perturb Europeans—and other Americans. If these are legionnaires in a new economic order, one nods recognition and gives full points—but where is the joy? These are cautious men, for they walk difficult ground—but where is the contagious verve? Once it was an American characteristic, a national strength.

After talking with a sympathetic and perceptive American in Holland, a reporter, as he reached the door to leave, turned and joshed, "Now, just once in a while you'll have to get out and be exuberant." The American smiled at the sally, but sadly; exuberance was something he and his fellows had given up.

Very slowly, as many interviews with American managers in Europe build, one upon the other, two realizations dawn. First, one comes to see that this is a sampling of a particular generation of Americans: men in their late thirties and mid-forties, the young men, the privates, sergeants, lieutenants, and captains (the generation of John F. Kennedy) who fought and came back from World War II. But these are not the ebullient ex-G.I.s one went to college with in 1946. Something besides the aging process has taken place. Something more has occurred of which Europe, Russia, the atom bomb, responsibility to and for the world, and the rise of the corporation are all a part.

The boisterous, cheerful, self-confident, glad-handing American has gone; if he was occasionally an embarrassment, one misses him. He is being replaced by a competent and self-restrained, perhaps slightly bitter, American, who is settling down for a long and not necessarily cheerful haul.

These old-young Americans in Europe are a mirror reflecting an America which has also changed. One recognizes in this generation abroad that Europe and the world closed in to age America before its time.

Meanwhile, these restrained Americans in Europe go on about their work.

AMERICAN "TYPES"

Inevitably, one tends to separate large groups of people into types or categories. After visiting with several hundred American executives in Europe, the author settled on the following. Each requires explanation:

• *The Outcasts*. In many companies it is not a case of "Whom should we send to Europe?" but "Whom can we get to go?" The senior vice-president two years from retirement (who is in the way) may go; the troublesome executive left over from a still undigested acquisition can be sent (he lacks political protection). At times, through misplaced kindness, a president may send a close-to-retirement executive to give him a few "nice years in Europe." Alas, these years are not usually so nice.

• *The Comers*. After a disastrous selection or two, a com-

pany finally faces up to "the challenge of Europe," picks a
"bright young man," and sends him out to "clean up the
mess." Sometimes he does. A few companies take great pains
to send highly capable people in the first place.

• *The Good Soldiers.* A great number of Americans in
Europe are there simply because their company sent them,
as they might have been sent to California, New Orleans, or
St. Louis for a tour of duty. Often these men go with a stipulation: "Okay, but you've got to promise it will only be for
two years."

People in these last two groups, the comers and the good
soldiers, fall into at least two further subcategories: One in-
cludes a fairly large number of men who do their job but
don't necessarily like it; in their minds they go into an emotional stasis, enduring the assignment, doing their best, but
hardly loving it. Then there are the men who discover and
like Europe and who also discover that, separated by three
thousand miles from an often indifferent or poorly informed
headquarters, they are in a position to "wheel and deal,"
"run their own ship," make decisions, gain experience, and
have a lot of fun doing so.

• *The Semi-independents.* Men who really like working
in Europe will quit their companies, take another job, or
start a business of their own in order to stay there. Again,
these break into subcategories. They include a number of
slightly sad and not very effectual postwar Americans who
have "gone native." They want nothing of competition, try
hard to explain Europeans to their fellow Americans, all too
often accept all too readily the multiple reasons a European
manager can give why something can't be done. Opposed
to these are a number of highly capable individuals who have
a knack for getting along with Europeans but who remain
highly American in drive and viewpoint—they just like the

excitement of growing Europe and of working in a strange environment.

Executives who do well in Europe usually end up describing themselves in frontier terms. They talk of developing new areas, eventually very important ones, which their fellows at home hardly know exist. They mention a sense of growth, rapid change, a different order and degree of risk which they must face on their own. In some ways the analogy applies. These people are very much *of,* but no longer *in,* the U.S. environment and they are penetrating and helping to change the European milieu—in a manner which in turn will eventually help bring about change in America.

The heroic image of the U.S. frontier all too often veils the fact that it was the incompetents and misfits there too who, to a considerable degree, peopled and advanced the frontier. It was not the prosperous, successful Europeans who came to America to stay. And those new arrivals who did well in America tended to stay in the East, dealing in trade, rum, and slaves, and building factories. It was the castoffs, the restless misfits, and the seeming incompetents who cut off their roots and moved to try again somewhere further west. Few of them were really successful, some of them never did stop moving, but in the process of trying they built a country and shaped many of its attitudes. Moving with these people there were always soldiers and their families who were there, not because they wanted to be, or because they had nowhere else to go, but because they were on a tour of duty.

Now, look back at the types of Americans we have been describing as peopling U.S. businesses in Europe: the men who were squeezed out, shouldered out to Europe; the men who, blocked at home, took this as a chance to break through into a fresh start or at least to get away from an old start; the restless, odd shoes; the competent but adventurous chance-takers; the good soldiers sent on a tour of duty, grimly doing their time. For a brief instant, like a drop of water forming, the analogy can hold—then it breaks of its own weight. "Europe isn't a frontier; it's a morass through which we're trying to build a couple of trails," says one marketing man of his own company. And, he adds, "the Europeans aren't simple Indians. They are complex sophisticated people; half of them are smarter than we are. And we're not fighting them—not in any frontier sense; we're all heading the same way." This same man says he is in Europe because he likes working in six very different countries at once, because it is Europe where growth and change is taking place, and because he can make decisions and try techniques no one would permit him to toy with in the U.S. "You can take the reins into your own hands here—as long as you're always, or almost always, right," he says. As he talks, the image starts to build up again. For some, the frontier is a state of mind.

PART V

AMERICAN LIFE ABROAD

CHAPTER 18

AMERICAN LIFE ABROAD [I]

"Emotionally, some of my parishioners never unpack. They go into a suspended state of animation until their tour in Europe is over. . . ."

THE MINISTER OF AN AMERICAN CONGREGATION IN GENEVA

What is it like living in Europe? There are some 40,000 American men, women, and children resident in Europe who are maintained by U.S. business. Some 14,000 of these people are in Switzerland. There are 10,000 Americans in Geneva. The other large concentrations are in London and Paris. Among such a broad sample of middle-class Americans one can find any combination of circumstances, attitudes, and reactions to life in Europe. There are no extensive studies or precise figures on these overseas Americans. At best, there are only estimates. But from what these Americans have to say about themselves, it appears that many (possibly as many as 20 percent, or one out of five) would like nothing more than to go home—right now. At least half the Americans in Europe deeply miss home, but are glad to experience life abroad. Of these more complaisant complainants, at least half again could be "persuaded" to take another tour. A minimum of one out of ten Americans abroad genuinely like living overseas and are in no hurry at all to go home. The people in this last group are not emotional expatriates—they are as American as apple pie—but for a mixture of personal reasons they enjoy working abroad. Almost all Americans, when they first go overseas, however, undergo a certain trauma.

THE SOCIOLOGISTS HAVE A WORD FOR IT

Culture shock is a phrase much used among, and applicable to, Americans abroad. Culture shock means a state of mind in which anything different from the norm at home becomes an irritant, something "wrong," almost immoral, "un-American." Cultural shock is a generalized trauma that extends from values to manners to work habits; from reaction to the way other peoples greet each other, snub each other, treat their children, or park their cars, to the way they mix their drinks or speak on politics.

"Don't tell me about culture shock. I know all about it. It's a lot of nonsense," says a 37-year-old American consultant in London. In the next instant he launches into an impassioned and detailed denunciation of British retailers and hotelkeepers—the shabby way they treat customers and the sheeplike patience of those customers. This man is reacting from behind the righteousness of cultural shock.

Another American, six months in Scotland, detachedly and amusedly describing his problems in getting his home heating system repaired during the Christmas holidays, is suddenly gripped by memory. Stopping in midstory, he throws himself down into his chair to mutter, "Boy you give up a lot when you come over here." He, too, deep in his chair, is deep in cultural shock.

When first transferred abroad, Americans find themselves being continually jolted and stirred out of the comfortable half-daze of predictable routine in which they lived and worked at home. Like the blind man who, stepping into his apartment, discovers that someone has moved every bit of furniture, a foreigner must constantly adjust to a series of little and big surprises. Overseas Americans encounter social and mental attitudes which force them to re-examine (and reaffirm or change) assumptions they grew up with at home. The status of women, the perquisites of classes, the etiquette of permissible lies, the valuation of children—all these and hundreds of other minor and major bits of a value system vary and must be adjusted to from country to country.

Americans who get over their first dose of cultural shock abroad can suffer a mild reverse dose of it when they come home. For instance, a onetime Indiana housewife took her family home on leave from Britain. After four years she had adapted rather well to life in misty, friendly Scotland. However, in her mind all things British, when weighed, were found wanting compared to increasingly golden memories of the States. "It took a trip home to settle me down," she says. Arriving in the U.S. with bag, baggage, and children, she found taxi drivers rude and unhelpful, waiters testy and impatient. Her old friends and neighbors, while friendly, appeared disinterested, uninteresting, and materialistic. "All they seemed to think and talk about were fancy new cars and houses," she says. Back in the heartland from a trip to the outside world, she found her old friends somehow narrow-minded. "All they see," she says sadly, "is America." And America, which had become the epitome of the virtues for her, came into new perspective.

This sort of two-way shock is not unhealthy. The second, home-culture shock, does not last more than a few weeks. Overseas-culture shock, while incurable in some cases, usually lasts little more than a year, and most Americans, with varying degrees of grace and ease, adjust to their new environments within this time.

MAKING DO

Like so many thousands of footsore, museum-besotted, U.S. tourists, many Americans in Europe (especially those there less than two years) are actually not as happy there as they will later recall; human memory is highly selective and usually kind.

But the men will have the fonder memories. Generally, American men in Europe are sheltered within the framework of their job. They hold responsible, interesting positions in offices where English is spoken and, as a result, they adapt to life in Europe much more easily and quickly than women. It is the woman in the family who must do the shopping, deal with deliverymen, maids, electricians, plumbers, and bills—in a foreign language. She has to discover that floor wax is sold at the place where you get pictures framed; that the stores (not open at night) close during lunch and early on Saturday; that her local grocer doesn't have any lemons on Wednesday; that meat at the butcher's, while not bad, is cut wrong (or, at any rate, differently than at home). She may find that family food shopping, which took four hours a week in the U.S., takes two hours a day in Europe. She may have a maid to help around the house and with shopping, but as one American woman in Milan says, "A washing machine, you push the button. A maid, you have to train." Many a U.S. newcomer, unaccustomed to maids, unsure whether to treat a maid as an equal, a chum, or as an individual brought in for supervised work, goes through several maids and suffers unhappiness in the process of discovering "the servant problem."

Essentially, however, the American woman's problem in Europe is that she is lonely—and bored. Her husband is often away on trips. She doesn't know what to do with her time, for ready-made distractions are scarce. In Switzerland, for instance, where there are many Americans, she finds she cannot join local charities or do hospital work. The local Swiss ladies, who make a fetish of this sort of thing themselves, are lined up six deep for available spots and want no intrusions from foreigners.

A young American husband in Lausanne says, "I'd like to do another tour; I'm learning a lot, and Europe is at an interesting stage of development." But he will soon return to the U.S. His wife, he says, has been awfully good thus far, but would not sit still for another tour. He explains, "You know, the women here don't neighbor much." In Switzerland this is an understatement. The Swiss don't neighbor much with each other—much less with foreigners. In Switzerland, a man who came to Geneva from nearby Fribourg as a child is still referred to by his neighbors as So-and-So, the fellow from Fribourg.

With variations and individual exceptions, the same holds true for most Europeans. Their close friends are their cousins and a handful of people with whom they went through school. Americans, who continually transfer into and out of the environment, are left to fend for themselves. One reason for this is that even those Europeans who would enjoy making friends with Americans are repulsed by the U.S. corporate habit of shifting management people around every few years. In every country in Europe one hears the same refrain: no sooner have Europeans actually come to know and like an American couple than these precious new friends are shipped home or to another country. Unaccustomed to making friends easily with strangers, Europeans, rather than make new overtures to persons who will be leaving in two, three, or five years, keep their distance. In Europe, incidentally, newcomers are expected to call on their neighbors rather than vice versa, as in America.

Then, there is the formidable barrier of language. It takes several years of practice to speak a language with sufficient fluency to convey any but the simplest facts and sentiments. "Let's face it," says the head of an American machine-tool company in Holland: "When we visit with Dutch friends who are having a party, everybody makes it a point to speak English most of the time, for our sake. They speak English very well, but there's much that doesn't get across. It is a strain communicating, and it's our presence that makes the strain."

For all these reasons the American ladies, especially the great majority who cannot or will not learn a language, are thrown upon each other for company. They turn to the local American Woman's Club, to that great international time-killer, bridge, and to dinner parties for other Americans. The Women's Clubs, especially for a newcomer, are invaluable. Some, as in Geneva and The Hague (Holland), provide new members with useful booklets and tips on shopping, schools, the care and cultivation of maids, and other vital bits. The clubs provide entree and company for the desperate. And, as one non-club-type woman explains it, "At least when you first arrive, the Woman's Club is a place to start." The clubs indulge in good works, arrange group tours, and invite guest speakers to provide the ladies with charities, sights, and culture in painless doses.

In Geneva, Paris, and London, where Americans are most numerous, one finds surprisingly little sense of community among American residents. Instead, social groupings tend to form on a company basis: Du Pont, Caterpillar, Chrysler, or Ford people clinging socially to—and caring for—their own. However, in Lausanne and in Milan, where the American communities are smaller, every American knows (or could know) almost every other American in the community, and there is an evident, general sense of belonging—even a cer-

tain local civic pride among the American community. Undoubtedly, whether and how much an American couple likes
Europe will depend in part on where they are stationed and
what friends they make. But the important thing in many
cases is that it is the wife's rather than the husband's
adaptability that determines whether or not a couple successfully adjusts to life in Europe.

This fact, widely noted in business literature, still seems
to be largely ignored by most companies. A few, like Procter
& Gamble, handle the problem indirectly, and probably
effectively, by doing overseas business via an international
company which recruits its own personnel. These recruits
are preadjusted to the idea of life abroad. Chrysler Corp.,
learning from experience, developed the practice of bringing
a husband and wife over to Europe for two weeks so they
could look things over, visit with residents, decide whether
they wanted to live abroad. Ford Motor provides language
lessons for overseas husbands and wives. But most companies
pick a man, send him over, cross their fingers, and hope his
wife adapts well or at least holds on for his and the company's sake.[1]

Most Americans in Europe, however, if not exactly ec-
static, are quietly pleased with their life there. These Americans feel important, are important, and live well.

---

[1] For all their long-range planning programs, and for all the scare
literature about wives passing muster at home, few companies seem to
survey their own people for overseas compatibility. It is generally
known that couples who do well overseas will happily spend hours
of their own time in the U.S. studying the history and language of
a country and area—if there is a probability that they will get there.
But few companies consciously seek out overseas-motivated personnel.

CHAPTER 19

AMERICAN LIFE ABROAD [II]

The Good Life and Keeping the Kids American

In America, the chiefs and certainly the second- and third-rank managers of relatively large corporations and organizations are, if they step outside their immediate social, industrial, and geographic environment, easily lost in the crowd. America is big. It is a country with multiple power centers. There are many large corporations; new ones keep evolving. Outside his bailiwick, a senior executive is just one more senior executive; middle managers number in the millions.

European countries, however, are small. Their social and power structures are easily identified. Their elite, few in number, are quickly spotted. There is high correlation between education, family connections, and positions in the social, governmental, and industrial hierarchy. With exceptions, of course, if a European heads a good-sized European company, it follows that he will have important, personal government and social contacts. He will have gone to school with, and be one of, the top people in his country. As a result, American managers of U.S. subsidiaries in Europe, because of their positions, are automatically placed well up on the local ladder. In their business and, to a degree, socially, they have easy access to elements of a country's elite. They find that government, business, and political figures will have a keen interest in American business activities and plans. Overseas, these Americans find they are not just another business couple; they are somebody important.

Most Americans admit they find it rather pleasant being bigger frogs in smaller ponds. Then, too, the automatic and formal deference a manager and his lady receive from subordinates at work or on the social scene, while at first a bit embarrassing, is pleasant. The other major attraction for many Americans in Europe is that they live well, better than they ever did at home. Many are touchy on the subject. Some have a tendency to bend the visitor's ear with tales of how hard their lot is. "Living well" demands a bit of explanation.

North Europe is damp, dark, and rainy most of the year. Houses are often chilly, the plumbing sometimes erratic (though this is improving). Americans often find they must live in apartments rather than in houses. To those Americans with a *Better Homes and Gardens* vision of the good life, North Europe is a hardship area.

However, most Americans in Europe receive cost-of-living and special expense allowances. Depending on a man's position, country of assignment, and family situation, allowances range roughly from $2000 to $10,000 extra a year. (The oil and chemical companies are particularly lavish.) The necessity of providing a house or apartment with central heating, U.S.-type schooling for the kids, and some American foods, during the period of post-World War II shortages, set the pattern of allowances for Americans overseas. Even now, in the prosperous new Europe, maintaining the American way of life (as some define it) is costly. If a family wants frozen orange juice and bacon and eggs, or pancakes with Log Cabin syrup, for breakfast, for instance, plus other American foods at other meals, these things are available in Europe—at a price. Living "just like at home" means paying an import price on many items—and there goes the special cost-of-living allowance.

A number of Americans in Europe, however, find they can get along with European foods and services and live comfortably, although differently than at home. One American in Geneva, for example, reports that his son's favorite condiment is Heinz Ketchup. The boy gets a bottle once a year, on his birthday. The father smokes European cigarettes, uses European shaving cream. This same man and his wife, having learned some French, use a French-speaking doctor and dentist instead of the more fashionable and thrice-as-expensive English-speaking equivalents. (In Milan one of the more popular English-speaking dentists keeps two price lists in his desk drawer: one for Italians, another for the rich Americans.)

Housing

Apartments and houses are a special case. Land is scarce in crowded Europe and building costly, especially in Paris, Geneva, and Milan, in that order. Anywhere in Europe, however, it is generally open season on transient Americans. As Parisians and Milanese explain it, the Europeans in these cities trade the old rent-controlled apartments among nephews, nieces, and cousins. New low-cost buildings are for laborers and clerks and this leaves the luxury apartments for Americans and status-happy European new-rich. The Americans can take some of the blame for these high costs. They and their companies, always in a hurry, thinking in dollars rather than francs or lire, willingly pay whatever the going rate seems to be—and more. One U.S. executive in Milan, looking over a recently completed apartment suite, found the rental was $4000 per year. He reportedly told the owners, "My rental allowance is $5000. Put in closets and cupboards and I'll take the place for $5000."

Meanwhile, when a 29-year-old assistant manager in Madrid casually mentions the swimming pool that goes with his company-rented house, one suspects that even in California a man his age might not do as well. And in Italy, as a hard-working American manager in his thirties complains of taxes on overseas incomes over $35,000[1] for persons who have been overseas more than four years, it is somehow difficult to sympathize; especially when his wife mischievously notes that their eight-room apartment, paid for by the company, is larger than the bungalow they owned in St. Louis. Life abroad has its sore points, but there are compensations.

Chief among overseas compensations, for those Americans who do not crawl into an emotional deepfreeze, is the fact it is easy to entertain. An open secret among old China hands is that "The mysterious lure of the Orient is the houseboy." In Europe, it is the maid. Baby-sitters, in the form of full- or part-time maids are still readily available in Europe (they do dishes, too), thus easing the mechanics of entertaining or going out to be entertained. Moved to Europe, child-chained American parents discover a heady social freedom they never knew before. In Europe, those evenings and weekends that husbands are home can be deliciously convivial.

NIGHT LIFE

In most major European cities (except London), for the price of an indifferent meal served in indifferent style in the U.S., one can be quietly presented with a dinner that shows

---

[1] The above is an extreme case. A much more common figure for U.S. middle-management salaries abroad would be $15,000 (plus) and special rent and education allowances of $2000 to $4000.

up many of New York's and Chicago's more pretentious expense-account restaurants.

"When I've got visiting firemen on hand from the States, we take them out to dinner at one of the fine restaurants," says the Paris-based chief of a $100-million-a-year U.S. operation in Europe. "We may finish up at 11:00, then we go home. If visitors want to play around town, that's their lookout." Others, not quite so crusty or self-confident, find themselves acting as tour guides, and for those who particularly enjoy the peekaboo of watching beautiful women taking off their clothes, or dancing about without them, Europe has much to offer. From Paris and the Lido on down, every major city has its clubs, shows, and "spots," some of them boasting dazzling displays. In fact, as *Fielding's Guide to Europe* discreetly notes, there is a great European industry geared to please those, accompanied or unaccompanied, who are "on the lookout." Americans in Europe soon learn that a clip joint is a clip joint and an international institution. Prices are also international ($1.25 and up for drinks), and the clientele in most places are European businessmen. Those Europeans who do make money spend it as fearlessly as Texas oil men.

But few American residents in Europe or veteran business visitors from the U.S. travel the flash-flesh-and-nightclub circuit. They travel their own business and international hotel routes. In every major city in Europe one finds the visiting American businessmen congregated in one or two, usually new, hotels. In these so-womb-and-room-alike, English-spoken-here way stations (where a man sometimes has to ask what country he is in) the busy visitor is shielded from cultural jolts of any kind. Here he can concentrate on his business. At the bar there are other Americans with whom he can talk, or not, as he wishes. There is a nightclub in the hotel, however, he probably goes to bed instead (usually there's an early meeting tomorrow). But if he wants company, this is a sophisticated hotel.

Since the greater number of American companies in Europe have two, three, or more subsidiaries in different countries, U.S. managers in Europe are often on the road visiting existing or potential ventures. What about the wives whose men are away so often and so long? Do they get romantically restless? In a town like Geneva or Paris one hears a few murmurs and hints, but not many. Overseas wives, like army wives and small-town matrons, tend to watch each other fairly carefully. Most European men are not particularly interested in American company women; they find their own are quite charming. There is little hanky-panky in Europe, certainly no more, and probably less, than in the U.S.

Another hypothetical question: what happens when American men travel and are away from home a good deal, when for the first time in their lives they can afford that cultural specialty, the mistress? Here again, the answer is: nothing much. There were rumors that one American company moved its European headquarters from Geneva to Paris because the company chief had developed personal interests there, but Americans don't keep mistresses, at least not for long. It is more in the American pattern to divorce one's wife and marry the mistress, which in any country usually meets with the approval of the mistress.

But then, again, most Americans have been in Europe only a few years. There is the language barrier. And this is a generation of discreet Americans.

Meanwhile, a consultant striding down a Brussels street affirms, "Here you're somebody a little out of the ordinary. It can be pleasant being an American in Europe." In this, he speaks for many innocent pleasures. He even speaks for numbers of American youngsters in Europe.

Looking out his window at a group of American teen-age boys awkwardly kicking at a soccer ball, Arthur Denyer, the British principal of the International School of Brussels, admits, "We haven't won a game yet." (Boys fresh from the U.S. can never match the Europeans in agility with their feet.) But most of his students, says Dr. Denyer, seem fairly pleased to be abroad. "Even after they go home it will mark them as something special, you know, to have been Americans living in Europe. They recognize this," says Denyer.

And, although it is American women in Europe who, more often than the men, decide they have had enough and want to go home, it is generally because of the kids—and their education—that Americans invited to take another tour abroad elect to go home.

KEEPING THE KIDS AMERICAN

The waking nightmares of American parents in Europe are peopled with College Board Examiners and high-school and grade-school certifying authorities. When Americans move abroad their worry is: Will the kids lose school time? Once overseas, it becomes: Can the kids be accredited to good schools at home.

There are hundreds of excellent schools in Europe. These schools are often more rigorous than the U.S. average for the same age level. But these schools are designed for Europeans. Apart from the language problems of getting a boy or girl into and through a foreign school, there is the matter of later accreditation to American schools. Since mose U.S. school bureaucracies are more red-tape than content conscious, presentation of European school credits can begin as a lost battle. Johnny may read and speak French and do algebra, but if he hasn't had civics he is in trouble. Unless they intend to stay in Europe for many years, most U.S. parents have to get their children into American or equivalent schools abroad. Then too, many parents feel that they want their children absorbing American values in American-like schools, living and socializing with a number of other American youngsters.

There were enough Americans and Britons in cities such as Geneva and Paris in previous decades so that U.S.- and British-accredited, English-language, international schools have been founded there. The present onrush of Americans to Europe, which started in the late 1950s, expanded these schools and spawned a spate of others around Europe. Like Dr. Denyer, of the Brussels International School, the majority of Europe's teachers-to-Americans are Britons. They come across the Channel better educated than, and at less than half the salary of, their Stateside counterparts. Many of these instructors are men, which makes for easier class discipline and possibly a more balanced and healthy *ambiance* than a child encounters in women-dominated U.S. schools (at least, numerous U.S. parents in Europe feel this way).

Day-school tuition ranges from $300 to $400 per year and is rising. Some companies, as Du Pont (for its U.S. employee-patronized schools in Holland), give extensive financial assistance to local American schools. Most firms, according to school-board members and principals, do very little. (Few U.S. chiefs in Europe would have authority for such gifts, and their superiors in the U.S. seldom see the virtue in bringing up such a point with company directors.)

However, because these U.S. managers' children tend to be above average in intelligence and because, outside of Geneva, Paris, and London, classes are usually pleasantly small, school *esprit,* and quality of work stay at a high level. The nearly 400-student Brussels International School, for instance, teaches fractions, decimals, and percentages to fourth-graders. Its first high-school graduating class all scored in the top half of the college board exams.

Because high schools demand much more extensive and expensive plants and equipment than grade schools, the smaller, newer U.S. business communities in Europe cannot afford them. They must send their older children to other cities or to boarding schools. There are, of course, numerous boarding schools in Europe, especially in Switzerland, and more are building; English-language schools are a growth industry there. International parents, escaping from their children, have been supporting some of these schools for generations. "But I don't want my kids growing up to be international snobs," says one firmly opinionated American father near Frankfurt, Germany; he has sent his oldest, high-school-age boy home to live with grandparents in Michigan. Generally, it is when children reach high-school age that parents in outlying, non-U.S. high-school areas of Europe begin signaling the home office that it is time to cut the European tour short.

Keeping the kids American in Europe, however, especially if they go to an American school, is no problem. In fact some American children abroad (like most U.S. Army and Air Force children in Europe) have little enough real exposure to the country in which they live. They study a European language four hours per week in school, ride European buses, read European signs, tramp European sidewalks. But their study time, leisure time, playmates, and preoccupations are twice-distilled American. Many return home virtually untouched by life abroad and speaking no new language. There are exceptions. Depending on location, their own age and personalities, and their parents' attitudes, children can pick up both the language and the "feel" of a country and its thought patterns. When they return home to high schools or colleges these youngsters will merge into the

American scene. But they will have memories, impressions, a familiarity with Europe and, often, a willingness or itch to return. To the degree that they have become bicultural, this will be good for Europe and America—and possibly a bit hard on the youngsters, unless they can reconcile in adult life the exotic advantages of their childhood.

Meanwhile, as the school principal in Brussels said, "It will mark them as something special . . . to have been Americans living in Europe."

The business Americans in Europe, scattered at random through some cities, living in prosperous ghettos in others, traveling the international hotels on business, entertaining each other, and attending their own schools, have little personal impact on the Europe in which they live. Like seeds sown in salt sand, they hold to themselves, extend no roots, and disturb no soil. They have little to do with the americanization of Europe.

And yet something called the "americanization of Europe" is obviously underway, stirring both excitement and deep resentment.

PART VI

THE AMERICANIZATION
OF EUROPE

CHAPTER 20

THE AMERICANIZATION OF EUROPE
What's Going on Here?

"Among older men you find highly emotional resistance to various twentieth-century phenomena which tend to be associated with the United States."

AN AMERICAN EXECUTIVE IN LONDON

An intensive tour of Western Europe can leave Americans much enlightened—and as much bemused by change as the people living there. The supermarkets and discount stores, frozen custard and frozen peas, ready-credit and ready-to-wear, instant coffee and instant hair (choose your own color, rinse with care), TV jingles that jangle but sell, roll-on deodorants, shaving cream, the roadside motel—all these "modern wonders" have come to Europe; and so has something else.

Walk through decorous Stockholm's well-lit Kungstradgarden park on a late summer's eve. You will see groups of youngsters loitering about in dark leather jackets. Such fair, clear-eyed young citizens as these are too clean-cut and mild to be troublemakers, but Stockholm's police will tell you otherwise. These kids are with it. They have social aggressions. They can give you lumps to prove it.

Drive a British weekend road. Whizzing around and through the traffic jams on the car-choked, two-lane roads are swarms of motor bikes. The black-jacketed, driver-impersonators of Mr. Death lean their cycles hard into the curves. Playing fighter pilot, strafing clotted convoys from their two-wheel putter pipes, they zip through traffic tie-ups. Upper-class Englishmen, trapped by prosperity, and their fellows on once uncrowded lanes, shake their heads at the bikesters and mutter, "Stupid clots those . . . bad for traffic . . . bound to kill someone . . . should not be allowed . . ."

But the black knights, damsels on crupper, roar truculent in new mobility. Shrinking their island, they blast through mist and rain from Glasgow, Scotland, to Carlisle, England, for Saturday dances. (They know or sense that in Los Angeles kids and factory workers long ago turned from bikes to super-souped-up hot rods.) At night they dream of cars.

In Germany, off-hours young workmen affect windbreakers which are a replica of U. S. Air Force flight jackets. With their close-cut hair, open shirts and jackets, it is hard to tell these men from their many Midwestern cousins stationed in Europe—until you look down and see narrow, pointed German shoes. A German market researcher reports that German stores selling U.S. western boots, shirts, and trousers have been doing land-office business. "Primitive Americanism," he calls it. In summer these working-class young Germans now vacation in Denmark, Italy, Spain, or where fancy takes them.

In France, blue jeans are now a standard teen-age garb. A disc jockey is seeking his fortune catering to teen-agers with their own magazine, *Salut les Copains* (Greetings, Buddies), and for years one of the most successful stage personalities has been an Elvis Presley-type rock-and-roll singer stage-named Johnny Halliday. French retailers are discovering that teen-agers represent a $1-billion market with tastes and styles of its own. Parents shake their heads in disapproval of this trend but cannot change it: youngsters look to their peers for guidance. Guitar sales (says *Business Week* magazine) are zooming.

All over Europe more and more pretty girls in form-fitting dresses and uplift bras are beginning to look as if they were poured out of the same bottle (their magazines tout the same dress and hair styles). All over Europe more and more kids seem to look and dress and slouch like the most publicized U.S. youngsters. All over Europe youngsters jitterbug to U.S. music. Sometimes the words to the music are French or German or Italian, sometimes they are English; it doesn't seem to matter.

There are national differences in dancing. American youngsters dance with stiff backs, concentrating hard on tight, precise, repetitive movements (automatic machines doing production-line steps), seldom swinging the hips except self-consciously. French kids dance more loosely, the girls swing rather than snap their hips, their backs are supple. The British have evolved a subform of Dixieland called "trad" (rhymes with dad), which is just off the driving Dixieland beat by laggard microseconds, but is popular with the young dancehall set, who gyrate to it with a studied jerkiness, the men bobbing forward from the hips in (unconscious?) mock formality. But these are minor differences. From Stockholm to Brindisi the dances and music of America and Europe are essentially identical. True, song hits and singers move both ways across the Atlantic, but the common veneer of the rising youth cults all over Europe are patently American.

Cool jazz, meanwhile, has been taken up long since by the smart sets everywhere. French pseudo-intellectuals, who have read up on their dogma, love to lecture on U.S. jazz. "Jazz is truly, purely an African thing," they like to say. Actually, nothing so sophisticated came from Africa. Modern U.S. jazz is a black-and-white-and-U.S.A. amalgam, with borrowings from Ravel and Debussy, but U.S. Negro musicians, who are mildly lionized in Europe, never argue the pure-Africa myth (why should they?) and neither do many others; it is a pleasant tale. What does jar Americans in Europe is that on any one radio program, U.S. music pours forth in a jumble of mood—hillbilly, popular, rock-and-roll, show tunes, or cool jazz. Europeans seem to exercise no discrimination in what they choose to play or hear—or from what period. One hears tunes and styles of the 1930s, the 1940s and of today in (to Americans) startling sequence.

It is not only the young people in Europe who adopt things American. Two French executives meeting at noon may agree that, while a *snack bar* is beneath them, they do want a quick *business lunch* where, taking *Coca-Cola* or *ginger ale* in place of wine, they can discuss *un deal* involving a *fifty-fifty* agreement with American partners. Later, one of them may announce that he plans to be off in his *sports car* for *le weekend* with *la girlfriend*.

All over Europe the language of ad men crackles with Madison Avenue jargon (and the language people use is said to shape their thought patterns). But the American impact does not stop at language: it spreads through a great spectrum of areas and activities.

In commerce, for instance, we know that German businessmen boast that they have adapted (and improved) U.S.-developed marketing techniques. One of the most fabulously productive North Italian appliance producers, Zanussi, set up its production system after study of U.S. models and systems. Giant corporations such as British Imperial Chemical Industries, Ltd., and Royal Dutch Shell Oil, Ltd., turn to U.S. consultants for help in major reorganization programs.

Moving away from the world of heavy industry, we see that on European television U.S. Westerns and private eyes are the most popular programs. For better or worse, American movies, now as before, are a major mass opiate or mass stimulation which, in the process of entertainment, conveys American attitudes, values, and styles—or at least those borne by television and theater films. (There is, of course, an important reverse flow of European films and ideas to the U.S.) In Germany, Holland, Switzerland, and Scandinavia current U.S. books, in English and in translation, are common. Among British intellectuals it became fashionable in the past decade to dote on certain U.S. authors.

In Spain, a painter, a member of the burgeoning modern school there, claims that "New York and Madrid are the only two places where new work, new schools of painting, are evolving." In Paris a Dutch painter and a South American painter several years resident are both thinking of moving to New York; Paris rents are getting steep and New York sounds exciting and fruitful. (America, incidentally, is the market for which most Paris art dealers buy.) In Amsterdam, over a bottle of the fierce local gin, two sculptors and a painter debate the undue influence the New York Museum of Modern Art exerts on their world when it does or does not decide to buy a particular style of art.

In Brussels, meanwhile, where the Common Market headquarters is established, the Common Market Commission's regulations are modeled on U.S. antitrust thinking and experience. (Where else in the world would there be any meaningful antitrust experience?) If, and when, Europe establishes an all-Europe investment capital and stock market, the U. S. Securities and Exchange Commission's organization and experience will be drawn upon for regulation and control of the new system. U. S. Internal Revenue and Census Bureau men are in demand as consultants in Europe (and Latin America).

AMERICA THE PROTOTYPE

It is all of the above, along with the spread of jukeboxes and ducktail haircuts, that Europeans and Americans refer to when they speak of the americanization of Europe. Many Europeans, captured—by the changes going on around them, give lip service to the cozy corner store but flock to shiny supermarkets. They decry American music but, like ourselves, find their feet tapping to, or their lips sounding, the catchy, silly tunes. Businessmen who frown on credit buying nonetheless tout installment plans (they are *so* profitable). And yet, americanization seen in these surfaces, and handled as a generic term is much too glib and pat an explanation of what is going on.

WHAT GOES ON HERE?

It happens that America got there first: it evolved the first consumer society. Now, the various countries of Europe are also creating consumer economies. However, America did get there first, for the most part. The Europeans, rather than invent new forms of products, production, distribution, organization, and distraction can easily borrow or adapt American forms. They do and why not? So the term "americanization" has a certain validity.

America is a dynamic, optimistic, relatively open culture with many attractions to many Europeans at various class levels. Americans have a missionary streak and love to export goods—and attitudes. So a degree of americanization is an inseparable and obvious part of what is going on in Europe—but it is only a part. If America did not exist Europe would still face many of the same problems it does right now.

For example, during this time of change a common lament among educated, well-to-do Europeans is the lack of taste or selectivity with which so many in Europe take to things American, or American-like. There are reasons why this happens.

In the old Europe, the relatively few people at the top of the social pyramid had the time and inclination to develop discretion in the use of goods and leisure. Many individuals at this level might lack sensibility, but they at least had careful training: they knew what they were supposed to like. This sense of propriety and taste filtered downward; poorer Europeans might have few possessions, but what was available to them and, therefore, what they had was usually sturdy, and though not always an aesthetic delight, attractive and highly treasured. The grandfather clock, father's pocket watch, gold-plated fountain pens, and the heavy, hand-carved furniture of another era were onetime symbols and signs of this economy and state of mind. This was a possessor rather than a consumer society.

But this old order is being turned upside down as suggested. The great mass at the middle of the social pyramid —the factory workers, office clerks, secretaries, and technicians—are replacing the elite as the principal clients and customers of commerce. Europe's masses, forgetting their place, are stepping up and reaching out to grasp at the good material things of life almost as if they were hereditary middle- and upper-class customers. However, there has been little time to educate these new consumers to consumption. Like children who reach for the brightest, most garish toys on the counter, some Europeans take most easily to tinsel, to flashing aspects of the neon society. Not only jukeboxes but bright pink-and-green sweaters, plaster-of-paris wall hangings, elephant-foot ashtrays, gaudy scarves, tinny tourists' toys, hung-from-the-windshield baby booties, dice, and kewpie dolls: all have come to Europe. The once uncluttered Costa Brava of Spain is starting to take on the garish ugliness of 1930s Miami Beach. Parts of Italy are as sign encrusted as California's once lovely Camino Real. The closest equivalent to present-day, plywood décor, "French provincial" roadside cafés, were America's mid-1940s roadhouses. Says an American soap salesman in Belgium, "If Europeans think so many Americans have bad taste, just wait till mass markets really get going over here."

For, where H. L. Mencken's Boobus Americanus, after several generations of education (via schools, papers, magazines, TV, and advertising) has actually begun to acquire a sense of taste, the Great Unwashed of Europe are only beginning to burst forth upon their fellows, rejecting, as we did, the old junk for new junk, and the old, handsome, home-grown styles.

What's more, in Europe the change is virtually a post-war, one-generation phenomenon. Like a small boy grasped by the hand and pulled along at a run, the people of Europe are moving faster than ever before and are almost off balance. The pace is exhilarating, frightening, and quite possibly dangerous. But the dangers in the change are home grown, purely European products with little relation to things American.

For instance, over an excellent lunch, with vintage wine, in a consciously nostalgic Louis Napoleon Parisian restaurant, an American investment banker points to problems: "There is a great shakeout going on in many industries and in farming here—and it could be dangerous. When these small farmers become laborers they won't be fiercely independent individualists; they'll become socialists or card-carrying Communists. And the old pattern of small family-held companies was not a socially unhealthy one."

This man feels that what is underway in France and throughout Europe is not just an economic revision but a massive social change which few influential Europeans, en-thralled by the possibilities of the new good life, have not yet faced. He also notes, quite correctly, that these socioeco-nomic changes have little to do with americanization as such, and are not only a matter of plastic products or business skills.

And yet, America and things American have long been a part of the European conscious and unconscious. Underlying the economic and resultant social changes going on in modern Europe it is possible to catch glimpses of attitudes and actions that might be called forms of americanization. They are the sort of thing one might casually encounter in almost any part of Europe. They are only hints, possibly misleading hints, but what they hint at is a particularly in-teresting American-European relationship. Let us look at a few.

FRAGMENTS OF AMERICANIZATION

In the castle-crowned Old Town section of Edinburgh, Scotland, for example, local impresarios, with the reluctant permission of the city fathers, occasionally book a traveling Cockney or Midlands jazz group. Here in a cellar or back hall, the musicians—conspicuously crewcut or "Ivy League," narrow-shouldered, three-button-suited replicas of U.S. combos—conjure up a Dixieland America where the *Muskrat Rambles* and the *Saints Come Marching In* slightly back of the beat. Here, not far from where John Knox's followers once burned witches and nonbelievers, Edinburgh's flaming youth (the males fueled on local whisky) now essay the Brit-ish trad. The more far-out youngsters self-consciously test themselves at the twist.

Not far away, down a dank medieval alley, is a back-stairs coffeehouse. Weak coffee, hard benches, black walls

and ceiling, dim light—someone's version of certain Bohe-
mian coffeehouses in New York and San Francisco.[1]

The above may be provinces-diluted second- and thirdhand
America, via London, courtesy of Hollywood, ASCAP, and
Telstar. But that is not the point. The thing to note is that
in America youngsters in changing Europe most readily find
behavioral patterns and postures they want.

Meanwhile, on the Continent, on September-October
evenings in the famous St. Germain-des-Pres district of Paris,
café crowds imbibing the fall auto fumes are entertained
irregularly by groups of strolling musicians. These performers
sing, clown clumsily, play abominably, pass the hat among
the good-natured crowds—and seem to do fairly well. As they
carry their live performance from café to café the entertainers
sometimes gain an entourage. Sidewalk-café patrons half a
block away smile and watch expectantly as the true-color,
three-dimensional sound show comes their way. It is a happy
sight, all amused good humor under electric light. It is something very "European" that one could not see in America.

These wandering minstrels are invariably Americans.

A Paris-based newspaper man says, "Every once in a while
a few French kids or other students take a crack at it, but
they can't seem to carry it off. The crowds like the Americans.
I don't know why."

One evening the entertainment is provided by a group of
four—a trombonist, a saxophonist, a hat passer, and a girl
singer. She is a fairly pretty girl and not professional, but she
doesn't mind and neither does anyone else. She has a nice

[1] Ironically, these U.S. coffeehouses, in turn, are distant second-
and third-generation derivatives of certain Parisian Left-Bank cafés.
And, while British trad musicians impersonate Americans, the Beatles,
a mop-headed, British caricature of U.S. rock-and-roll singers, have
stormed America. (Like intermixing wavelets in a pool, folk culture
now washes back and forth across the Atlantic.)

grin (American girls grin, European women smile). She is enjoying herself. This enjoyment is reciprocated by the audience, which fact overwhelms her a bit and, in turn, delights the friendly crowd. Student or itinerant, what her hang-up is, what she is running away from or chasing, is nobody's business but her own. Right now she is having a ball. Yet there is nothing brash or brassy here. These American performers are so patently amateur, ever so slightly embarrassed and yet just relaxed enough (not worried about loss of face), that they and the audience have a game together. The crowds like the Americans, or at least they are fond of this particular unpretentious aspect of the Americans.

It seems that America and Americans, by turns, fascinate and horrify, attract and repel the people of Europe. In New York a young German girl ten months in the city is, with reason, frightened of walking through the streets to her West Side apartment at night. But she also says that in America she is discovering a feeling of personal release, emancipation, or perhaps individuality (she is not sure which) that she had never known before.

In Denmark, a 34-year-old Dane, two years resident in Copenhagen after living six years in Detroit, says he is moving his family back to the U.S. Partly this is because he can earn more in America. But also, he says, "I miss the energy and gusto there. Somehow, I don't know why, I felt that my personal horizons were much wider in the States. Here things are too bland and constricted."

This man, whose sense of his own value or place in the universe was somehow changed in the U.S., has contracted the American infection. All over Europe, American businessmen report that those European managers who have previously worked at least two years in America (for a U.S. company) are more restless, active, socially ambitious, and willing to try new approaches than most of their fellows.

Europeans also notice and comment (not always kindly) on the sea change that affects their fellows who cross the Atlantic. Even the solid, stolid, static Swiss are reportedly caught.

Whatever heady essence it is that percolates along with the smog in America's cities, what continuously fascinates many Europeans in Europe about Americans is that the Americans are such obvious, distorted mirror images of the Europeans themselves. Europeans talking with an American with whom they establish some rapport, especially if the American is of the same extraction, sometimes watch him, noting similarities in attitudes, observing differences, sometimes pondering: "There, had some restless ancestor emigrated, go I, my cousin, or my cousin's cousin. How strange, how similar, how different this person is. How does he think?"

"What is this America?" At the close of a three-and-one half-hour interview a worldly German in his thirties, who matured young in postwar Frankfurt, leans forward in his chair and pours out puzzlement. He says, "No one can tell us what America really thinks. We only know what we see: we see rockets, factories, and goods. You have a tremendous network of technology, but no structure beneath it of logic or mores. It must exist, but we know nothing of your thought processes. All we see is delivery of clichés and propaganda. All we really get over here in Europe are products and techniques."

But in West Berlin, in November 1963, some 25,000 young Germans gathered to form a torchlight funeral procession, and 300,000 Berliners massed to mourn an assassinated John F. Kennedy.

Something more than Cold War propaganda or industrial techniques was working then.

For far longer than they consciously realize, great segments of the peoples of Europe have had America under their skin.

Thus far, what we have is a kaleidoscope of facts, comments, and impressions both economic and cultural. Is there a pattern here? I believe there is. The pattern is as seemingly chaotic as that in some modern abstract paintings. It is as elusive as the relationships between sub-atomic particles in matter, but it exists. The pattern is one of mass consumer societies. It transcends national states and to find a parallel we have to turn to medieval Europe.

Led by Henri Pirenne of Belgium, historians over the past generation have been revising their views of what they once called the dark ages of Europe. In the Europe of Charlemagne and the Holy Roman Empire they now see great continuity with the Mediterranean civilization of Rome—as well as the roots of modern Europe. Early Europe, for all its tribes and petty principalities, had a unity which was gradually and inevitably overlaid by the rising particularism of national states. Now, responding to the impelling technology, modern commerce, transportation, and communication that shape our lives, the West is reweaving something like the old pattern of economic and cultural unity that marked its beginnings. However, the new pattern is a far broader one being woven in new circumstances of which America is a vital part.

America, for long eras affected (and still much affected) by Europe, is increasingly affecting the mother culture. Nor is this something entirely new.

THE AMERICAN DREAM COMES FROM EUROPE

The central fact of the matter is that America is, or has been for long, Europe's dream, a dream evolved from an ancient distillate of European philosophies and hopes. And all Europe (opinion pollsters and passing political passions notwithstanding) has affection for and a proprietary interest in this strange pan-European dream, the American Experiment, which has for so long been Europe's alter ego and goad.

The fact is that, for generations now, America has been Europe's favorite fable, with the amazing added attribute that, like few fables, it is at least partly real and lies just across the ocean.

For years America was Europe's land of gold, where the Dick Whittingtons and the restless could go, where an L. B. Johnson and a Dean Rusk could rise from quite modest origins to national prominence.

For years, too, America was Europe's social safety valve. To fill her own cities, she took in Europe's crowded people, a most useful service to Europe's elite.

But from its beginnings, for all its harsh flaws, America was also a standing accusation and moral annoyance to Europe's ruling groups. As the first nonaristocratic republic and relatively open society, America, merely by existing and surviving, gave the lie to restrictive social and political dogmatists.

What's more, thrice now—in World War I, World War II, and after—America, like a tyro playwright's *deus ex machina*, came out of the West: twice to prevent Europe's being united by the bayonet, and then to serve as shell-shocked Europe's shield and source of badly needed plasma of all sorts—monetary, technical, humorous escapist.

By careful arrangement of the major facts, America's recent roles in Europe can be made very much to resemble those of some of the heroes in the TV and film Westerns followed so avidly by many Europeans. Something like, say, the classic Shane, who comes out of the West to be useful around the beleaguered ranch—with one unpardonable difference. When Shane had done his woodchopping and villain trouncing, he had the good manners to ride off into the sunset and back into dreamland; America and the Americans did not.

There are many facts about America that Europeans find disconcerting. One, for instance, is the realization that the American dream has its nightmare content. The realization that:

• In America organized crime flourishes. It is a factor in city and state politics. It even achieves a form of acceptance, from citizens who turn a blind eye to its activities.

• Only in American dry (no alcoholic beverages) towns and counties can one find the compartment-minded, righteous hypocrisy with which bluenose prohibitionists join forces with bootleggers to defeat legalization of the drinking in which most adults in the region more or less openly indulge.

• Some of those individuals and organizations in America which inveigh most loudly against government, a few Europeans cynically note, seem to be those that nonetheless gain most from direct or indirect government subsidies or contracts.

Then, too, America's seething elections alarm many Europeans (and a few Americans), who do not realize how much venom and pressure is thus being vented and dissipated. (In some countries such strong feelings might steep and mount for generations or turn to revolution.)

Lately, the most discomfiting realization about America (for some Europeans) is that, like the *Arabian Nights* genie who refused to get back into the bottle, America is not settling back across the Atlantic. (Not only does it turn out that Shane picks his teeth and dribbles gravy on his vest, but he has bought the ranch next door.) For many years most Americans wanted nothing more than to retire back across the Atlantic to their own affairs. Power politics, technology, and the needs of commerce, however, have not permitted this.

Today, when new technology can cross the Atlantic in some six months to a year, an armored division in sixty hours, a new joke in twenty-four hours, and a guided missile in half an hour, more and more Europeans are discovering that parts of the once distant American dream are no dream at all—they are everyday reality in Europe. This is awakening the Europeans to just how much they, while remaining themselves, are changing, becoming part of what is now a joint American-European experiment.

WHERE IS EUROPE?

A most important thing about the new Europe is that it grows out of the old Europe. In the Palace Hotel in Copenhagen, a transient German businessman (who has lived six years in the U.S.) sits comfortably at his table chatting easily with a number of Norwegian and Danish fellow guests—in English. His American accent and colloquialisms are almost perfect. An American might think this was a countryman.

When a German friend in joining him at table makes a number of remarks in German, our businessman pointedly answers him in English. Twice. His associate switches to English.

This businessman later admits that in once occupied countries he finds life simpler, things a little smoother, if it is assumed he is an American.

Our German businessman in Denmark, who is the managing director of a U.S. company with headquarters in West Berlin and business throughout Europe, is, almost by definition, in and of the new Europe. But the new Europe is also the old Europe—with all of old Europe's memories, national and class attitudes, and prejudices. Frenchmen and Englishmen, Germans and Frenchmen, Catholics and Protestants, workers and managers still eye each other askance. Political parties still tend to represent class and religious groupings.

In Europe, for example, the popular American footrace with the Joneses is also run—but only among tightly restricted, specific peer groups. Energy is devoted also to keeping those below one on the social scale in their place. Since a man is a child, and usually a prisoner, of his culture, those effectively kept in their place cannot help feeling and reacting as if there were a proper "place" to which they were assigned by fate and "breeding." Not everyone "adjusts." At the bottom of the social scale the embitterment, the bottled-up sense of injustice, the feeling of being locked out of the core of one's society—as it shows up in, say, a British or French union organizer's feelings—has to be seen and heard to be appreciated.

But changes, like vines growing through and around a trellis, are underway. New technologies and new (or changed) organizations, loyalties, and values are taking hold and swarming up and through the old social structures of Europe. Large-scale manufacturing and distributive systems, for instance, are creating thousands of new kinds of jobs— and a new importance for those who hold them. The *petit bourgeois* corner store and tiny, costly factory, meanwhile, are being left behind, if not eliminated, by the surging economy. The large and growing organizations of the new Europe, badly in need of managers and technicians, recruit whatever people they can and, even while disclaiming it, bestow whatever corporate honors and promotions they must to develop new personnel and new loyalties. As a result, society is opening to all manner of lower- and middle-class Europeans.

Then too—and in the long run, most important—the new Europe needs a much greater number of trained, well-educated people than the old Europe was producing. As a result, those keys to the society, those highly reliable mind conditioners and social filters, Europe's school systems, are being modernized in many countries (notably Britain, Holland, France, and to a lesser degree, Germany) and opened up to lower-class entrants. Some of the invisible bars to social mobility are being lowered, although not thrown aside. In Italy, in the name of scholastic integrity and quality, the classicists have reportedly managed to keep the school system as a prime segregator and bulwark of the upper and middle classes. But this defensive system is cracking. Eventually it will be breached.

The old social structure of the old Europe is still very much there (and will stay there for the forseeable—if there is such—future), but those "lower" classes, promised so much and given so little by the French Revolution, are reaching a stage of sophistication and education where they can begin to achieve. Marx *is* having his revolution, but it is no more purely Marxian than it is purely American or democratic. The socialists are in sight of their original (often obscured) goal of equal opportunity. This is happening, not through state ownership of business or a leveling of the elite, but by increased productivity and education, by a new social order that elevates the lower classes into the middle classes, and that alters the middle classes.

There is strong emotional resistance to change both from the Right (Europe's elite have a history of holding fast to their prerogatives) and from the Left (for some members of the Left, orderly class integration offers neither the romantic satisfactions nor the personal power that class war promises). But the pressure is on. A card-carrying Communist workman would really rather be middle class than revolutionary. The stiffly conscious-of-their manners lower middle class want nothing more than to be middle middle class, and in the new

Europe this is becoming possible. For this, class war can take a back seat.

Meanwhile, unless Europe's elite settle down to an intensive and creative job of training and leadership of their masses, they are likely to find themselves swamped in mass bastardized culture by disc jockeys. Europe's present elite will have to accept the challenge of joining and educating the new society growing up around them—or be left behind by it. In part, it is the realization that they must join a mass society and lose something of their own present very special pampered status that explains why so many European intellectuals of the Left and Right react so bitterly against the so-called americanization they see around them. But in Europe the old verities of place and station are becoming meaningless, and new ones have yet to be concocted. It is the seeming rootlessness of Americans which disturbs many Europeans. But this same rootlessness, this lack of a definite social slot, is affecting Europe.

To call what is happening an *americanization* of European society is to take the easy way out. And yet, to say that the American Evolution has come to Europe might not be so far off the mark. What is happening is that an American society much evolved from its beginnings, and a Europe which has also changed happen to be drawing closer together.

Think of time as a vast, many branched river flowing through low country. America and Europe, after traveling two parallel arms of that river for a period, are flowing together. The confluence is where the gradient is steepening. This faster flow is creating crosscurrents of turbulence and anxiety. There are Americans even more disturbed and confused by the changes going on around them than the Europeans. An as yet unnamed phase of the Industrial Revolution, is upon us—Americans and Europeans alike.

PART VII

THE ESCAPING CORPORATION

CHAPTER 21

THE ESCAPING CORPORATION

The Paris offices of the National Cash Register Co. of Dayton, Ohio, are situated at the foot of the famous Champs Elysées. It is a choice site. Along this lovely boulevard pass all ceremonial processions on the way to Napoleon's Arc de Triomphe.

In the stark summer of 1940, however, as the conquering German armies swept through France and into Paris, they too made a triumphal procession up the famous way. At that time National Cash's French staff, bleakly eying the Teutonic tide from behind their windows, were startled to see a tank detach itself from the ordered mass to roar purposefully up the circular driveway of their office. Climbing out of the machine, a German strode to the door and rapped loudly. When the French manager, with some trepidation, came to the door he saw a major who, clicking his heels and bowing, presented his card and introduced himself as manager of National Cash's Berlin office. If, during the immediate pressures of occupation, his colleague at anytime had need of his services, said the Berlin manager, he had only to call. The German gave his unit and location, hopped back into his tank, and clanked off to catch up with the passing parade and the pressing business of war.

This little tale is a favorite with National Cash executives, who pride themselves on their company spirit. However, it shows something not only about National Cash but about international companies as a whole, for international companies, more and more, tend to transcend national barriers and prejudices—even those of war.

In fact, one of the nagging problems increasingly confronting national governments in future years is going to be that of relations with once purely national companies that have become international. For when a company grows in other countries (to the degree that it internationalizes), it escapes the control of any one government. More and more companies are going international. In the process, they are laying the foundations of a new extrapolitical order.

What is happening is that many national societies, whose thought patterns, until recent times, have centered around the largely self-sufficient and insular social, economic, and political affairs of one country, are adjusting to life on a much larger stage. Not just companies but whole industries are becoming international, interconnected, and interdependent. The process is largely irreversible. It is also hauntingly familiar. Partly, this familiarity is because the process has actually been underway for a long time. Also, something very similar to this happened once before and long ago. It occurred in Europe during the early and later Middle Ages. How it happened is worth a sketchy review.

In early Europe—a rude area of dukedoms and petty principalities, of tribal enclaves and rudimentary fiefs of conquered land—when the idea of nationhood was barely beginning to have meaning, local merchants were active, if unconscious, "internationalists." Over the years, trading and manufacturing groups, while nominally subservient to their local lords, created the cities, laid the commercial networks, and supplied the money, manpower, and technology that did much to bring Europe's fledgling kings to centralized power and its nations into being.

This was a long, drawn-out process; it took fifteen and more generations. During this time local merchants, while considering themselves no less Burgundian or Lancastrian or Flemish for doing so, conducted business beyond local realms, and spread out their investments and risks so that no one lordling could rise in sudden wrath to ruin them. Over-all, for their own reasons, they tended to back the stabilizing influence of the Crown against that of the quarrelsome nobles. If they could not achieve a city republic, which some did, then they would opt for a strong monarch who supported trade. In the eyes of local princes the attitudes and activities of the merchants were upstart if not outright traitorous. To our own differently biased eyes (since it is the merchants who prevailed) it is obvious that the burghers, while meanly involved in the lowly business of trade and manufacture, had the broader vision, all along, or, had at least woven their designs to a far broader pattern than their liege lords and warrior masters.

Turning to the present, today's individual businessmen, it turns out, may be chauvinists, but once their companies undertake multicountry operations these same men undergo a sea change. The international logic of the multicountry company comes to coexist with that of nationalism. An international business manager feels himself no less a German, Englishman, or American when he tries to remove existing tariffs and controls in order to most easily and profitably move goods, money, and personnel from country to country. And, as they establish themselves in several countries, companies, in a dozen minor and some major ways, undergo metamorphoses. The changes are most evident among companies with no more than one third of their business in any one country. But even companies tentatively testing themselves in multicountry operations are affected. These companies slowly begin to make more and more decisions not in terms of national needs and priorities but in response to a wider international logic and logistics. They learn to shop for materials and components abroad. They ship parts and funds between countries (creating gold-flow problems). Invariably they find some of their own self-interests at variance with the interests of the governments of the countries where they set up plants and do business—or of the home country. (Ford's payments to secure its English company were directly contrary to the interests of the U.S., with its critical imbalance of payments, argues Bernard Nossiter.)

For its own economically sound reasons, a multicountry company in the new Europe, for instance, may decide to move a subsidiary (i.e., weaken part of a nation's industry) from France to Italy. Another firm may create or expand a technologically based subsidiary in Holland or France (thus strengthening a national industry). But the company itself will be thinking not of national industries but of supplies of labor, cost of parts, where the new subsidiaries fit into a Europe-wide or worldwide pattern of trade. The company will also think of possible nationalist reactions to its moves, but multicountry companies soon find they can play off the demands and pressures of one government against those of others. Again, by careful arrangement of prices between and profits among subsidiaries in various countries, international companies also manage to pay minimum taxes in any one country while maintaining maximum cash flow within the firm. And, given rigid controls or punitive measures in one country, an international company can often sidestep them by compensating adjustments of trade and operations in other-country operations. Finally, unlike a purely national company, a company with operations in, say, twenty-four countries, while it can be hurt, is not easily ruined by that ultimate government threat, expropriation. In fact, international companies or associations of companies can occasionally even find means to retaliate against governments (by withholding vital parts or needed supplies, or through control of patents).

Until recently, because there were few such international companies in existence, their effect, while annoying or perplexing to national governments, could be ignored or treated as a "special case," or be written off as one more instance of economic imperialism or power politics in corporate disguise. For, assuming these companies are "tools" of another nation, they would not, of themselves, seem a real challenge to national authority. But this concept misses the point. Over the coming generation a great many companies, enough to create a new politico-economic environment, will be turning international, or *supranational*. It will not be possible to ignore them. Or to easily categorize or control them.

Thus, while it would be dangerous to carry the analogy too far, there are basic similarities between early evolutions of life and trade in ancient Europe and portions of the modern world. At present it is difficult to predict in any detail just what form these allegiances evolving around us will finally take. But just as an experienced engineer, by looking at the substructure and a few standing girders of a building under construction, can make an intelligent guess as to its eventual size and general structure, so we can see something of what's ahead by looking at what is around us.

THE WORLD AROUND US

Up till now we have been thinking and talking of international industrial organizations as private corporations. In general this is realistic, for private companies are the main economic engines of the West and the most active developers of international trade. It is true that in some countries groups distrustful of private corporations have developed nationally owned organizations to supplant or compete with private concerns. However, to the degree that they get into actual multicountry operations, these government entities, like private companies, tend to adopt an internationalist point of view.[1] Even more important, any country's government officials and citizens tend to be suspicious of, and hostile to, foreign-government-owned companies operating within their national boundaries. In fact, it is because of the alacrity with which private corporations move to take care of their own "private" interests that these corporations will continue to be the principal form of international company: as between countries they are more likely to be neutral.

Meanwhile, to make themselves more attractive to local nationalists (and to further free themselves from home-country restraints?), multicountry companies are seeking ways to get their stock more widely held in those countries where they do much business. Often, these are mere token gestures, but sometimes they are in earnest. Tokens, under the right circumstances, have a way of turning into the real thing. At least one New York-headquartered international company, irked by U. S. Government controls and pressures over its international flow of funds, is looking for

[1] E.g., the Italian Government-owned gas, oil, and chemicals combine, E.N.I. Reportedly, even before its founder, Enrico Mattei, died, the more this organization got involved in multicountry deals and operations, the more it started to think and act like just one more international company—with special home-market advantages. In time, the career "professional" managers who run such organizations as E.N.I start to think less in national and more in terms of vital organizational needs and problems. What is more, it is specially interesting that E.N.I., through its contributions to the coffers of various political parties, was able to influence the very government of which it was theoretically a tool!

some way to escape these "arbitrary" restraints. Says a senior aide of this company: "Of course, it is only a matter of washroom speculation, but we did wonder about the possibility of registering ourselves as a Swiss Corporation." This was, as he said, speculation, but one generation's idle speculation can sometimes be another's determined course of action.

If, through a series of acquisitions, mergers, and exchanges of stock, what was once a 90 percent American- (or German-, English-, Italian-, or French-) owned company becomes 30 percent American, 20 percent British, 20 percent German, 20 percent French, and 10 percent Italian—what is it then? Is it American, British, German, French, or Italian? Is it Ameropean? Or would it be something entirely apart from its ownership and national registrations? Such companies are actually developing. Corporations are outgrowing their government; they are "escaping!"

Keeping in mind our analogy of merchant groups in ancient Europe and looking about us, we can see other important characteristics of international companies. One is that they tend to ride out, fairly successfully, many forms of national upheaval. Throughout a series of government changes in Iraq, for instance, petroleum companies and many other operations there were little affected. Through mid-1964 international organizations in Argentina, Brazil, and Peru continue to survive government upheavals. Even in Indonesia and Egypt certain international companies have continued to prosper. Like ancient Europe's merchant burghers, they were too necessary and too well connected for local lordlings to crush.

International companies are also resistant to international wars. Like colonies of beavers whose dams and connecting ways are completely destroyed by flood, international concerns, seemingly smashed by war, almost invariably rebuild a new and stronger structure.

The National Cash Register Co. of the United States —and a dozen other countries—is an interesting case study of the survival characteristics of world companies. At the advent of World War II, National Cash's manufacturing and maintenance facilities in Japan and Germany were nationalized. With the fall of France, properties in that country were taken over. Facilities in England were converted to war work. The teams of men who managed these subsidiaries were scattered through the armed forces of their various countries. As an international company, National Cash no longer existed. Within months after the cessation of hostilities, the surviving members of National's subsidiaries were back at work picking up the pieces, contacting their opposite numbers in recently belligerent nations as well as the parent company, and turning out products. The same held true of the widespread Holland-based Unilever and Philips company operations. The war was a grim episode, but life and the company of which these men were a part went on. This holds even for companies with roots in countries that lose a war. A number of German companies whose overseas holdings were sequestered by the Allies have quietly retrieved some of these pieces or created new ones.[2]

SOMETHING NEW IS BEING ADDED

These international companies bring new wealth, new problems, new responsibilities—and new types of diplomatic alternatives to the countries in which they operate.

For example, through pressure on national governments

---

[2] During World War II some citizens in Frankfurt, Germany, were eager to move to homes near the I. G. Farben headquarters. They felt that this key member of prewar Europe's chemicals cartel would not be bombed. As it turned out, the I. G. Farben headquarters were not damaged. They were turned into U. S. Army headquarters.

—and because of pressure from these governments—the international oil companies have created a worldwide system for the orderly marketing of petroleum. This system permitted the smooth resumption of Iranian oil flow to world markets after a sudden stoppage in 1956. During this Suez Crisis, these companies arranged for a continuous flow of oil to Europe from the Western Hemisphere. Today, as new oil sources are developed in Libya and the Sahara, this consortium, by absorbing the extra flow, has prevented various forms of diplomatic and economic chaos.

Admittedly, oil companies are a special case. Dealing as they do in billions of dollars of one of the prime energy sources of our era, they are important to all governments. Invariably, oil companies find themselves dealing not only with local industries and customers but, extensively, with local governments. To help in this task, they create extensive politico-economic intelligence networks and expert diplomatic staffs (which, of course, are never formally identified as such).

The idea of private corporations bargaining with governments on a quasi-diplomatic level can be disturbing to citizens and to diplomats. It represents a seeming loss of control of affairs by "statesmen." What is more, businessmen, with a few exceptions (as in some oil companies), have, to date, developed little reputation or evident skill in the sensitive field of political economics. But if oil (or some other commodity) is vital to a country's interests and if that government closely controls or protects its local industries, who else are such firms to deal with?

Oil, a power industry in more ways than one, is, as suggested, a special case; but the point is that, as more and more companies of all types go international, more and more "special cases" are developing. One sees this, for instance, as developing nations drive towards modernization and industrialization. These usually small, always poor countries must treat almost any capital investment, whether it be a giant chemical plant or minor consumer-goods factory, as a special case. Meanwhile, it is indicative of how much the world has changed in fifty years, and of the new role international companies are playing in it, that the governments of many new nations often find they are dealing with concerns whose total annual budgets are as big or bigger than the governments'.[3] Among developing nations this immediately leads to talk of economic imperialism, for it is popularly assumed that companies reflect the policies of their countries of origin. Sometimes this is true. Sometimes the reverse is true, wholly or in part; that is, countries reflect the policies of some of their major companies. But neither assumption is always correct. Much depends upon the particular company, its industry, its country of origin, and the extent of the company's involvement in multicountry operations. What is more, the trend among multicountry companies is toward less nationalism and more transnationalism and independence of action. What happens is that in a company with vital interests in many countries, countervailing forces can develop so that no one national interest always predominates. Thus, a third alternative is arising.

One could go on and on projecting the characteristics of international companies in the future from bits of evidence available today. For instance, as they become more numerous and more experienced at multicountry operations, international companies will gradually do away with at least one tenet almost all of them consistently and often sincerely

[3] This imbalance of power is not limited to new national states. As Robert Heilbroner has observed, General Motors' *profits* in a recent year were larger than the national income of Greece.

preach but which a few top firms do not practice. That the personnel of an international company's various subsidiaries be 100 percent, or nearly 100 percent, nationals of each subsidiary's country, is highly attractive to supernationalists in a country, but such a system, of compartmentalization by nationality, is inefficient. It blocks able men from rising easily in the international company's hierarchy. Government officials are also coming to realize that this in turn means that nationals of subsidiary companies have less effective influence on over-all decisions of the international company. They are not in a position to counter possible nationalistic decisions from other countries' nationals. Also, tight compartmentalization means that these men are not as quickly or as broadly trained as they might be.

That is why among some of the most experienced and effective international companies, one begins to find teams of executives and technicians of all nationalities working in various countries. Except among the more pathologically nationalist and unsophisticated governments, this sort of cross-pollination is increasingly accepted.

Because of nationalist pressures upon the spreading international companies, it is possible that, in future, a significant number of their local subsidiaries will be quasi-government-owned. This is seen already in Argentina and Italy. In time, as major countries' governments become more sensitive to the role and impact of international companies, they may try to get special representatives on the central boards of such concerns (where their effect could be to cancel each other out).

Meanwhile, a number of multicountry companies, wondering about their own status in a changing world, have been musing about the value of seeking a United Nations corporate charter sometime in the future.[4] For the fact remains that,

[4] An attractive form of supplementary financing for the U.N.

though they may deal with governments, international companies are not semisovereign entities. Though they may operate freely in the never-never land between governments, they can be carefully policed or harassed within any one country, and it is quite easy for groups of governments to gang up at anytime on international companies. Of course, effective control of supranational companies calls for supranational agreements, watchdog organizations, and the beginnings of a supranational government. This is something few goverments are willing to consider at this time. And yet, it is obvious that something new is building here whose final form we do not yet know.

We do know that what is happening is that a Western invention, the corporation, which is a legal entity, is spreading around much of the world: more and more corporations are becoming citizens of more and more countries. A corporation as a legal entity cannot vote, but it does create jobs and wealth, it pays taxes, and it creates lobbyists within governments. As multicountry corporations take on citizenships in more and more countries, they in effect tie those countries closer and closer together in one economic community.

We also know these companies are creating a long term challenge to cherished nationalist concepts the world over. Like their predecessors in ancient Europe they may be laying parts of the basis of a new world order.

Like swarms of bees which in their search for honey pollinate and fertilize the flowers in a dozen separate fields, international businessmen, intent on profits, trade, and their personal careers, are effecting this new order.

If a similar process, which saw the rise of national states in ancient Europe required over fifteen generations to bear fruit, it will take, even in these accelerated times, four or more generations to establish a firm pattern of economic and social development for the coming era. But, it is our generation which is plowing the ground by first breaking down the old fences.[5]

[5] Incidentally, a power problem which Americans (for one) are just beginning to wrestle with at home will be greatly accentuated throughout the world by the rise of multicountry companies. This is the problem of the great direct and indirect power wielded by the cadres of "professional" (i.e., nonowner) managers of important and highly influential corporations. What is more, there are signs that it hardly matters whether these organizations be private or government owned; such organizations respond to a logic of their own. In private international corporations, however, the situation is highlighted. Given a multicountry company whose ownership is widely scattered, whose decisions can be momentous to various countries, and whose managers are self-selected and virtually autonomous, to whom can, or should, these managers be made answerable and to what degree?

SOME ATLANTIC COMMUNITY
WAGE-COST-VOLUME RELATIONSHIPS

For years U.S. businessmen, politicians, and labor leaders have shared an identical nightmare in which boatloads of cheap-labor-produced European goods flood through the country to unbalance the home economy. In fact, one of the unmentioned reasons some American companies set up European operations was to offset part of this possible threat; if European goods were to invade the U.S., they wanted to be manning the landing craft and directing the troops. In many instances, however, things have not turned out that way at all and are not about to. European wages may be lower (generally one fourth to one third those in the U.S.), but in many industries total European production costs approach or are higher than those in America. There are several reasons why.

One obvious factor equalizing European-U.S. costs is rising wages. In Germany they climbed 10 percent per year for three years till 1963, when key unions kept the pressure on for smaller but still significant raises. In Italy, at the start of 1963, workers in the metal trades demanded a 20 percent increase, and all over Europe shortages of skilled personnel are sending some key costs within distant hailing range of U.S. rates. A chemical company in Switzerland reports it is paying 75 percent of the U.S. base wage for top graduates of technical schools (five years ago it paid less than 40 percent the U.S. rate), and the head of an American petrochemical plant design team notes, "This only happens on a spot basis, mind you, but we just got some design bids from a New York firm that are cheaper than those in Europe. The American company probably has some slack periods and wants work, but three years ago this could not have happened at all."

Another factor affecting costs is productivity and pace of work. There are European plants where productivity is higher than in the U.S., but they are rare. An American company assembling complicated, measuring equipment in Holland finds that it takes 1.7 Dutch workers to equal the production of one U.S. worker. "You may hear a lot about the hard-working Germans and Dutch, but don't take it too seriously. These fellows work well, but there is nothing in this world that will hurry them," says the American manager of this plant. After allowing for differences in equipment and length of product run, many U.S. plant managers in Europe report similar production lags. An American heavy-equipment producer that owns plants in partnership with numerous European companies finds that it takes 100 man-hours to produce a given product in the U.S., 180–200 in Britain, 250 in Belgium, 250–260 in France, and 240 in Germany. A U.S. engine manufacturer reports that labor productivity in Europe is presently 75–80 percent of that at home. Another heavy-equipment producer, with three European plants, produces at about 60 percent of the U.S. rate.

The most important cost factor of all, however, is size of markets—and the mechanization that this permits.

Before and after World War II, America was known as the land of mass production, the Mecca of advanced tooling and design. This is no longer the case—at least not to the same degree. The Renault assembly line in France is the envy of the industry. Germany's Volkswagen trundles out over one million cars per year from an effective and continuously improving plant. Ignis, the Italian refrigerator manufacturer, has conveyorized production equipment that is modeled from, and an improvement upon, older U.S. systems. An American industrial consultant, recently back from a trip through a number of Italian plants, was dazed to discover that invest-ment-happy engineers were writing off and replacing major items of equipment in three years. There have been changes. The best equipment in Europe today is as good as, or better than, much of the best U.S. equipment.

But, strangely, this modernization, this increased capital investment, can help bring European and American costs closer together. This is because in factories where almost equally expensive equipment is used—and where direct fac-tory labor becomes an increasingly minor portion of the final cost of a product—wage differences between two companies or two countries become less and less important.

To further see how volume can help offset wage costs, let us look at a specific example. French refrigerator manu-facturers, hurt in pride and pocket by a 1962 influx of Italian machines, got a 12 percent temporary tax imposed against this "unfair" competition from "cheap" Italian labor. The Italians admitted that their labor costs were 10–15 per-cent lower than the French, but claimed it was full utilization of better, newer production equipment that permitted them to sell their machines at 22–25 percent below the lower-volume, high-cost French plants. In Italian refrigerator plants direct labor accounts for less than one third of the final product cost, and the way the arithmetic works out this means that only 4 or 5 percent of the Italian price advantage was due to lower costs. In other words, if the Italians had had the same labor costs as the French, they could still have undersold them by 17–20 percent. In fact, as long as they could find markets to keep their production lines at capacity, the Italians could have paid one and a half times the French wage rate and still have met the French price.

By the same token, U.S. companies churning out products for the biggest single market in the world can sometimes pay three and for times the European wage and keep as low a unit cost as European competition. This is one of the factors that makes cross-Atlantic and cross-Europe competition feasible.

So it is not merely wage rates, but a complex and shifting combination of a series of wage, productivity, volume, capital investment, shipping, tariff, technological factors which determine where it might be best to produce a given product for particular markets. In 1962, for instance, one out of six of the farm tractors sold in France came over the tariff wall from Britain. Volkswagen, of Germany, finds its largest single export market for cars in the U.S., but in 1962 a Ford Motor Company official reported that the lowest bids (including shipping costs) for bumpers and some other parts for Ford's highly successful, German-built Taunus car, came from manufacturers in Michigan. Proctor-Silex found its U.S.-made toasters selling well in Britain. Dozens of U.S. small-appliance manufacturers who exhibited at the December 1962 U.S. trade show in Frankfurt, Germany, were pleased and surprised to discover that they could ship goods to Europe, pay tariffs, and still meet or beat the European prices. I.B.M. finds it is still cheapest to ship some parts to Europe from its high-volume U.S. plants. Burroughs Corp., however, ships adding machine parts to the U.S. from Scotland.

Then, too, close as they are in industrial technology, U.S. and European industries are often on different investment cycles. As of mid-1963 numbers of American companies were getting ready to make a new jump, move to a new phase. Speaking of the metalworking industry, John Fry, then managing editor of the trade journal *American Metal Market,* noted:

The past two years of fierce price competition in U.S. industry are going to change the world market outlook. U.S. plants are going to be a lot more competitive as they learn to live with lower prices and as more and more output comes onstream from the big automated production lines and machine tools. There's no doubt that the visiting European and Japanese business people who see what's happening are a bit awestruck. I think they see where the world market competition is going to come from in the next few years.

In effect, Europe has completed its postwar expansion and will be operating for a while now with its existing modern plant and tools. The present (1963–64) cycle of U.S. investment, though, will put in even more productive equipment. As more and more uneconomic equipment is retired from production here, and as the new stuff comes in, Europeans are going to take fright at the competitive monster across the pond. Here's one straw in the wind; I was up at a Connecticut Valley fabricating mill the other day. The company has been typical of many such concerns—rather inefficient, plenty of fat in the executive ranks. But I talked to the next president. Besides new equipment he speaks of cutting overhead, trimming staff functions, getting "lean like the European mills."

FADING BAD DREAM

Meanwhile, the U.S. nightmare of floods of efficient goods produced cheaply by overseas labor (while it has proved all too real for some U.S. companies) has not been as fearsome and widespread as predicted. Heartened by wage rises in Europe, U.S. businessmen (in America) find they can look at labor demands (in Europe) in a strange new light. In someone else's country, it seems, wage demands and inflation, while potentially dangerous, are not necessarily the moral and economic sins they are at home.

It also seems that where there is enough competition so that wage hikes are not immediately passed on to consumers, pay boosts can perform a vital dual function. First, they force management to invest money—and, even more important, thought and energy—in the new cost-saving equipment or systems that increase productivity. Second, by giving a work force more spending power, wage rises expand Europe's mass markets—which is what her present prosperity is all about.

Evidently it is not competition alone, but a hard-to-maintain balance of competition and aggressive labor that keeps managements alert, on the lookout for improvements and new markets. There is slippage in the system. Productivity does not rise hand in hand with wages, but Europe's recent history has proved that wages and wage rises are an expense —and an investment. They have been a productive form of income redistribution which created new markets. In most European industries there is plenty of room for improvement in productivity both in manufacturing and distribution. If they do not run too painfully and quickly ahead of industry's capacity to reinvest in better, or to invent new, systems, rising wages in a competitive economy can bring about productivity and income improvements. They create an uncomfortable but very healthy business atmosphere, one that is new to much of Europe.

As Europe's wage levels and productivity rise, its various national economies will come closer and closer to the U.S. level. Cross-Europe and Cross-Atlantic interpenetration of goods and services will continue to climb sharply.

MORE THAN MEETS THE EYE

But the above interactions and relationships are part of something else. For parts of the steel, aircraft, heavy equipment, office machines and (increasingly) other industries the Atlantic Market is not merely a concept: it already exists. European and American industries are outgrowing their national markets. Over the next ten years, as more and more European companies realize it is not Europe-wide but Atlantic-wide markets in which they must now compete, they will (as so many U.S. companies have done) set up operations on both sides of the Atlantic. Politics, strain, conflicting demands, or whatever, the Atlantic Economic Community is abuilding.

INDEX